≺≻

# AVUNCULARISM: CAPITALISM, PATRIARCHY, AND NINETEENTH-CENTURY ENGLISH CULTURE

# AVUNCULARISM

## CAPITALISM, PATRIARCHY, AND NINETEENTH-CENTURY ENGLISH CULTURE

*Eileen Cleere*

STANFORD UNIVERSITY PRESS
STANFORD, CALIFORNIA
2004

Stanford University Press
Stanford, California
© 2004 by the Board of Trustees of the
Leland Stanford Junior University
Printed in the United States of America

Library of Congress Cataloging-in-Publication Data

Cleere, Eileen.
    Avuncularism : capitalism, patriarchy, and nineteenth-century
English culture / Eileen Cleere.
    p.  cm.
    Includes bibliographical references and index.
    ISBN 0-8047-5025-4 (acid-free paper)
    1. English fiction—19th century—History and criticism.
2. Capitalism and literature—Great Britain—History—19th century.
3. Literature and society—Great Britain—History—19th century.
4. Great Britain—Civilization—19th century.  5. Moneylenders—
Great Britain.  6. Pawnbrokers—Great Britain.  7. Social classes in
literature.  8. Father figures in literature.  9. Patriarchy in literature.
10. Uncles in literature.  I. Title.

PR868.C25 C56    2004
823'809355—dc22                                          2003025201

This book is printed on acid-free, archival-quality paper.

Original printing 2004

Last figure below indicates year of this printing:
13   12   11   10   09   08   07   06   05   04

Typeset at Stanford University Press in 10/13 Trump Mediaeval

*For my parents,*
GERARD R. *and* JOYCE CLEERE,
*who let me read novels at the dinner table*

≺ ≻

# Acknowledgments

I am so grateful to the many people who helped this book along at all of its various stages. At Rice, where it began as a dissertation, my teachers Robert Patten and especially Helena Michie were (and continue to be) its most incisive critics and staunchest champions. Joseph Childers and Robyn Warhol were early readers of the manuscript, and their extremely valuable, generous comments were essential to its eventual publication. At Stanford University Press, Norris Pope made all obstacles finally disappear.

This project has also benefited from the support of several institutions. Rice University and Simmons College were generous with travel money that made early archival research possible. With the significant financial help of the Brown Foundation, Southwestern University provided me with that most valuable commodity—time—in the form of a junior sabbatical that allowed me to complete the manuscript. I would also like to thank my Provost, Jim Hunt, and my colleagues in both English and feminist studies for their ongoing belief in the importance of faculty scholarship at the liberal arts institution. Moreover, university-wide, my colleagues and students at Southwestern have encouraged my research and writing with support far beyond the financial.

Various friends, at various times, in various ways have nursed this project and its author through the vicissitudes of the production process, and I would especially like to thank Mike Levine, Melinda Dougharty, Julie Sims-Steward, Rebecca Stern, Keith Gorman, Pam Bromberg, and Reneé Bergland. Elizabeth Green Musselman, Lisa Moses Leff, and Kimberly Smith were latecomers to the scene of writing, but their confidence and humor propelled me through the final stages with more serenity than I thought possible. Shannon and Matt Diamond have reminded me constantly that there are worlds beyond the academy where intellectuals live and work. With her customary wit, intelligence, and style Caroline Levander has, from the very beginning, been the best friend a girl and her book could have. And, most importantly, I am grateful to John Pipkin, who always knew this book would happen and who would tolerate no other assumption.

I am grateful for permission to reprint parts of this book. A version of Chapter One was published as "Reinvesting Nieces: *Mansfield Park* and the Economics of Endogamy" in *Novel* 28.2 (1995). A version of Chapter Two appeared under the same title I use here in *Genders* 24 (1996).

# Contents

<>

AVUNCULARISM:
CAPITALISM, PATRIARCHY,
AND NINETEENTH-CENTURY
ENGLISH CULTURE

≺ ≻

# Introduction

LIFE WITHOUT FATHER: UNCLES IN HISTORY,
THEORY, AND LITERATURE

"Avuncularism" (as the experienced reader may comprehend) means "recourse to a pawnbroker"—popularly
called "my uncle."

William Michael Rossetti, *Ruskin,*
*Rossetti, PreRaphaelitism*

Who that cares much to know the history of man, and how
the mysterious mixture behaves under the varying experi-
ments of Time, has not dwelt, at least briefly, on the life of
St. Theresa, has not smiled with some gentleness at the
thought of the little girl walking forth one morning hand-in-
hand with her still smaller brother, to go and seek martyr-
dom in the country of the Moors? Out they toddled from
rugged Avila, wide-eyed and helpless-looking as two fawns,
but with human hearts, already beating to a national ideal;
until domestic reality met them in the shape of uncles, and
turned them back from their great resolve.

George Eliot, *Middlemarch*

≺ I ≻

*Psychoanalysis, History, and "New" Historicism*

This book begins with a simple assertion that has potentially far-
reaching ramifications for feminist, literary, and cultural studies:
while the concept of the "nuclear" family has crucially informed
our understanding of patriarchy, and has been fundamental to a
variety of oppositional theories and practices, it has also functioned to normalize or negate a spectrum of cultural discourses
that resist father-centered vocabulary and standard psychoanalytic
form. In the field of nineteenth-century British studies, I will ar-

gue, this normalization has been so effective that the "avuncularism" defined by William Michael Rossetti in my first epigraph has
been largely forgotten or overlooked by contemporary scholarship.
Moreover, within the structuralist paradigms that have dominated
studies of the Victorian family in history and literature, "the
shape of uncles" in the second epigraph from *Middlemarch* is only
intelligible if analogized to the law of the father, thus becoming an
archetypal prohibition in both anthropological and psychoanalytic
contexts. Between Freud and Lawrence Stone,[1] the perimeters of
nineteenth-century private life have been rigidly measured: "nuclear" in shape, "companionate" in disposition, "affective" in
temperament, and of course, "patriarchal" in organization. If these
terms are now more accurately recognized as ideological constructions rather than historical conditions, they still have the power to
monopolize critical interest and theoretical regard, and consequently to enforce static impressions of the cultural work performed by familial tropes in the Victorian period. Given that any
contemporary understanding of the nineteenth-century social
world is already based upon assumptions about the doctrine of
separate spheres, the cult of domesticity, and the "rise" of industrial capitalism, nuclear tropes and terminology seem the obvious
and only way to make sense of the past. Add to this the fact that
psychoanalytic, feminist, and post-colonial critics rely heavily on
a concept of patriarchy to explain both global and local forms of
oppression, and the nuclear family becomes a practically impermeable axiom of Victorian culture.

In other words, although the Victorian family as a nuclear, father-centered unit is a recognized ideology, *as an ideology* it continues to maintain its intellectual authority, tailoring even the
most sophisticated discussions of nineteenth-century kinship to
the narrow contours of a nuclear unit. This tyranny is especially
remarkable in the field of literary criticism, even though the stark
absence of biological parents is a nearly ubiquitous paradigm of
nineteenth-century British fiction. One reason for this apparent
contradiction is that psychoanalytic methodology can convincing-
ly convert all paternal and maternal absence into a particularly
eloquent and indicative narrative presence. The Freudian family
romance can make sense of parental dissonance throughout the
nineteenth-century canon, classifying novels like *Mansfield Park*,

*Jane Eyre, David Copperfield, Bleak House,* and *Wuthering Heights* as archetypal foundling tales or bildungsromans. It is also the case that Lacan's "law of the father" can transform the paternal absences of *The Woman in White, The Moonstone,* and *The Mill on the Floss* into paradigmatic narratives of paternal prohibition and repressed sexual desire.[2] While psychoanalytic theory has certainly inspired some of the most compelling criticism on literary families to date, the compulsion to discover psychological traces of the missing father in the nineteenth-century British novel obscures a most important and pervasive thematic: although few fathers can be found, the uncles proliferate.

Of course, psychoanalysis is not the only methodology that repeatedly uncovers a father paradigm in nineteenth-century literature. For example, Catherine Gallagher's important and influential *The Industrial Reformation of English Fiction* also inscribes the nuclear family at the heart of "new" historicist Victorian studies by privileging the nineteenth-century philosophy of social paternalism over all other family/society metaphors. Gallagher explains,

According to [Arthur] Helps and other nineteenth-century social paternalists, society could be regenerated by reduplicating the family's benevolent hierarchy: by acting out the roles assigned in a metaphoric equation between society and the family, masters and workers could bring themselves into a harmonious productive relationship. If employers would act like wise fathers and workers like dutiful children, antagonistic class interests would disappear, along with the extreme poverty and the class separation that accompanied early industrialism.[3]

Gallagher further argues that this affective, patriarchal family provided a "natural" prototype for all brands of civil interaction in nineteenth-century culture, directing the plots of industrial novels like Elizabeth Gaskell's *North and South* and Dickens's *Hard Times* to familial solutions that simultaneously promoted social reformations. While it is difficult to disagree with such a convincing analysis, I would argue that Gallagher's historically attentive book also ratifies the primacy of psychoanalytic terminology in literary criticism, and renaturalizes an image of patriarchy embodied by the father. When patriarchal oppressions are read only in terms of the mythic "law of the father," a spectrum of cultural imperatives that cannot be styled "patriarchal" or "paternal" are prematurely elided. Beginning with Rossetti's helpful reminder to the "experienced reader," and continuing with a variety of texts ranging from economic essays and political pamphlets, to conduct books and fiction, *Avuncularism* contends that nineteenth-century ideologies of kinship are more fractured and contradictory than twentieth-century interpretive strategies have traditionally assumed. The father-child bond may have been a dominant metaphor of the nineteenth-century social world, but its inadequacies or failures as a universal metaphor were sometimes registered by alternative ideologies of kinship: systems of signification that exceed the theoretical possibilities provided by nuclear family paradigms.

In fact, while Arthur Helps was certainly in favor of patriarchal order in social relations, he describes not the paternal, but the avuncular order of contemporary fiction in his 1849 book *Friends in Council*. "In novels," Helps writes, "one's uncle in India always dies, opportunely. To be sure, the thought occurs, that if this novel life could be turned into real life, one might *be* the uncle in India and not the hero of the tale."[4] Helps's literary analysis is both satiric and surprisingly accurate: a host of novels of the period indeed employ the convention of the conveniently deceased or soon-to-be-deceased foreign Uncle, a family connection valued for his timely infusion of wealth and status among the protagonists. In *The Australian Uncle; or, Help in Time of Need*, the significance of avuncular intervention is rather transparent, but the subtitle of this 1871 novel could just as easily illuminate Anna Maria Hall's *Uncle Sam's Money Box* (1848), Frances Trollope's *Uncle Walter* (1852), S. C. Bridgeman's *Uncle George's Money* (1884), or Leslie Keith's *The Indian Uncle* (1896). These little-known novels are ubiquitous in imagining a striving middle-class British family transformed by colonial wealth, an economic boon that enters the family horizontally through a conveniently widowed, childless and aged Uncle. The money he bestows is different from the paternal legacy because it is the profit of successful capitalist enterprise rather than hereditary wealth. As Rossetti has explained, money from "my uncle" is a departure from familial economic systems: such wealth is not subject to the vertical laws of patrilineage, and can transform the economic identity of even the most insignificant younger sons and impoverished, orphan daughters.

The most canonical example of such commercial transformation is, of course, Charlotte Bronte's *Jane Eyre*, published a year before *Uncle Sam's Money Box*, and two years prior to Helps's *Friends in Council*. In light of foundational twentieth-century feminist readings that identify suppressed paternal dictums and subversive maternal narratives in Jane's rich dreams, artworks, and storytelling devices,[5] it is easy for us to forget what Helps's cultural immediacy discovers: Bronte's novel actually maps the heroine's struggle for individualism against the absent presence of neither fathers nor mothers, but three recently dead uncles. During her childhood at Gateshead, Jane's imprisonment in Uncle Reed's death-chamber initiates her first emancipation from her cruel Aunt and cousins; after leaving Thornfield Hall, Jane is able to enter Moor House on terms of equality with its also orphaned siblings due to her Uncle Rivers's recent demise; and, most significantly, the death of Uncle Eyre, a Madeira wine merchant, leaves Jane with a modest inheritance that allows her to marry Rochester with financial independence.[6] To gloss these uncles as mere variations on the theme of patriarchal oppression is to repress an alternative paradigm of economic individualism that emerges not only from *Jane Eyre's* teleology, but also, as Helps suggests, from a wide variety of nineteenth-century British novels.

Of course, questions about what I am calling (after Rossetti) "avuncularism" in nineteenth-century fiction are somewhat easier to ask in the wake of Michel Foucault's poststructuralist analysis of "polymorphous techniques of power."[7] Although Foucault doesn't directly critique the historical narrative that locates the genesis of the nuclear family at the end of the eighteenth century, he suggests that psychoanalysis intensified the notion of the nuclear unit by asserting "that one would find the parents-children relationship at the root of everyone's sexuality."[8] Additionally, Foucault warns that any theoretical paradigm that enforces a notion of power that "has its central point in the enunciation of the law"[9] obscures an entire network of power relations which emanate from a variety of partial and unstable sources. Foucault's impact on multidisciplinary studies of kinship can be imperfectly gauged by the way texts as varied as Juliet Flower MacCannell's *The Regime of the Brother*, and Lynn Hunt's *The Family Romance of the French Revolution*, have, in the last decade, begun to insist upon more nuanced and culturally specific interpretations of what is normatively deemed "patriarchal" oppression. Intervening in contemporary feminist debates about the current objectives of patriarchal critique, MacCannell argues that the post-Enlightenment promise of equality was a ruse, and that what has taken the place of the Patriarchy is a more invidious, more oppressive "regime of the brother."[10] Hunt's research is more historically centered, but she comes to similar conclusions about the inherent instability of family/society tropes. Using the Freudian family romance as a theoretical backdrop, Hunt argues that the French desire to get rid of political "parents" during the revolution generated a whole new set of family metaphors based on a seemingly fraternal, seemingly egalitarian order of the brother.[11]

Both MacCannell and Hunt present important challenges to the hegemony of patriarchal theory, but their brother-centered arguments still privilege a psychoanalytic model of kinship that is economically and racially homogenous. More attuned to differences of class and race within the seeming hegemony of patriarchy, Anne McClintock argues in her 1995 *Imperial Leather: Race, Class, and Gender in the Colonial Contest* that Lacan's "Name of the Father" has prevented all "historical investigation of why there is not one patriarchy, but many":

Committed to the economy of one, Lacan's Name of the Father cannot account either descriptively or analytically for historical contradictions and imbalances in power between men. Nor can it account for the history of masculine powers that are not invested in metaphors of paternity; nor for hierarchical relations between fathers and the state—a relation of particular historical importance for black, colonized and otherwise disenfranchised men.[12]

As McClintock calls our attention to historical moments that challenge the seamlessness of psychoanalytic accounts of patriarchy, it may be useful to recollect Arthur Helps's satiric analysis of mid-Victorian fiction. The uncle who "always dies in India" is one possible manifestation of the alternative masculine power described by McClintock: in most cases, a non-procreative younger brother who owes his "patriarchal" status to colonial commerce rather than to English patrimony. It will be my contention in this book that the figure of the uncle in the nineteenth-century British novel marks an important cultural and historical schism in the concept of patriarchy, a schism provoked by significant historical events from the onslaught of industrial capitalism, to colonialism, to the demands of a newly global economy. By shifting the focus from the father to the uncle, from the nuclear family to a more broadly based topography of kinship, this book attempts to theorize the avunculate as an important narrative inscription of evolving nineteenth-century commercial imperatives, especially as they pertain to accounts of gendered subjectivity and social development.

Post-Foucauldian historians of the family have been rethinking these commercial imperatives as well, revising the cause and effect teleology that has stationed the nuclear family at the baseline of industrial capitalism. For example, Leonore Davidoff's and Catherine Hall's 1987 book *Family Fortunes* thoroughly reassessed Stone's "rise of the nuclear family" paradigm, and destabilized the psychoanalytic family's cultural primacy in the late-eighteenth and nineteenth century. *Family Fortunes* argues that the boundaries of the middle-class family were always porous, and concludes that "technical and organizational developments" of the late eighteenth century actually nurtured relationships among members of extended families: "Increasing literacy, the introduction of the postal service, fast and relatively cheap travel by coach, steamer and later railway, all encouraged family and friends to keep in touch."[13] While I discuss this technological aggrandizement of kinship more specifically in my fifth chapter, on the Victorian post office, the thesis that organizes *Family Fortunes* is crucial to my project as a whole: "If the focus shifts from individual nuclear families to the group as a whole, then it becomes evident how such patterns contributed to the survival and enhancement of the middle class, given the uncertain, even hostile economic and demographic environment."[14] Davidoff and Hall insist that it was quite common for married couples to take in nieces or nephews to live with their families, although many aren't visible in census reports because they are listed by function: "apprentice, shopman, manager or some other occupational designation within the family enterprise."[15] As the experienced reader may comprehend, such an intermingling of kinship and commerce suggests a radically different anthropology of middle-class family life than the one Freud bequeathed to us. Just as "avuncularism" signifies "recourse to a pawnbroker" in the nineteenth century, "uncles," as I will be arguing here, come to stand for a set of economic possibilities enabled by capitalist enterprise.

≺ II ≻

*The Monkey's Uncle*

Unlike history or psychoanalysis, anthropology, and especially feminist reinterpretations of the anthropological family, has offered a discourse of the avunculate that, in turn, allows broader speculation on how ideologies of the family took non-nuclear forms in the Victorian period. In a short chapter of *Psychoanalysis and Feminism* entitled "Patriarchy, Kinship and Women as Exchange Objects," Juliet Mitchell invokes Claude Lévi-Strauss in order to "make some tentative links between the myth that Freud has deduced from his analysis of the individual's unconscious and what we know from anthropological studies that confirms this."[16] In trying to recuperate Freud for feminism, Mitchell attempts to show how Freud's theories do not discount the fact that individual, nuclear families are situated within larger social structures, social structures which are necessary on a practical level if the incest threat is ever to be deflected from the core family. Lévi-Strauss's analysis of the exchange of women between men indicates that it is not the nuclear family that is the primary element of society; the law of exchange requires that we view not the terms themselves, but the relationship between the terms as the primary site of socialization. "In order to establish the socio-cultural break with the circularity of the biological given of two parents and their child," Lévi-Strauss explains, "a fourth term must intervene. This is where the mother's brother comes in, and he comes in with the very inauguration of society, he is essential to it."[17] Because he first exchanges his sister with his brother-in-law, and later mediates between the parents and their children, the mother's brother, for both Lévi-Strauss and Mitchell, is the "true atom of kinship. . . . Nothing can be conceived or given beyond the fundamental requirements of its structure, and, in addition, it is the sole building block of more complex systems."[18] This theory of the avunculate serves Mitchell's purpose because it suggests that the Oedipus complex is not really "about the nuclear family but about the institution of culture within the kinship structure and the exchange relationship of exogamy."[19]

Mitchell's appropriation of Lévi-Strauss is pregnant with possibilities—possibilities that remain dormant within the scope of her project because she still wants to view the Oedipus complex as a universal paradigm that became visible with the onslaught of industrialization. Nevertheless, Mitchell connects the avuncular function with exchange, a link that proves especially provocative within the rich and contradictory nineteenth-century discourse of family life under capitalism. Mitchell's chapter on Lévi-Strauss is cited with great frequency in various types of feminist analysis; however, the avuncular term is usually avoided. Most recently, in *The Law of the Father?: Patriarchy in the Transition from Feudalism to Capitalism*, Mary Murray discusses Mitchell's appropriation of Leví-Strauss only to foreground the act of exogamy as it pertains to women as property.[20] Although Murray argues for a broad, non-localized definition of patriarchy as the economic, political, sexual, and ideological source of female oppression, she does not mention Mitchell's use of the avunculate as a potential fracture in patriarchy's apparent seamlessness. To my knowledge, Craig Owens was the first critic to explore these ramifications of Mitchell's suggestive analysis, as the uncle interestingly resurfaces in his 1987 article on gay men in feminism.[21] Owens has two tentative paragraphs about what theorizing the avunculate might mean for gay studies, an aspect of Lévi-Strauss's theory that Mitchell certainly does not address:

Although the role of the maternal uncle varies from society to society, it appears to be especially important in groups which practice institutional or ritual forms of "homosexuality." In New Guinea, for example, where initiation into manhood often requires the ingestion of sperm from adult males, the most important relationship is that between a boy and his mentor—ideally, *his mother's brother.*[22]

By suggesting that uncles are positive alternatives to the compulsory heterosexuality demanded by fathers within traditional oedipal models, Owens argues that avuncular relationships might provide anti-homophobic paradigms of social development for queer theory.

This is a line of reasoning that Eve Kosofsky Sedgwick followed while discussing Oscar Wilde's "The Importance of Being Earnest" in her 1993 book *Tendencies*. Sedgwick's summons to "Forget the Name of the Father" as well as the deeply laid psychoanalytic consciousness that the phrase immediately and necessarily invokes, indicates that it might be something more than a matter of semantics to address the differences between daughters and nieces, fathers and uncles as crucial to our understanding of the social development of the family.[23] "Think about your Uncles and Aunts," Sedgwick advises, arguing that a more inclusive definition of the family would redress both contemporary social and legal limitations placed on kinship, and historical assumptions about the past that define the family in the narrowest sense:

> The easiest path of argument from some of my starting points here would be advocacy of a more elastic, inclusive definition of "family," beginning with a relegitimation of the avunculate: an advocacy that would appeal backward to precapitalist models of kinship organization, or the supposed early-capitalist extended family, in order to project into the future a vision of 'family' elastic enough to do justice to the depth and sometimes durability of nonmarital and/or nonprocreative bonds, same-sex bonds, nondyadic bonds, bonds not defined by genitality, "step"-bonds, adult sibling bonds, nonbiological bonds across generations, etc.[24]

This expansive assessment of the use value of avuncular reading has the potential to dislocate or at the very least disrupt the nuclear family paradigm wherever it has been naturalized. From a contemporary perspective, it is important to question any narrative that privileges a nuclear family at the expense of other family types. From an historical angle, moreover, it becomes possible to view the extended family as a site of material changes in nineteenth-century discourses of individualism, productivity, and value.

Although Sedgwick's work on the avunculate provides an empowering developmental model for gay male identity, her celebratory equation of avuncular behavior with "kindness" may be dangerous to feminist studies. If queer theory can afford to imagine uncles as benign, less oppressive alternatives to fathers, feminist theory should not passively accept Sedgwick's suggestion that patriarchy itself is now an anachronism. At the close of her argument Sedgwick writes:

> You will have noticed a certain impatience in this reading of *Earnest*, with the concept of the Name of the Father. That is partly because I see

what may have been the precapitalist or early-capitalist functions of the Name of the Father as having been substantially superceded, in a process accelerating over the last century and a half, very specifically by what might be termed the Name of the Family—that is, the name Family. (Within this family, the position of any father is by no means a given; there are important purposes, including feminist ones, for which the term "familialism" may now usefully be substituted for "patriarchy.")[25]

Sedgwick's parenthetical diminishment of the value of "patriarchy" as a theoretical term is, on the one hand, well-taken: as Sheila Rowbotham pointed out more than a decade ago, the word "returns us to biology—and thus it obscures the need to recognize not only biological differences, but the multiplicities of ways in which societies have defined gender."[26] While "patriarchy" has come to signify an institutionalized form of gender oppression that exceeds the boundaries of the family, it maintains a father of mythic proportions at its center of power and obscures the particular agents of its aggression.

Unlike Sedgwick, however, I would argue that the local forces of patriarchy are not necessarily rendered benign just because they have curtailed size or jurisdiction. Although my interrogation of the avunculate provides a fundamental challenge to the rhetorical and actual hegemony of the nuclear family, it does not ignore the gendered imperatives that have been central to feminist work on patriarchy. After all, Sedgwick's interest in "The Importance of Being Earnest" necessarily limits this particular assessment of avuncular kindness to a male-centered developmental narrative. Within nineteenth-century novels that foreground female development, however, uncles are, at best, ambivalently situated within debates of ideology versus resistance. For example, the non-homophobic possibilities Sedgwick finds in Wilde are absolutely reversed in Charlotte Bronte's 1849 Shirley, where the heroine's masculine name and romantic friendship with Caroline Helstone do appear, initially, to challenge the law of compulsory heterosexuality.[27] Like Jane Eyre, Shirley Keeldar is an orphan, but she is also an heiress who lives with her Uncle Sympson's family until she comes of age. The reader is first introduced to Shirley when she gains control of her fortune, and watches as she makes a series of choices that imply she is a heroine in control of her own sexual destiny: Shirley renames herself Captain Keeldar, infiltrates the male world of business, and quickly develops a reputation for affecting "masculine manners" (217). Yet with the return of Uncle Sympson to Shirley's life, the reader is retrospectively made aware that Shirley's "true" femininity and "innate" heterosexuality had been previously constituted by lessons learned in her Uncle's house. Her former tutor/suitor Louis Moore is revealed to be the predetermined object of Shirley's desire, and the moment that the marriage plot becomes inevitable for Shirley, her subversive sexuality collapses along with her previously impermeable bodily health. In *Shirley*, the return of Uncle Sympson is the return of compulsory heterosexuality, a circumstance actually more in keeping with traditional interpretations of patriarchy than with Sedgwick's proffered "familialism."

Even nineteenth-century novels that better reflect Sedgwick's hypothesis that the bachelor Uncle is an inscription of the homosexual Uncle do not invite the possibility of heterosexual subversion as an option for their heroines. In Wilkie Collins's 1860 *The Woman in White*, for example, Uncle Frederick Fairlie's extreme hypochondria, misogyny, fastidiousness, and aesthetic pretension are recognizable as phobically stereotyped accoutrements of homosexuality, yet his subversion of a traditional patriarchal model in no way liberates the two nieces in his keeping.[28] Indeed, the relationship between half-sisters Laura Fairlie and Marian Halcombe is subversively sexual, and at first Uncle Fairlie's passivity and invalidism allows the intensity of their relationship to thrive.[29] But Uncle Frederick's inadequate patriarchal governance eventually recapitulates the heterosexualizing law of the father by failing to prevent the arranged marriage of Laura to the evil Sir Percival Glyde—a marriage that was Laura's father's dying wish. Certainly the novel foregrounds the abject failure of patriarchy and its metaphoric equivalent, paternalism, when it reveals Sir Percival's abuse of both Laura and her illegitimate, working-class half-sister, Anne Catherick. Laura is ultimately returned to Marian, but not in a triumph of feminist solidarity or sexual subversion; in fact, Laura is in such a diminished mental state that Marian merely becomes a necessary and permanent appendage to Laura's heterosexual life in her second marriage to Walter Hartright. Perhaps the marital threesome that emerges from *The Woman in White* is subversive, and denounces the original law of the father; on the other hand, it ultimately services the demands of heterosexuality, the new middle-class patriarchy, and the Victorian marriage plot.

Indeed, *Jane Eyre* may seem the strongest argument for the benign and even benevolent role of uncles within nineteenth-century fiction, but it is also the case that Jane's uncles must be dead before they are actually useful to her. The ghostly apparition that the child Jane takes to be Uncle Reed is not a particularly comforting spirit, moreover, and Uncle Eyre's coincidental friendship with Richard Mason suspiciously links his colonial fortune with the more sinister aspects of Rochester's wealth. In fact, the avuncular "Indian" legacy identified by Arthur Helps is a perennially troubling trope in the nineteenth-century novel of all genres, from the gothic, to the sensation, to the realist novel. In Collins's 1866 detective novel *The Moonstone,* Uncle John Herncastle bequeaths his niece Rachel Verinder an Indian diamond seized during his violent participation in the 1799 British storming of Seringpatam.[30] The diamond first takes its revenge on British nationalism by eroding the patriarchal order from within the confines of the aristocratic family: the disappearance of Rachel's "jewel" from her bedroom in the middle of the night coupled with the telltale stain on her cousin Franklin Blake's nightgown transforms the discourse of Victorian cousin-marriage into a violent narrative of ritual endogamy. Rachel is prematurely sexualized by this encounter, afterwards shocking her cousin, Miss Clack, with her "absence of all ladylike restraint in her language and manner," and seeming to be "possessed of some feverish excitement which made her distressingly loud when she laughed, and sinfully wasteful and capricious in what she ate and drank" (244).[31] While it is indeed the case that the threat of racial otherness represented by Uncle Herncastle's legacy will eventually challenge British heterosexuality, such avuncular intervention is scarcely benevolent or liberatory within the context of *The Moonstone.* When the three Indian Brahmins who have been sent to retrieve the diamond attack both Godfrey Ablewhite and Septimus Luker "from behind," their clearly racialized violence evokes the unmistakable image of anal penetration:

He [Godfrey] had just enough time to notice that the arm round his neck was naked and of a tawny-brown colour, before his eyes were bandaged, his mouth was gagged, and he was thrown helpless on the floor by (as he judged) two men. A third rifled his pockets, and—if, as a lady, I may venture to use such an expression—searched him, without ceremony, through and through to the skin. (239)

While the avuncular legacy unleashes a definitive threat to the patriarchal order in *The Moonstone*, challenging normative notions of female sexual purity as well as male heterosexuality, any subversive potential of the avunculate is demonized by its association with racial otherness, and is finally returned to its colonial context along with the yellow diamond. As implied by Helps, the trope of avuncular inheritance in *The Moonstone* is defined by the historical imperatives of British colonialism in the Victorian period, and the threat that racial otherness posed to white patriarchy.

While *Avuncularism* attempts to foreground such culturally specific manifestations of the avunculate in order to refuse a definition of patriarchy that has been univocal and ahistorical, it does not engage anthropological methodology in order to institutionalize yet another monolithic archetype in Lévi Strauss's "true atom of kinship." More recent anthropological studies have suggested that the avunculate is instead a kinship unit that alters in function and temperament under different historical conditions. Robin Fox explains that in cultures and historical periods where paternity cannot be proven, the uncle

crops up like other atavistic memories, sometimes friendly, sometimes frightening, but always a powerful potential lurking behind our rational calculations and cultural certainties. In cultures that turn him into an authority figure, he can even be hated; in those where he is not, he is the refuge from paternal hates. But he is always there, if only in the shadowy background, waiting to step forward when social systems decay and we are forced back to those primitive equations of kinship that are as much our creators as our creations.[32]

Although many anthropological models of kinship tend to produce metanarratives of a culturally ubiquitous family, Fox's work on the avunculate opens up a space for studying historical interventions and ideological shifts: moments when the avunculate is thrown into relief by the disorder or erosion of a father-centered society. Similarly, the psychoanalytic possibilities for the avunculate that motivate Mitchell, Owens, and Sedgwick are less compelling for me than Lévi-Strauss's original hypothesis that the place of the uncle is at the mainsprings of exchange, at the threshold of an economically driven social order. By proposing that the avunculate in *Jane Eyre*, *Middlemarch*, *The Moonstone*, and a variety of other nineteenth-century texts carries this economic valence, I am positing a difference between fathers and uncles that psychoanalytic and feminist criticism normatively denies: if fathers are the benchmark of hermetical family models, uncles are a familial trope fundamental to narratives of social and economic exchange.

### ≺ III ≻

### *Literature and Material Culture*

This opposition between fathers and uncles is clearly mapped in George Eliot's 1860 *The Mill on the Floss*, a novel that looks back at a crucial transitional moment in the history of industrial capitalism.[33] At first glance, the novel fits the Freudian paradigm identified by feminist critics like Margaret Homans where a fundamental paternal prohibition can be read as an attempt neutralize the threat of incest within the nuclear family.[34] Attempting to forestall what he sees as an inevitable teleology of generational displacement, Mr. Tulliver takes every possible step to prevent his son Tom from inheriting the Mill that has been in the Tulliver family for generations.

I don't mean Tom to be a miller and a farmer. I see no fun I' that: why, if I made him a miller an' farmer, he'd be expectin' to take the Mill an' the land, an' a-hinting at me as it was time for me to lay by an' think o' my latter end. Nay, nay, I've seen enough o' that wi' sons, I'll never pull my coat off before I go to bed. (16)

Mr. Tulliver denies his son a traditional place in the social and economic hierarchy, and hence a patriarchal position in relation to the women in the family: his mother and his sister, Maggie. Tom is sent to school, but is soon recalled home when his father's failure to understand changing economic conditions (such as the shift in water power to an irrigation-based system) causes him to lose the Mill in a lawsuit over water rights. In line with psychoanalytic expectations, Tom is determined to transgress his father's initial prohibition, planning to get rich and "buy his father's mill and land again," and thus find a way to "keep my mother and my sister" (229). Yet in a crucial shift from the Oedipal drama, Tom turns to his Uncle Deane, a prosperous banker and capitalist, for temporary assistance in the shape of a job, and eventual help repurchasing the Mill from the disreputable lawyer, Wakem. In *The Mill on the Floss*, the role of the Uncle is to rectify an outmoded and anachronistic paternal legacy by reconsolidating the father's goods for his nephew through capitalist enterprise.

More needs to be said about the role of the avunculate in *The Mill on the Floss*; after all, the myriad aunts and uncles that descend on the Tulliver family in Book First are particularly indicative of the way specific nineteenth-century commercial imperatives were given narrative shape through the figure of the uncle. Most of these avuncular connections are related to the Tullivers through its female line, and are part of a vast kinship network known as the Dodsons. Dodson traits are wholly alien to Maggie, but "partly latent in Tom" (44); significantly, the Dodson clan habitually subsumes the sentimental ties of family to economic bonds that are fundamental to kinship, distilling all family interaction to the legacies, inheritances, and dowries that measure the historical passage of money from one member to another. Moreover, when Aunt Glegg lends money to Mr. Tulliver it is secured through an usurious rate of interest. In fact, as industrial capitalism begins to reshape St. Oggs's economic system, usury becomes the defining feature of the Dodson clan in general; while the Dodsons had been happy enough in the past to make their fortunes slowly through the old-fashioned, "inalienable habit of saving as an end in itself" (121) they are willing now to seek a faster profit and a higher interest rate by financing Tom's plan to form a partnership with his old friend Bob Jakin, now a thriving packman. Answering consumer demand for domestic good in towns at a distance from land routes, Bob has taken to shopping his "packs" up and down the river Floss, providing rural women with slightly damaged but fashionable fabrics and laces at a discount. In spite of the "risk" that is endemic to this new capitalist enterprise, the Gleggs provide their nephew with money for his initial speculation; Tom's father, on the other hand, has resorted to hoarding the money Tom slowly earns in a tin box, unwilling "to put the money out at interest lest he should lose it" (311). It is the suc-

cessful speculation of the extended family, however, that ultimately clears Mr. Tulliver's debts, and puts Tom on the road to
economic individualism: a commercial status that represents the
fundamental promise of the avunculate.[35]

Given that such a reading of uncles begins to interrogate the
material underpinnings of nineteenth-century ideologies of family
life, my project obviously shares some objectives with Marxist
criticism. Not only has the distinction between exchange and use
value provided an essential tool for understanding the economic
distinctions between daughters and nieces in representations of
working- and middle-class households, but Marx's careful analysis
of the process of exchange importantly prefigures Lévi-Strauss's
economic anthropology. In *Capital*, Marx indicates that the "reciprocal isolation and foreignness" necessary for commercial alienation "does not exist for members of a primitive community of
natural origin, whether it takes the form of a patriarchal family, an
ancient Indian commune or an Inca State."[36] Instead, Marx argues,
"the exchange of commodities begins where communities have
their boundaries, at their points of contact with other communities, or with members of the latter."[37] Like Lévi-Strauss, Marx recognizes that alienation is impossible in the closed sphere of the
patriarchal family and that the inception of exchange is coterminous with the "inauguration of society." On the other hand, contemporary Marxist-feminist work on the family tends to rely too
heavily upon the equation of the rise of the nuclear family with
the rise of industrial capitalism, failing to account for Marx's
analysis of the "reciprocal isolation and foreigness" endemic to
narratives of exchange. It is my contention that a concept of the
avunculate—by granting wider theoretical latitude both to the literal and metaphoric significance of the extended family under industrial capitalism, and to patriarchal imperatives that are not coterminous with the "law of the father"—has the capacity to dis-
lodge the normalizing dialectic of the nuclear family that has been
produced and reproduced by both psychoanalytic and Marxist
models of kinship.

This book's greatest debt to Marxism is finally its debt to Frederic Jameson, most specifically, Jameson's Althusserian argument
in *The Political Unconscious* that history, as an "absent cause," is
only available to us through textual representation. In the spirit of

Jameson's assessment of the novel as a vehicle not just of cultural dissemination, but of production, *Avuncularism* makes use of fiction as a primary document of nineteenth-century social history: "The 'objective' function of the novel," Jameson writes, "is . . . the task of producing as though for the first time that very life world, that very referent . . . of which this new narrative discourse will then claim to be 'realist' reflection."[38] Like critics such as Gallagher, Nancy Armstrong, and also Mary Poovey,[39] I understand nineteenth-century literature not only as a set of responses to political, economic, scientific, theological and philosophical debates, but as texts that perpetually invented and reinvented the terminology—and teleology—of the debates themselves. At the same time, this book interrogates the avuncular economy of nineteenth-century literature and culture not as a family configuration that gives us greater access to the "real," but as a set of discursive practices that exposes the complicated negotiations between family and society throughout the nineteenth century, and, consequently, at the end of the twentieth. By reintroducing the contradictory discourses and ideologies of Victorian family life to embattled anthropological narratives of kinship, I am using history to expand and revitalize the rigid paradigms of contemporary theoretical models, and using theory to hopefully enrich a set of historical practices that has come to distrust the very possibility of cultural studies.

Moreover, because historical scholars from Stone to Davidoff and Hall have placed such heavy emphasis on the rise of industrial capitalism in the changing shape of the family, this book begins not with the beginning of the Victorian period, but with a handful of earlier texts that attempt to account in some way for the transition between the eighteenth and nineteenth century.[40] George Eliot was particularly interested in this transitional moment, hence my brief discussion of both *The Mill on the Floss* and *Middlemarch* above, and my extended interrogation of *Adam Bede* in the second chapter. Yet it also seems crucial to examine texts that represent this proto-capitalist moment without the retrospection that necessarily shapes Victorian novels. Despite Sedgwick's assumption that early nineteenth-century novels do not reflect specific investments in the avuncular function, the mannered Regency world of Jane Austen's *Pride and Prejudice* has something to tell us about the benevolent power of uncles, and about evolving notions of kinship and commerce that make their power tangible. More than a hint of the historical instability of patriarchy under capitalism resides in the Bingley sisters' mock-distress at the thought of Jane Bennett's marital prospects, and their pseudo-aristocratic repulsion at the idea of "their dear friend's vulgar relations":

"I have an excessive regard for Jane Bennett, she is really a very sweet girl, and I wish with all my heart she were well-settled. But with such a father and mother, and such low connections, I am afraid there is no chance of it."

"I think I have heard you say, that their uncle is an attorney in Meryton."

"Yes; and they have another, who lives somewhere near Cheapside."

"That is capital," added her sister, and they both laughed heartily.

"If they had uncles enough to fill *all* Cheapside," cried Bingley, "it would not make them one jot less agreeable."[41]

Indeed, the existence of this uncle *is* capital: Uncle Gardiner is a respectable tradesman and Cheapside a thriving commercial district of London. The fact that Bingley's high regard for the Bennet sisters is proven by his willingness to countenance such a bewildering proliferation of uncles suggests a latent anxiety about the extension of kinship across classes, and the relatives who are suddenly rendered "vulgar" by their extant connections with a quickly rising middle class.

Despite Bingley's strong testimony, however, these Cheapside uncles can and *do* deter his marriage to Jane: when Colonel Fitzwilliam unknowingly cites "some very strong objections against the lady" in explanation of Bingley's romantic defection, Elizabeth Bennet correctly surmises "these strong objections probably were, her having one uncle who was a country attorney, and another who was in business in London" (122). These very uncles will also deter Elizabeth's marriage to Darcy. While jealously teasing Darcy about his early preference for Elizabeth, Miss Bingley again touches upon the social inferiority of the Bennet family in the idiom of avuncular anxiety: "Do let the portraits of your uncle and aunt Philips be placed in the gallery at Pemberley. Put them next to your great uncle the judge. They are in the same profession, you know; only in different lines" (36). The possible domestication of Elizabeth's Uncle Philips, the attorney, within the family portrait gallery at Pemberley suggests that commercial changes in pre-Victorian England are already threatening to forge new family "lines" from professional connections as well as from marital ties.

Yet Austen will eventually reveal such anxieties to be unfounded: in *Pride and Prejudice*, one's middle-class uncles are the saving grace of a patriarchal system in decline. Mr. Bennet's significant failures as a father are directly linked to the more general failings of paternalism, and are largely remedied by timely avuncular intervention.[42] Uncle Gardiner cleans up after his youngest niece Lydia's sexual misconduct, negotiating a generously dowered marriage for her with the economic assistance of Mr. Darcy. This commercial transaction forges a kinship between the two men that predates Elizabeth's marriage to Darcy, a marriage that Uncle Gardiner will again be instrumental in negotiating. When the Gardiners' excursion to the Lake District is curtailed by avuncular trade obligations, Elizabeth instead visits Pemberley and develops a taste not for the Romantic poets and their landscape but for the more material benefits of what it would mean to be Mrs. Darcy.[43] Most significantly, Elizabeth rightly perceives that Darcy's introduction to the Gardiners is a watershed moment in his feelings about her more vulgar relatives: "It was consoling, that he should know she had some relations for whom there was no need to blush. She listened most attentively to all that passed between them, and gloried in every expression, every sentence of her uncle, which marked his intelligence, his taste, or his good manners" (162–63). It is indeed important that *Pride and Prejudice* shapes a parable of capitalism's ostensible "rise" as a narrative of avuncular kindness, but the avunculate in Austen's novel still finally enables a series of sexually normative marriage plots. Moreover, while this equation between the extended family and economic aggrandizement can be found elsewhere in the Austen canon, its sprightly optimism about kinship and commerce diminishes significantly in later novels.

Avoiding any strict periodization that would separate Austen from later nineteenth-century British writers, my first chapter begins not in the flush of those Victorian values perennially linked to the Freudian family, but with Austen's 1814 *Mansfield Park*: a novel that is like *Pride and Prejudice* in clearly belying the idea of a rising nuclear family at the outset of the nineteenth century. It is also the case that the twentieth-century critical history of *Mansfield Park* is one of persistent psychoanalytic normalization, and provides a compelling example of the pre-emptive hegemony of patriarchy within literary interpretation. Following my premise that attention to the avunculate makes alternative models of kinship visible, family relationships that are economically rather than affectively maintained, Chapter One argues that extended kinship ties under industrial capitalism are not traces of what Lawrence Stone has termed "obsolete" family models, but emergent middle-class ideologies of work, production, and reproduction. Reading *Mansfield Park* against not only contemporary domestic economy tracts such as Maria Edgeworth's *Practical Education* (1801), and Hannah More's *Strictures on the Modern System of Female Education* (1809), but also coterminously published essays on agricultural and estate improvement by T. R. Malthus, William Cobbett, Arthur Young, and Humphry Repton, this first chapter foregrounds the way the hyper-affective ritual of cousin-marriage is underwritten by early nineteenth-century economic strategies for the conservation and aggrandizement of British resources.

In this context, Chapter One argues that endogamy itself becomes an exemplary economic strategy in *Mansfield Park*, a strategy that borrows its idiom and its imperatives from zealously conservative domestic regulations put forth by new systems of land and household management. That is, if domestic economy involves making the most of the family's resources, of meeting the basic needs of the household by using and reusing materials that the family already possesses, then incest at Mansfield Park has its own status as a principle of waste-prevention. Under the influence of a general national fervor for the cultivation of "internal resources," Sir Thomas finally discovers that Fanny Price is more economical than a daughter because she is the perfect compromise of exogamous trade and incestuous self-sufficiency: the domestic commodity that can be both produced and consumed at home. The bad father and faulty paternalist is transformed into a good uncle, and the story of capitalism's "rise" in *Mansfield Park* becomes a narrative of familial extension and investment rather than atomization.

When the second chapter continues to question the centrality of the nuclear family to narratives of rising industrial capitalism, it does so from the mid-Victorian perspective of George Eliot: while Chapter One upsets the affective veneer of nineteenth- and twentieth-century discursive constructions of incest, Chapter Two argues that *Adam Bede* privileges an avuncular model of family interaction in order to disrupt an idiom nearly ubiquitous to novels of industrial development, the rhetorical program of social paternalism. By foregrounding the extended Poyser family at the onslaught of industrial capitalism—the transition between the eighteenth and nineteenth century—Eliot's narrative of extended family development is mapped out against a working-class crisis of economic individualism that ostensibly forced a fledgling middle class into existence. Focusing again on the figure of the niece, and especially on the way this figure is located at the fringes of the traditional affective family, I argue that Hetty Sorrel's illegitimate and invisible pregnancy becomes an emblem of economic and familial crisis in *Adam Bede*, an emblem that registers thematically and metaphorically as a failure of ownership. The tenant-farming Poysers may have adopted Hetty in order to possess her labor and the fruits of her economic productivity, but their niece's blooming body is finally like the richly fertile Hall Farm: owned and appropriated by a rapacious landlord class.

While turn-of-the-century debates about agricultural improvement are equally important to the economic program of *Adam Bede*, Eliot's focus on tenant farmers rather than landowners will necessarily point to an alternative understanding of Sir Thomas's celebrated project of home-consumption. Renewed interest in England's internal resources also set into motion a series of arguments about the legal and philosophical status of "tenant-right" under an increasingly capitalist social order. The mutual moral obligation of landlord and tenant was anachronistic to agricultural writers like Arthur Young and James Caird, who described the shift from feudalism to capitalism as a transition from metaphoric paternalism to literal paternity: in other words, an economic imperative for the "productive" classes to put the needs of the biological family ahead of any former duties to the social one. Thomas Malthus's 1798 *First Essay on Population* also furnishes a cultural and historical backdrop for my reading of the mathematical (and misogynous) rhetoric of population, production, and labor that shapes the turn-of-the-century economic program of *Adam Bede*. Obsessed with one side of the Malthusian drama—the production and consumption of food—the Poysers finally cannot keep up with the inexorable teleology of the population principal.

Nineteenth-century novels that foreground female development have historically been central to feminist literary scholarship and to our understanding of patriarchal authority; accordingly, the first two chapters of this book are dedicated to a purposeful dislocation of the "law of the father" from two women's texts that have been repeatedly interpreted from a psychoanalytic perspective. Both *Mansfield Park* and *Adam Bede* situate the niece at the contested center of evolving definitions of ownership and private property in the early nineteenth century, and look to the avunculate for a new model of patriarchy under capitalism. With the third chapter, however, the book begins to look beyond the teleology of the individual novel for broader signs of cultural investment in the avunculate, isolating and interrogating a particular node of nineteenth-century culture where Lévi Strauss's "true atom of kinship" intersects with an economic and social menace. Such intersection is particularly visible in that 1859 letter from Dante Gabriel Rossetti to Ford Madox Brown, expressing relief at being "saved from further avuncularism" by the sale of two drawings, thus prompting his brother to supply the editorial gloss that explains my choice of title.

Avuncularism is not so well defined in an 1851 essay called "My Uncle" that appeared in *Household Words*, but Dickens and co-writer W. H. Wills are able to more fully celebrate the wisdom, commercial prowess, and widespread popularity of "The most remarkable man of any age or country" by describing a few of the banking transactions Uncle managed for members of the working-class:

What the Bank of England is to her Majesty's Government . . . that My Uncle is to the De Montagues, the artisans, the labourers, and the poor of London and the suburbs generally . . . Take the case of Phelim O'Shea, bricklayer's labourer. A wet week or a defaulting brick-maker has thrown Phelim O'Shea temporarily out of employment, and his stock of cash is inadequate to meet his current expenses. Yet . . . He has a coat—a loose blue coat, long in the cuffs, with a swallow-tail, and brass-buttons rubbed black in the center. He converts that coat into a bank deposit, and My Uncle advances him a sum of money, which enables him to meet contingent demands . . . In like manner, Mrs. Lavers, the char-woman, is short of shillings; but she has a fender; so her neighbor the washerwoman, has no money at all, but is, thanks to My Uncle, a capitalist while she possesses a flat-iron.[44]

Before Dickens's signature irony begins to overpower the cultural significance of this characterization, it is important to isolate the dramatic and widespread resonance of the metaphor in its historical context: as early as 1756, for reasons unspecified by the OED, "uncle" was a common euphemism for pawnbroker.

Illustrating the way that Victorian debates about pawnbroking took their cue from larger philosophical arguments over economic individualism and social paternalism, Chapter Three materially reinforces the larger argument of the book that the avunculate provided an important commercial metaphor within nineteenth-century literature and culture. Moreover, by interrogating the rhetorical equation between pawnbrokers and uncles, Chapter Three continues the project of Chapter Two in isolating yet another point of fracture in the ideological program of social paternalism. Examining well-known texts from the Dickens oeuvre, but also from a host of less canonical sources, this third chapter engages a methodology that is more reflective of the myriad strategies of New Historicism. In part this has to do with the internal architecture of my project: while the first chapters of this book use a theory of the avunculate to destabilize our late twentieth-century feminist expectations about the hegemony of paternal law in canonical nineteenth-century novels, later chapters foreground the way "Uncle" took on broader cultural significance as he moved through the nineteenth century, resonating more widely across classes, races, nations, and literary genres. Yet the very process of moving the book toward a more metaphoric understanding of "avuncularism" should also enable us to look back at the familial economies of the first two chapters, and to novels like *The Mill on the Floss*, with heightened recognition of the persistent correlation between uncles and the commercial sphere of usury throughout the nineteenth century.

In fact, as avuncularism begins to expand conceptually, the broader implications of my argument should also become more apparent: under industrial capitalism, a socioeconomic philosophy founded upon the law of the father was threatened by a competition-based commercial code that took its shape from the law of the uncle. A similar shift in family/society tropes has been traced by Benjamin Nelson's twentieth-century analysis of the sociocultural history of usury, and of the non-tribal doctrine of "otherhood" that had taken the place of "brotherhood" in the industrial age. Borrowing from the work of Max Weber, Nelson argues that the spirit of capitalism was founded upon the repudiation of the Deuteronomic commandments on usury: the first which forbid taking interest from "thy brother," and the second which permitted taking interest from "a stranger."

Originally, two opposite attitudes toward the pursuit of gain exist in combination. Internally, there is an attachment to tradition and to the pietistic relations of fellow members of tribe, clan and house-community, with the exclusion of the unrestricted quest of gain within the circle of those bound together by religious ties; externally there is absolutely unrestricted play of gain spirit in economic relations, every foreigner being originally an enemy in relation to whom no ethical restrictions apply . . . As soon as accountability is established within the family community, and economic relations are no longer strictly communistic, there is an end of the naïve piety and its repression of the economic impulse. This side of the development is especially characteristic in the West.[45]

Because capitalism could not mature under the conditions imposed by the Deuteronomic code, what Weber refers to as "accountability" invaded the sanctified space of the family, replacing affect with economics, brotherhood with otherhood. An image of the disaffected family took its place within an already abundant set of nineteenth-century metaphors and tropes, everywhere marking and measuring the impact of "gain spirit" on interpersonal relationships.

If we return to Middlemarch's "Prologue" in this context, and make inquiry about "the shape of uncles" that thwarts the pilgrimage of child-saint Theresa, we are inevitably struck by the significance of pawnbroking within the novel that follows. Over the years, Mr. Bulstrode, Rosamond's uncle and former London pawnbroker, has striven to launder his ill-gotten fortune by investing in legitimate and even charitable concerns (another of the novel's many oppositions between commercial realism and humanitarianism): for example, he has established a fever hospital in Middlemarch for the treatment of the coming cholera epidemic. Cholera made an appearance in England in the 1830s (the time

frame of *Middlemarch*) and in the 1860s (*Middlemarch* was published in 1871), and as historians of pawnbroking have noted, during this second wave of the epidemic, it was feared that the circulation of infected clothing and bedding through pawnshops was
causing the disease to spread more rapidly in poorer areas of the
country.[46] Reading historically, the social crime represented by the
pawnshop in *Middlemarch*, the moral illness that ultimately infects everyone associated with Bulstrode—from the orphan Will
Ladislaw who discovers he is the grandson of Bulstrode's business
partner, "a thieving Jew pawnbroker" (829), to Dr. Lydgate whose
desperate acceptance of Bulstrode's money looks like a bribe to
keep silent about the banker's former occupation—is at the root of
the literal disease that endangers the entire community. Not only
is Bulstrode's construction of the fever hospital more holistically
related to the cleansing of the pawnshop from his past than he realizes, the avuncularism of *Middlemarch* emphasizes the ineffi-
cacy of social paternalism by exposing the usurious beginnings
(and endings) of humanitarianism, idealism, and even sentiment.

Indeed, when we think more specifically about the avuncular
injunctions laid upon our latter-day Theresa, Dorothea Brooke, it
makes sense to remember how her own humanitarian endeavors
are perpetually stymied by guardian Uncle Brooke's appeals to political economy: "that never-explained science which was thrust
as an extinguisher over all her lights."[47] Although the cultural significance of avuncularism is explored in later chapters as a widespread and ideologically profound opposition between capitalism
and paternalism, otherhood and brotherhood, it remains a useful
tool for feminist reading of female subjectivity and bodily integrity
in key nineteenth-century texts like *Middlemarch*. Another good
example is Thomas Hardy's late Victorian *Tess of the d'Urbervilles*, a novel that makes subtle capital of the avuncular metaphor
when Tess Durbeyfield is sent to The Slopes to "claim kin" with
her aristocratic paternal family. Initially struck by the shiny new-
ness of the supposedly ancient d'Urberville property, Tess will
eventually learn that her own family is in fact the last, lingering
remnant of the ancient clan.

When old Mr. Simon Stoke, latterly deceased, had made his fortune as an
honest merchant (some said money-lender) in the North, he decided to
settle as a country man in the South of England out of hail of his busi-

ness district; and in doing this he felt the necessity of recommencing with a name that would not too readily identify him with the smart tradesman of the past, and that would be less commonplace than the original bold stark words. Conning for an hour in the British Museum the pages of works devoted to extinct, half-extinct and obscured and ruined families appertaining to the quarter of England in which he proposed to settle he considered that *d'Urberville* looked and sounded as well as any of them: and d'Urberville accordingly was annexed to his own name for himself and his heirs eternally.[48]

Simon Stoke-d'Urberville takes Bulstrode's cleansing impulses even further, divesting himself of a usurious past by purchasing the accoutrements of patriarchal heritage and constructing a "reasonable" family tree for himself, "framing intermarriages and aristocratic links, never inserting a single title above a rank of strict moderation" (42). The usurer's uninhibited revision of paternal history erases the Durbeyfield right to "claim kin," placing the doubly unprotected Tess in the "barbaric" hands of Simon's son, Alec d'Urberville, who disingenuously corrupts "cousin" to "cuz" in his attempt to gain access to Tess's body. If the compromise of exogamy and incest in *Mansfield Park* yields a healthy and economically productive middle-class marriage, such compromises in *Tess of the d'Urbervilles* merely underscore the multiple failures of paternity and paternalism: under industrial capitalism, the defunct law of the father has been appropriated and rewritten by the highest bidder, exposing Victorian heroines like Tess Durbeyfield, and, as we will see, Hetty Sorrel, Esther Summerson, and Gwendolyn Harleth to false families and a range of potentially dangerous "cousinships."

While such local, novel-centered interventions in cultural history have been recently devalued, I would argue with Eve Sedgwick that there are "important phenomenological and theoretical tasks that can be accomplished only through local theories and nonce taxonomies," and that the relation of these "weak" theories to the strong ones produced by Foucauldian historicism has yet to be articulated.[49] Though this book takes issue with Sedgwick's earlier claim that avuncular reading necessarily reveals non-homophobic narratives of pleasure, its revision of patriarchal methodologies—in itself a queer pursuit—depends much on such local interventions. My consideration of individual novels in the first two chapters is a deliberate attempt to use such weak theories to unseat the weighty methodologies of psychoanalysis; similarly, when I return to consideration of a single novel in Chapter Four, it is to use weak theory to interrogate a surprising phenomenological contradiction between Victorian narratives of usury and our most enduring Western stereotypes about the usurer. As should be apparent from my brief overview of Chapter Three, the Victorian tendency to represent usury, pawnbroking, and moneylending as cultural synecdoches for capitalism all but banished the *Jew* usurer from nineteenth-century textual representation. Displaced from *Middlemarch* before the novel even begins by the young Calvinist pawnbroker, Brother Bulstrode, the Jewish pawnbroker makes his return in George Eliot's *Daniel Deronda* long enough for a deliberate wedge to be driven between usury and its stereotypical Jewish façade.

While non-literary documents are surprisingly discrete about the racial identity of pawnbroking, a reading of *Daniel Deronda* suggests that spiritual Judaism is in pawn to Jewish economic identity, held hostage to ideologies that work in concert with the logic and rhetoric of nineteenth-century capitalism rather than with the religious inheritance of the Jews. This is most literally the case when Daniel finally locates Mordecai, the consumptive heir to Jewish spirituality and historical consciousness, in Ezra Cohen's pawnshop wasting away amongst the stoppers and teaspoons of other disintegrated households. Yet it is also made apparent by the metaphoric significance of the avunculate when Daniel realizes his own Jewish heritage has been similarly placed under erasure by his Christian Uncle, Hugo Mallinger. By revealing the way that "conversion" functions as a kind of commercial transformation, Chapter Four argues that Eliot's pawnshop mimics not only the work of the Dickensian avunculate, but Karl Marx's analysis of political economy, especially his description of commodity circulation as a capacious and capricious mill stone, grinding the consecrated artifacts of religious history into the uniform, socially ambiguous "money crystal."

This reading of *Daniel Deronda* in the cultural context of Victorian pawnbroking allows me to begin my fifth chapter with a better understanding of how the capitalist was eventually distinguished from the criminal within Western, Christian work ethics, and how the avunculate began to stand in for a democratic con-

cept of economic autonomy that may have its logical culmination
in the American icon of Uncle Sam. Both Edward Said and Anne
McClintock have observed the decay of "filiation" that accompanied middle-class economic aggrandizement in the mid-Victorian
period, and the consequent transition to "a compensatory order of
affiliation, which might be an institution, a vision, a credo, or a
vocation."[50] While the circulation of money and commodities enables a variety of important alternative "affiliations" in nineteenth-century cultural representation, government agencies in
the mid-nineteenth century were also imagined to be powerful
compensations for or extensions of family life: entities that would
enable the British family to multiply and conquer under the tri-
umvate forces of capitalism, colonialism, and Christianity. Recalling Davidoff and Hall's analysis of the aggrandizement of the extended family under myriad nineteenth-century technical ad-
vancements, Chapter Five will expand the metaphoric significance
of uncles within dominant family/society tropes, and argue that
the government takes up an avuncular identity when it domesticates itself as one of the family and establishes itself as the technological linchpin of exogamous, extended networks of kin. This
again necessitates an engagement with strong theory, especially
when the fifth chapter begins by exploring a site of Victorian social reform that has been virtually ignored by historians and literary critics: the 1837–1840 agitation for Penny Postage. Rowland
Hill published *Post Office Reform: Its Importance and Practicability* in 1837, a tract which identified high postal rates as a griev-
ous obstruction to not only the social and intellectual improvement of mankind, but to the affectionate and morally uplifting intercourse between parent and child. Hill's idea of penny-postage
was almost universally received as a relatively simple solution to
many of the social and economic problems caused by rapid industrialization, especially the break-up of the working-class family
caused by migratory employment. By stemming the perceived tide
of "disaffection" that was spreading among working-class family
members, reformers from Queen Victoria to Harriet Martineau to
Henry Cole also hoped to curtail female sexual and economic independence, and prevent other "revolutionary" hostilities from
eroding the hierarchical, paternalistic design of the social order.

Although the Queen's institution of penny postage in 1840 was

ostensibly a democratic triumph, this chapter argues that the rise
of the penny post marks a significant reinvention of government
control in Victorian England: a Foucauldian transformation of government by violence into government by affective discipline. Appearing to give up power and authority in the name of democracy,
the British monarchy exchanged a tangible, vertical method of social control for a more covert and horizontal mechanism of ideological manipulation: the invisible, but apparently unlimited appa-
ratus of the Post Office. As the essential connective tissue of the
post-industrial family, the British Post Office provided an anthropological answer to a political anxiety, and used its naturalized
identity as the "true atom of kinship" to regenerate family feeling
beyond domestic borders. As a "postal" concept of affective family
life began to extend far beyond the "nuclear" unit—to the community, to the nation, and eventually to the colonies—the language of paternalist government also underwent a significant shift,
and a specifically Postal avunculate began to take credit for the
sentimental reform of British empire in texts as varied as Margaret
Oliphant's 1861 novel *The House on the Moor* and Elihu Burritt's
cheap postage tract *Ocean Penny Postage: Its Necessity Shown
and Its Feasibility Demonstrated*. While this chapter first explores
the anthropological architecture of Victorian postal reform in a variety of cultural materials, it culminates in a closer examination of
one-time postal worker Anthony Trollope's dual identity as a man
of letters, and in his deployment of affective postal ideologies in
two novels in particular: *The Claverings* (1867) and *John Caldigate*
(1879). In both novels, Trollope indicates that postal reform is indeed synonymous with anti-paternalism, and the newly developed
pillar-box perpetually liberates his heroines from the rigid sexual
surveillance of their parents; however, Trollope also links postal
communication with the dangerous and criminal cousinships that
can now be spawned by blackmailers, forgers, and a variety of
highly literate commercial speculators.

For better or for worse, a "Universal Family of Man" was the
imagined result of penny postage for social reformers, and "My
Uncle, the Pawnbroker" was replaced in our collective cultural
memory by a different form of benevolent avuncularism in England and America. One hundred years after the home-trade arguments of William Cobbett and Arthur Young became public rec-

ord, a series of tracts would be published with an appeal to a similarly internalized form of commerce: a system of trade that would eliminate the middleman class entirely, and bring producers and consumers together in a "Brotherhood of Man" ensured by combination, organization, and "Universal Co-operation." What we might understand in contemporary terms to be a socialist or pseudo-socialist co-operative store or a credit union is described by one writer who signed himself "Uncle John's Nephew" in the idiom of extended kinship, as a financial institution that could govern working-class society by transforming it into a familial collective.

Still an agent and purveyor of capital, by the end of the century Uncle John is no longer a symbol of greedy individualism and anti-familialism: he is a "fair capitalist" who enables the working classes to empower themselves as a family as the wealthy have done for centuries. It is no accident that "Uncle's John's Nephew" published his anonymous tracts through the New Parcel Post Publishing Company, and, as I discuss in my conclusion, that he cites the far-reaching and egalitarian channels of the Post Office as the best model for his co-operative banking system, "Uncle John's Millions."

Each chapter in *Avuncularism* makes a set of claims about how nineteenth-century novelists, essayists, economists, and propagandists intervened in and manipulated the developing commercial theories of industrial England through the metaphor of the extended family. Playing out the national drama of political economy within the microcosm of individual life, the story of commodity circulation was written and rewritten within the localized systems of the community, the family, and even the human body. That Victorian narratives of kinship performed important cultural work has been proven by critics such as Gallagher, Armstrong, and Poovey; that these narratives adapted themselves to changing economic conditions, forging new ideologies of the family, society, and nation, is the argument of this project. My ability to make these assertions about the past is partly informed by the present, especially by the iconic representative of American government, Uncle Sam, our own alternative to the law of the father's colonial and patriarchal rule, who still shapes the interstices of private life and national identity, domestic production and foreign trade, free will and social determinism. The avunculate provided (and continues to provide) a particularly elastic term for understanding the intersection of the commercial world with the affective family: unhampered by paternalistic imperatives of either affective benevolence or unilateral oppression, the avunculate stood in for a variety of social directives that came to life under industrial capitalism. In the wake of poststructuralism, it is the responsibility of feminist criticism to question the architectural limitations of psychoanalysis, even when those limitations are the very bedrock of feminist methodology. Moreover, at a time when the legal concept of family is becoming less reflective of patriarchal, heterosexist values, it is important to develop a historical recognition of the instability that has always resided in ideologies of family life.

# Home Trading

## 'MANSFIELD PARK' AND THE ECONOMICS OF ENDOGAMY

It is the maxim of every prudent master of a family,
never to attempt to make at home what it will cost
him more to make than to buy.
Adam Smith, *The Wealth of Nations*

UNLIKE THE commercial interventions of Uncle Gardiner in *Pride and Prejudice*, the enabling role played by Uncle Bertram in the final marriage of *Mansfield Park* has been widely discussed. In fact, Sir Thomas Bertram's belated discovery that his niece Fanny is "indeed the daughter that he wanted"[1] has encouraged many Austen critics to harness the metaphorical power of nuclear family terminology for their assessment of the novel's close. Avrom Fleishman's venerable book-length study of the novel, for example, cites King Lear's attempt to choose "one daughter among three"[2] as the obvious archetype for *Mansfield Park*. In a similar manner, David Kaufman insists that Austen intended to draw a parallel between the initial "account of the three sisters, the Misses Ward," and the concluding "history of the next generation, centering on, again, three sisters (in fact, if not legally)."[3] While Kaufman repeatedly acknowledges that Sir Thomas is actually Fanny's uncle, he still cannot resist slipping into the seductive idiom of fathers and daughters, and ultimately ends up likening Sir Thomas to a feudal patriarch who attempts to exert the power of a "father-figure" over his "vulnerable daughter" Fanny.[4] This "vulnerable daughter" is also the central figure in Paula Marantz Cohen's *The Daughter's Dilemma*, and Fanny is among her examples of nineteenth-century heroines that function in "the regulatory role of psychosomatic daughters, who, through their symptoms, help to establish equilibrium and closure for their families."[5]

Just as Fanny's shift from niece to daughter has occasioned a considerable amount of speculation about nuclear family relationships in *Mansfield Park*, her contingent move from cousin to sister to wife in relation to Edmund Bertram has generated a large body of criticism about the novel's depiction of sibling incest. By using Lawrence Stone's history of family development as a backdrop for her daughter-centered reading of *Mansfield Park*, Cohen argues that the novel's endogamous marriage plot reflects "a new affective order for the family in which a marriage between cousins will perform a much-needed structural role."[6] While Cohen challenges Freud's nuclear family model, she does so only to posit Fanny as a "developing daughter" who fractures the father-son Oedipal dynamic. Glenda A. Hudson similarly concludes that because Fanny and Edmund "have been raised as brother and sister under the same roof . . . their endogamous union preserves the inviolability of Mansfield and excludes risks attendant on marriage outside the family—to the Crawfords, for example."[7] A more romanticized Fanny "yearns in isolation for a brother-mate, repelling the Crawfords above all because they are so different as to constitute virtually another species" in Nina Auerbach's work,[8] and Ruth Bernard Yeazell concludes her article on the spatial and temporal boundaries of *Mansfield Park* by neutrally observing, "It is not surprising that the final marriage at Mansfield Park should assume [the brother-sister] form. Edmund Bertram brings back to Mansfield 'my only sister—my only comfort now.'"[9]

Like Sir Thomas Bertram, Austen's critics have been repeatedly seduced by the neat closure supplied by nuclear family discourse. Yet by reducing all variety of family interaction to a presumptive nuclear core, such father-centered criticism tends to obscure the socioeconomic factors that condition family development, and to limit discussions of incest to presumptions about affect. Psychoanalytic paradigms (like Freud's) and historical narratives (like Lawrence Stone's) have mutually reinforced the hegemony of the nuclear family within literary criticism, and have been especially effective at naturalizing the shifting significance of kinship at its intersection with the more material claims of domestic history and social class. This is an oversight that feminist critics such as Jane Gallop and Helena Michie have attempted to address. In *The*

*Daughter's Seduction,* for example, Gallop insists that "the closed, cellular model of the family used in psychoanalytic thinking is an idealization, a secondary revision of the family."[10] Gallop's own search for a "seducer" within the family is not complete until the nuclear unit itself is fractured, forced to reveal its element of dissonance in the lower-class "threshold figure" of the governess/ nurse/maid. Although psychoanalysis would subsume the presence of the governess under the category of "mother-figure" to reassert the hegemony of the closed nuclear cell, the economic difference between the two figures cannot finally be ignored.

By suggesting that a more material understanding of adoption and endogamy is necessary in an early nineteenth-century novel like *Mansfield Park,* I do not want to argue that concepts such as affect or sexual desire are unimportant. On the other hand, the psychoanalytic hegemony of these terms tends to hoodwink discussions of family formation before the economic facets of proto-capitalist endogamy can be sufficiently interrogated. While the rapid deployment of domestic ideology in the final pages of *Mansfield Park* has all the revisionary power of psychoanalysis, the novel's historically resonant narrative of family aggrandizement ultimately resists complete assimilation by nuclear family paradigms. Like Gallop's governess, Fanny is indelibly marked by an economic function that relegates her to the threshold of the Bertram house, reinforcing Davidoff and Hall's argument that adoption under industrial capitalism is as likely to signal commercial investment as familial benevolence. Sir Thomas ultimately concludes that his indigent niece Fanny is the daughter he always wanted because she is *more economical* than a daughter, and this first chapter argues that his change of heart reflects and enacts a more pervasive ideological shift in England's commercial philosophy during the trade embargoes imposed by the Napoleonic Wars. Exemplifying the myriad benefits of economic isolationism as represented by early nineteenth-century proponents of the "home trade," Sir Thomas realizes that Fanny is a neglected commercial resource: a latent, domestic property that can be exchanged and retained simultaneously. If such a transformation seems to modern critics like a sentimental evolution from uncle to father and from niece to daughter, that is because the ultimate goal of home trading was, at least metaphorically, an apparent return to the nuclear family through a renewed social faith in the affective benevolence of paternal government.

It is also the case that political economists from T. R. Malthus to Arthur Young were calling for an improved internal economy to remedy commercial instabilities rooted in French aggression at the very moment home trading was becoming a widely purveyed sentiment in those tracts most emphatically dedicated to the science of domestic conservation and retention. Designed for female use, the conduct literature put forth by more conservative writers encouraged an internal cultivation, productivity, and general *improvement* in British women that similarly provided defense against dangerous French influences: in this case, French fashion, music, literature, and other wasteful and incendiary novelties. In other words, the discourses of domestic and political economy merged in the early nineteenth-century around the concept of home trading, subsequently producing a set of strategies for waste management that lend an important cultural context to *Mansfield Park*. While it has been widely noted that the term "improvement" in Austen's 1814 novel references both revised systems of female education *and* controversial estate renovations recommended by agricultural engineers and landscape gardeners like Humphry Repton, these discourses have not been jointly mapped against growing anxiety about the fate of England's foreign commerce. In fact, within the early nineteenth-century clamor for home trading in its various forms, Fanny's "improvement" from niece to daughter can be read as a definitively nationalistic strategy for better domestic management. Marked as uncultivated waste or excess at the beginning of the novel, Fanny eventually represents savings to Sir Thomas; in a time of dwindled resources, an historical moment when both plantations and daughters are imperiled by foreign markets, Fanny is the interior resource who finally cannot be thrown away.

Indeed, the definitive economic lesson of the novel may well be administered by atrocious Aunt Norris, whose perverse delight in the regulatory device of domestic economy expresses itself as an hysterical desire to prevent "waste" within the Bertram family, and to always "mak[e] the most of things" (128). While Nancy

Armstrong points out that the nineteenth-century domestic woman's most important qualities included this ability to oversee and regulate household expenditure,[11] Aunt Norris is eventually expelled from the family because she is guilty of "mismanaging" another domestic commodity: her nieces. If she has failed to "make the most" of Maria and Julia Bertram, she has also failed to capitalize upon Fanny's hidden value; after repeatedly refusing to "claim her share in their niece" (20), she cannot reap the same "rich repayment" that is Sir Thomas's final reward. Fanny's conservative economic function is fully realized by her union with her cousin: as Joseph Litvak points out, by marrying Edmund instead of Henry Crawford, "Fanny . . . helps Sir Thomas to consolidate his empire and to protect his property from dispersion at the hands of outsiders."[12]

By focusing here on the economics of family aggrandizement, and on the material factors that underwrite the seemingly affective space of the family, this chapter argues that endogamy itself becomes an economic strategy in *Mansfield Park*, a strategy that borrows its local vocabulary from Aunt Norris's zealous domestic regulations. Like the flood of eighteenth- and nineteenth-century economic tracts that explicitly denounce wastefulness as the cardinal crime of British households, *Mansfield Park* punctuates its story of family formation with the very commercial principles codified at the beginning of the century by Hannah More's *Strictures on the Modern System of Female Education* (1799) and Maria Edgeworth's *Practical Education* (1801), and reproduced by later texts such as Sarah Stickney Ellis's mid-Victorian *The Daughters of England*. "The absolute waste of material," writes Ellis, "in whatever is manufactured, prepared or produced, is an evil of a distinct nature, and can never be allowed to any extent, where it is possible to be avoided, without a deficiency of common sense, or of moral rectitude."[13] In keeping with the ideological work performed by such conduct manuals, *Mansfield Park* identifies the daughters of England themselves as sites of potential spoilage, and in the process of mingling Bertrams and Prices puts forth a narrative of endogamy similarly concerned with the evils of waste. That is, if domestic economy involves making the most of the family's resources, of meeting the basic needs of the household by using and reusing materials that the family already possesses, then incest at Mansfield Park will gain its own status as a principle of waste-prevention.

Through this particular illustration of home trading in *Mansfield Park*, this chapter is able to make a series of local observations about domestic conservation strategies that gesture toward the larger argument of *Avuncularism*. It is important that renewed attention to the British home trade reflected an imagined return to the paternalistic values of feudal society, when the responsibility of a wealthy landowner included the moral and material enrichment of the tenants and laborers under his benevolent protection. Years of successful and profitable foreign commerce, it was believed, had eroded this paternal model, and under economic embargo the country was especially vulnerable to the kind of internal violence that had overthrown the monarchy in France. At the level of the state, a healthy and productive domestic economy would ward off the threat of revolution by reinstating the lost values of affective paternalism to the social hierarchy. At the level of the family, moreover, the decreased availability of dangerous French luxuries would initiate a moral change in children made rebellious and disrespectful by an economy of commercial exchange and lavish display.

With reference to *Mansfield Park*, Sir Thomas Bertram has been guilty of neglect on both levels; as Maaja Stewart has argued, Sir Thomas's money is derived from a West Indian plantation economy that cannot finally support a persona of benevolent paternalism.[14] Although the domestic economy of a country estate tends to disguise how wealth is produced, it can't entirely hide its dependence on foreign commerce within an aura of falsely assumed self-sufficiency. Yet with revenues from his colonial holdings in decline, Sir Thomas makes commercial autonomy his new order of business, converting his foreign exchange into a home trade to avoid the dangers and instabilities of exterior markets. In this way, Fanny's movement from niece to daughter also marks the Bertram family's internalization of "accountability" as theorized by Max Weber; as I discussed in my Introduction, capitalism can only mature when unrepressed gain spirit dissolves the "naïve pieties" that originally protect the affective family from the laws of economic exchange. Under this philosophy of accountability in

*Mansfield Park*, the sphere of the family and the sphere of commerce become openly coterminous, transforming brotherhood into otherhood, incest into economic self-sufficiency, and Sir Thomas's obsolete and dysfunctional model of paternalism into a thriving avuncular home trade.

≺ I ≻

## Political Economy

Sir Thomas's sudden interest in the latent value of his domestic holdings is understandable, given the economic climate of the early nineteenth century. As early as 1779, free-trade advocate Adam Smith was describing the "natural uneasiness" which a merchant feels "at being separated so far from his capital," believing that "upon equal or nearly equal profits, the merchant naturally prefers the home trade to the foreign trade of consumption."[15] In fact, according to Smith, a merchant will always, if possible, convert "his foreign trade of consumption into a home-trade" to save himself "the risk and trouble of exportation":

Home is in this manner the center, if I may say so, round which the capitals of the inhabitants of every country are continually circulating . . . a capital employed in the home trade . . . necessarily puts into motion a greater quantity of domestic industry, and gives revenue and employment to a greater number of the inhabitants of the country than an equal capital employed in the foreign trade of consumption.[16]

Even before the French wars threatened England's international commerce, political economists like Smith lauded fair-price home consumption as a way for merchants to alleviate the instabilities of the foreign marketplace. By the early part of the nineteenth century, moreover, a series of economic events had indeed conspired to make a conversion to home trading increasingly appealing: not only did Napoleon's control of European ports and shipping channels threaten to bring Britain's foreign commerce entirely to a halt, America closed its ports to most British goods in 1806. Moreover, the profits from British colonial plantations were rendered completely unstable by both internal rebellions and uprisings, and economic and political events like the bankruptcy of Antigua's local government in 1805 and the Act for the Abolition of

the Slave Trade in 1807. If these particular events help contextual-
ize Sir Thomas's difficulties with his West Indian plantations, his
sudden appreciation of Fanny on his return from Antigua resonates with the isolationist solution proposed by British newspapers, periodic publications, and economic tracts and journals
from the early years of the nineteenth century. Reflecting a host of
anxieties prompted by the immanent decline of British commerce,
economists urged a pre-emptive strike against international trade
through the internal cultivation, improvement, and development
of long-neglected English resources.

Adam Smith's early assessment of the dangers of foreign exchange was recalled at the turn of the century by economists like
Thomas Robert Malthus, who argued that England's current problem was inevitable given the improvident trade practices of the
past few years:

It is the nature of things that a state which subsists upon a revenue fur-
nished by other countries, must be infinitely more exposed to all the ac-
cidents of time and chance, than one which produces its own. . . . Dr.
Smith justly observes that the Navigation Act, and the monopoly of the
colony trade, necessarily forced into a particular and not very advantageous channel, a greater proportion of the capital of Great Britain than
would otherwise have gone to it; and by thus taking capital from other
employments, and at the same time universally raising the rate of British
mercantile profit, discouraged the improvement of the land.[17]

England had completely neglected her own agricultural resources
during the period of flourishing international commerce, so an
improved "home trade" was heralded as the most obvious solution
for imposed economic isolation. Following Malthus, reformers
such as William Cobbett and Arthur Young encouraged landowners to embrace a variety of improvements designed to invigorate
the internal economy through, among other things, the expedient
enclosure and cultivation of England's interior waste lands. Rather
than characterizing such a strategy as a defeat of British commerce, home-trading philosophy suggested that a revival of domestic agriculture would also revive a sense of responsibility in landowners and respectful subservience in farmers and laborers, diffus-
ing benevolent effects throughout the economic hierarchy.

William Spence offered the most sustained argument for the
home trade in his 1807 tract *Britain Independent of Commerce*,

beginning with the declaration that it was both "humiliating and distressing" for England's vigor to depend on a system of commerce entirely beyond domestic control.[18] Spence argued that it was only a matter of time before both West and East Indian possessions were retaken by rebellious indigenous populations "assisted by the military skill and knowledge of our European enemies."[19] With the colonial trade so seriously at risk, renewed attention to the home trade is Spence's primary objective; yet rather than eliminate the concept of commerce entirely, Spence's goal is an economic system in which production and consumption are safely contained within England's borders. Spence explains:

It is the increase of our consumption of luxuries fabricated at home which I contend for, not of foreign luxuries . . . the moment our manufacturing class is deprived of its foreign market, we ought to cease our consumption of them, and supply the place of that market, by an increased use of home products.[20]

Spence's analysis was not entirely lost on the *Weekly Political Register*, where editor William Cobbett published a series of his own articles called "Perish Commerce!" More vituperative than Spence, Cobbett was also less able to make Spence's subtle distinction between foreign and home trading, and his essays primarily consist of the repeated declaration that England would lose none of its essential strength by being thrown back upon past resources and practices: "Pitt is gone, commerce, as the foundation of a system of politics, will soon follow him, and, let us hope that Englishmen will once more see their country something like what it formerly was."[21] Yet agricultural reformer Arthur Young responded more fully to the ideas outlined by Spence, describing the concept of home trading within the agricultural sector in a series of letters to the Editor of the *Political Register*. Following Spence, as well as Smith and Malthus, Young argued that domestic resources were the foundation of England's national prosperity, and that an expedient enclosure of waste land would allow England to eschew foreign commerce, and raise its corn entirely at home. Citing statistics on British corn importation, Young confessed "that such an importation seems to be an enormous evil, and which calls for more attention than all the sugar colonies and distilleries that ever existed . . . if such an importation does not call for a general enclosure of our wastes, the voice of reason can no longer be heard."[22]

As recommended by Young, agricultural improvement of neglected soil was a doubly appealing proposition: on the one hand,
it promised sustenance for a population that, Malthus argued,
would soon outstrip its food supply, and it simultaneously returned the country to a paternalistic model of social relations that
external trade had appeared to exterminate. If the current French
blockade made the prospect of starvation an immediate concern,
the recent French Revolution had increased anxiety about a similarly violent dissolution of England's ruling class. Again, attention
to and cultivation of England's internal resources provided the
most expedient solution: as a Mr. Marshall insisted in his 1801
tract *On the Appropriation and Inclosure of Commonable and Intermixed Lands*, "the present distresses of the people, led to acts
of violence, by a want of the necessaries which these lands are capable of furnishing, might be a sufficient warrant to bring them
immediately into cultivation."[23] In order to ward off violent revolution from within and gradual economic destruction from without, England's waste lands were to be converted into food for the
enervated, demoralized, and hungry home trade.

In 1812, after nine years of war with France, reformers were
still calling for the reclaiming of waste lands as a way to remedy
the immanent extinction of foreign commerce, and to "approach a
perfect independence from our neighbors."[24] However, writers like
the anonymous "Agricola" were seemingly less concerned with
the possibility of violent revolution than they were with other foreign challenges to British paternalism. Remembering the lessons
of another fallen empire, Agricola argues for a proud and virtuous
isolationism based on honest agriculture rather than an "immoral-
izing" foreign commerce:

. . . although trade is the source of riches to the mercantile part of the nation, yet it has its concomitant disadvantages; for instance it is the
means of introducing foreign vices and politics, the bane and influence of
which tend to diminish our regard to the genuine interests of our country: and it may be observed and must be strongly imprinted in the minds
of historical readers, that when Rome was poor . . . and contented herself
with cultivating the principles of virtuous poverty she was able to withstand all efforts to subdue her, and for a time to triumph over her opposing enemies. To what are we in reason to ascribe this but to her inhabitants having individually an interest in her soil, that naturally strength-
ened the *amor patria* which forms so conspicuous a feature in the Roman

character. [Eventually] Commerce had acquainted her with luxury, and she . . . exerted her fascinating and dangerous influence at the ready beck of every rich, designing and powerful man. By an easy figure the observations may apply nationally to us. Should an overruling providence permit our commerce totally to be destroyed, . . . and compel us to live on our own resources, England might not, I admit, maintain the proud mercantile preeminence she has been accustomed to, but she would still be great and respectable within herself as a nation. By the simple practice of employing the refuse of trade in agriculture, and by gradually weaning ourselves from foreign luxuries, for which we so dearly pay, and by depending on the bounty of providence for the conveniences of life, the zest for foreign superfluities soon would relax and vanish.[25]

I have quoted at length from Agricola's interesting and *Concise Essay on the British Constitution* in order to display certain associations as they unfold: not only does foreign commerce erode our "*amor patria*," it does so by decreasing our interest in the soil and removing our capital from agricultural development. Conversely, by "employing the refuse of trade in agriculture" England can actually convert its waste into profit, its exchange value into use value, while re-educating its disaffected citizens in a patriotic love of home and country.

Yet perhaps the most pertinent aspect of Agricola's essay lurks at the center of the above passage in the form taken by the anti-paternalistic figure of Commerce, who exerts "her fascinating and dangerous influence at the ready beck of every rich, designing and powerful man." Not only did the figure of the prostitute provide a powerful icon of illicit commerce in a variety of literature of the period, as Catherine Gallagher has argued more generally, "the sphere of exchange as opposed to that of production, is traditionally associated with women."[26] While Agricola uses the seductive woman to give metaphoric emphasis to the dangers of perpetual foreign exchange, conduct books and domestic novels reversed the teleology of the metaphor, attributing sexual aberrance in women to the vices of foreign commerce and, by the same logic, female purity and domestic sanctity to the virtues of home trading. Here, indeed, the discourses of internal cultivation and improvement inevitably merge, as the prevention of internal waste becomes a subject of anxiety for all managers of England's domestic resources.

≺ II ≻

*Domestic Economy*

Not only did early nineteenth-century conduct books produce a
revulsion for foreign exchange by forging deliberate connections
between trade and female misconduct, French commodities and
anti-paternalism, these guides inspired a nationalistic preference
for internal productivity through myriad recipes for household
thrift and waste prevention. This assertion may seem to challenge
Nancy Armstrong's formidable argument that because "eighteenth-century conduct books ceased to provide advice for the care
of livestock or the concoction of medicinal cures . . . producing
goods to be consumed by the household was apparently no longer
their readers' concern."[27] Yet while it is certainly true that the prescriptive household practices Armstrong describes are less prevalent in eighteenth-century conduct materials, their suppressed
mercantile idiom resurfaces within a new set of prescriptions for
female behavior, education, and self-regulation. A virtual economics of conduct began to shape late eighteenth-century prescriptive
literature for women, an economics that redefined family life
within categories previously reserved for a more political brand of
domestic economy, insisting upon strategies of retention rather
than exchange, consumption rather than exportation.

At the turn of the century, both Maria Edgeworth and Hannah
More were noting the shifted focus of conduct materials Armstrong mentions, a shift they interpreted as the end of an era of
"useful" female occupations and the beginning of a modern era
concerned only with female display. This vacillation was in some
minor ways admitted to be an improvement over past prescribed
behaviors in the sense that the kind of accomplishments women
were now expected to possess gave them a repertoire of "sedentary
occupations" which, Edgeworth writes, are "valuable to those who
must lead sedentary lives."[28] Affixing some kind of value to these
sedentary occupations is one of Edgeworth's initial concerns in her
1801 treatise *Practical Education*, as she evaluates the economic
argument in favor of female display put forth by the purveyors of
modern notions of female education:

Accomplishments, it seems, are valuable, as being the objects of universal admiration. Some accomplishments have another species of value, as

they are tickets of admission to fashionable company. Accomplishments have another, and a higher species of value, as they are supposed to increase a young lady's chance of a prize in the matrimonial lottery. Accomplishments also have value as resources against ennui, as they afford continual amusement and innocent occupation.[29]

While female economic function had been, in the recent past, located in the "useful" nexus of household management, the modern emphasis on display laid bare the fact that middle-class female value under capitalism increasingly resembled aristocratic female value, and was hence derived from objectification and from exchange. After making this point, Edgeworth launches her critique, a critique designed to show the diminishing returns of the modern system, and to suggest that the successful production of English domesticity relied upon a more efficacious production of useful daughters, wives, and mothers.

If what has been said of the probability of a decline in the public taste for what are usually called accomplishments; of their little utility to the happiness of families and individuals; of the waste of time, and waste of the higher powers of the mind in acquiring them: if what has been observed on any of these points is allowed to be just, we shall have little difficulty in pursuing them further.[30]

As the accomplishments that Edgeworth previously described in terms of value are gradually revealed to be waste, female education itself takes on an economic function, and the family begins to assume the responsibility of producing and reproducing its own domestic happiness. Yet with accomplishments identified as waste, the defining factors of female value were again thrown into question, necessitating a new cultural interpretation of female utility, and the construction of a kind of domesticity that was not at odds with burgeoning middle-class ideologies of femininity.

Fellow conduct book writer Hannah More approached the reorientation of female value in ways similar to Edgeworth, initially according the new female accomplishments a modicum of static, "sedentary" value, but eventually revealing her suspicions about their limitations:

Let me be allowed to repeat, that I mean not with preposterous praise to descant on the ignorance or the prejudices of past times, nor absurdly to regret that vulgar system of education which rounded the little circle of female acquirements within the limits of the sampler and the receipt book. Yet if a preference almost exclusive was then given to what was merely useful, a preference almost exclusive also is now assigned to what is merely ornamental. And it must be owned, that the life of a young lady, formerly, too much resembled the life of a confectioner, it now too much resembles the life of an actress; the morning is all rehearsal, and the evening is all performance.[31]

As I will later turn to the private theatricals at Mansfield Park as a primary site of female wastage, I would like to briefly call attention to the above theatrical analogy and its place within More's distinctly economic understanding of female conduct. If the cultural shift from female utility to display prompted Edgeworth to locate a limited form of economic value *within* female accomplishments only to then redefine that value as waste, More's idiomatic movement from confectioner to actress, from use to display, signals a creation of a third category of utility that was neither the hands-on drudgery of household production nor the artificial production of theatrical talents. Production, in fact, had to go underground entirely in More's new formulation of female utility, as, in Armstrong's words, "a woman educated in the practices of *inconspicuous* consumption"[32] became the new domestic heroine. Instead of producing any kind of tangible commodity open to exchange or alienation in the social marketplace, a woman's education was to be an end in itself: a commodity produced entirely for domestic, and hence invisible, forms of use. More writes,

The chief end to be proposed in cultivating the understandings of women, is to qualify them for the practical purposes of life. Their knowledge is not often like the learning of men, to be reproduced in some literary composition, nor ever in any learned profession; but it is to come out in conduct. A lady studies, not that she may qualify herself to become an orator or a pleader; not that she may learn to debate, but to act. She is to read the best books, not so much to enable her to talk of them, as to bring the improvement which they furnish, to the formation of her habits. The great uses of study are to enable her to regulate her own mind, and to be useful to others.[33]

Denied the "reproduction" of knowledge allowed to men in the form of scholarship, the new domestic woman transformed her knowledge into conduct, thereby internalizing the superficial "acting" of theatrical display as the more sincere "acting" of cultivated behavior. In this way, the whole definition of economy was transformed by writers of conduct manuals, who, like More, needed—simultaneously—to identify the use-value of female labor while rendering inconspicuous its function *as* labor:

Economy, such as a woman of fortune is called on to practice, is not merely the petty detail of small daily expenses, the shabby curtailments and stinted parsimony of a little mind operating on little concerns; but it is the exercise of a sound judgment exerted in the comprehensive outline of order, of arrangement, of distribution; of regulations by which alone well governed societies, great and small, subsist. She who has the best regulated mind will, other things being equal, have the best regulated family.[34]

By regulating itself, the female mind would mysteriously regulate the order and arrangement of the family, making the economics of the household virtually indistinguishable from the economics of female knowledge.

This internalization of economic function in the shift from female display to use is certainly seen by Armstrong as having significant political implications: "Under the dominion of such a woman," Armstrong writes, "the country house could no longer authorize a political system that made sumptuary display the ultimate aim of production. Instead, it proposed a world where production was an end in itself rather than a means to such an end."[35] Yet I would extend the cultural significance of Armstrong's important observations, and argue that the domestic woman's new skills and abilities were defined by contemporary discourses of home-trading that called for a more widespread internalization of England's commercial practices. Indeed, considering that the goal of the conduct book was to seal production and consumption within strict domestic boundaries and to make the regulation of the family wholly dependent upon the regulation of female behavior, it seems inevitable that More would eventually use language that might be more familiar to students of political than domestic economy. "That kind of knowledge," More announces in her chapter on "The Practical Use of Female Knowledge," "which is rather fitted for *home consumption* than for *foreign exportation* is peculiarly adapted to women" (emphasis mine).[36]

At the very moment the domestic woman's economic functions become most vague, the commercial language used to describe them is, conversely, most precise. Again More posits a distinction between female use and exchange, this time tapping into a discourse of trade relations borrowed from writers like Smith,

Malthus, Young, and Cobbett, making clear the extent to which conduct manuals like *Strictures on Female Education* began to filter modern ideas about female behavior through contemporary economic concerns. It becomes increasingly obvious that More was using her own anxiety about female commodification to reference economic debates about how open British markets should be to foreign trade when we discover More's apparently nationalistic objectives in penning such a hard-hitting critique of English women: "to expose the weakness of the land as to suggest the necessity of internal improvement, and to point out the means of effectual defense is not treachery, but patriotism."[37] As commodities produced by English soil, women were subject to the same risks likely to befall more tangible forms of capital when employed in foreign trade. Just as turn-of-the-century political economy lauded home consumption as a way for merchants to alleviate the dangers of foreign commerce while increasing both domestic industry and *amor patria*, turn-of-the-century domestic economy recommended its own version of home trading as the safest and most lucrative outlet for female knowledge. The seductive danger of perpetual exchange represented by the prostitute or actress is banished by both systems of economic logic, and the commodity consumed at home rather than abroad replenishes the family and the nation, effecting patriotism and domestic harmony simultaneously.

≺ III ≻

### Home Trading in 'Mansfield Park'

The "shabby curtailments" and "stinted parsimony" censured in More's *Strictures* should now lend some context to the brand of bad economy represented by Aunt Norris, while the laurels of More's "best regulated mind" will necessarily fall to Fanny Price, the inconspicuously consumed niece and consuming domestic heroine of *Mansfield Park*. Because they constantly call attention to their own machinations, because they insist upon the visibility of their own operations, because the "details are continually present" and the economist "is overwhelmed by their weight, and is perpetually bespeaking your pity for her labours, and your praise for her exertions,"[38] Aunt Norris's frugal domestic practices—

while eventually banished from the economy of Mansfield Park—will lend us an idiom of consumption, waste, and expenditure long enough to make Fanny's inconspicuous economic function visible within Austen's novel.

In fact, Aunt Norris's bad domestic management skills are evident from the opening pages of *Mansfield Park*, as her ignorance about the economics of endogamy, her blatant misunderstanding of the laws of home consumption, is revealed by her plan to "adopt" one of her Sister Price's daughters, and raise her with very little expense to herself alongside of the Bertram's four children. Initially, of course, endogamy is not an economic strategy Sir Thomas is over-willing to practice, and he abhors the thought that Fanny's entrance into his family will resemble a premature marriage transaction. Yet Sir Thomas's semi-articulated anxieties about "cousins in love" are quelled by his sister-in-law's now infamous assertion that cousins who are raised as siblings are morally incapable of forming incestuous attachments:

Suppose her a pretty girl, and seen by Tom or Edmund for the first time seven years hence, and I dare say there would be mischief. The very idea of her having been suffered to grow up at a distance from us all in poverty and neglect, would be enough to make either of the dear sweet-tempered boys in love with her. But breed her up with them from this time, and suppose her to have the beauty of an angel, and she will never be more to either than a sister. (4–5)

Aunt Norris's reasoning here would seem less faulty if Sir Thomas actually intended to raise Fanny as a daughter. On the contrary, Fanny's admittance into the Bertram family is contingent upon a collective recognition of her inferior social status, and her own daily consciousness that "she is not a *Miss Bertram*" (8). Sir Thomas is resolute about the class division that must be erected and maintained between Fanny and her cousins, and his vanity prevents him from realizing that these intentions would seem to negate the conditions of his sister-in-law's prior argument: "I should wish to see them very good friends, and would, on no account, authorize in my girls the smallest degree of arrogance towards their relation; but still they cannot be equals. Their rank, fortune, rights and expectations, will always be different" (8).

If we return for a moment to Jane Gallop's non-nuclear family romance, and by extension to Hannah More's distinction between use and exchange, Sir Thomas's anxious need for a discernible "difference" between his daughters and his niece becomes more provocative. In fact, the different "rank, fortune, rights, and expectations" granted to Fanny as a niece in the Bertram's home is perpetually assimilated to the economic and sexual difference usually reserved for the governess. It is easy to forget the unobtrusive Miss Lee while she is an inmate of Mansfield Park, but once the governess has departed the house she becomes a haunting emblem of Fanny's threshold status within her uncle's home. At Aunt Norris's suggestion, ten year-old Fanny is given "the little white attic, near the old nurseries" (7) for a bedroom, a space that is both perpetually infantilizing, and is connected—geographically and socially—with the rooms occupied by Miss Lee and the housemaids. As an adult Fanny is granted access to another room, "more spacious and more meet for walking about in, and thinking" (135), and this new chamber continues to link her with the phantom governess:

It had been their school-room; so called till the Miss Bertrams would not allow it to be called so any longer, and inhabited as such to a much later period. There Miss Lee had lived, and there they had read and written, and talked and laughed, till within the last three years, when she had quitted them.—The room had then become useless, and for some time was quite deserted, except by Fanny, when she visited her plants, or wanted one of the books, which she was still glad to keep there, from deficiency of space and accommodation in her little chamber above;—but gradually, as her value for the comforts of it increased, she had added to her possessions, and spent more of her time there; and having nothing to oppose her, had so naturally and so artlessly worked herself into it, that it was now generally admitted to be hers. (135–36)

If Fanny's gradual appropriation of an otherwise "useless" space, a room "nobody else wanted" (136), isn't enough to reinforce her identification with waste and excess, the sparse furnishings of the room include "a faded footstool of Julia's work, too ill done for the drawing-room, three transparencies, made in a rage for transparencies . . . and a collection of family profiles thought unworthy of being anywhere else" (137). Going to waste with all the other rejected trappings of Bertram family life, Fanny "naturally" enters the governess's room as she approaches adulthood, thereby confirming her social displacement within the Bertram family: if Fanny does not have children to educate, she is still required to fill

Miss Lee's place as a companion to her indolent aunt, "naturally bec[oming] every thing to Lady Bertram during the night of a ball or a party" (30). Even the role that temporarily falls to Fanny in the Mansfield production of "Lovers' Vows" was to have been played by the governess at Ecclesford, and Mr. Yates explains that the Ecclesford company "all agreed that it could not be offered to anyone else" (121).

"By fulfilling the duties of the domestic woman for money," Nancy Armstrong argues, the governess called "into question an absolutely rigid distinction between domestic duty and labor that was performed for money,"[39] making, I would add, the economic logic of domesticity even more legible in a novel like *Mansfield Park*. With Fanny's difference from Maria and Julia Bertram understood as the socioeconomic liminality of a Miss Lee, Fanny's family value is increasingly derived from her utility as a form of domestic labor. The accumulated "possessions" in Fanny's sitting room seem oddly limited to a "table between the windows . . . covered with work-boxes and netting-boxes" (138), the unnecessary redundancy of the items forming a veritable shrine to unpaid and unappreciated female work, the kind of "useful" labor women were expected to undertake in the past, as well as serving as a constant reminder of the "amount of debt" (138) Fanny is somehow under obligation to repay. Fanny works out this debt in the service of her aunts, sitting "at home all day with one aunt, or walk[ing] beyond her strength at the instigation of the other" (31), in addition to all the stooping, cutting, stitching, and message-carrying she is forced to do during her tenure as a niece. Yet Fanny's role is not the only one at Mansfield Park that carries an economic valence: if nieces are emblems of household utility, daughters are the promise of family aggrandizement through exchange. Although Sir Thomas is made uneasy by the "extravagance" of his eldest son, his "daughters he felt, while they retained the name of Bertram, must be giving it new grace, and in quitting it he trusted would extend its respectable alliances" (17).

Luce Irigaray's analysis of female commodification lends a twentieth-century feminist perspective to the categories of female value formulated by the conduct literature of Hannah More and Maria Edgeworth. As commodities, women draw their value from the "cult of the father," to use Irigaray's phrase, and can be measured as a form of wealth as long as their use value is subordinated to their market value. She writes:

*Women-as-commodities are thus subject to a schism* that divides them into the categories of usefulness and exchange value; into matter-body and an envelope that is precious but impenetrable, ungraspable, and not susceptible to appropriation by women themselves; into private use and social use.[40]

Just as the difference between foreign exportation and home consumption defined two separate and unequal varieties of female education in More's *Strictures*, the difference between daughters and nieces in *Mansfield Park* begins as a "schism" between the social use to which Sir Thomas can put his daughters, and the private use to which he relegates his niece. Even though Fanny seems to have already entered circulation in her move from the Price's home to the Bertrams', the symbolic power of the Name of the Father has invested Fanny with no Price at all. Fanny's own mother is "surprised that a girl should be fixed on, when she had so many fine boys" (9), and Aunt Bertram soothes Sir Thomas's difficulties with her plan by insisting that there can be "no difference" between two girls in the family and three (7). Although all of the Price children fall under the heading of "superfluity" (3), daughters represent negative value, a form of internal waste that the Portsmouth family can give up without much regret.

At Mansfield Park, however, the value of daughters is significantly higher, and when Sir Thomas finds it financially necessary to make an extended visit to his plantation in Antigua, he regrets leaving "his daughters to the direction of others at their present most interesting time of life" (28). Maria and Julia are both emblems of their father's economic worth and important extensions of his power, and at eighteen and seventeen respectively, they are "most interesting" because they are at the threshold of marriageability: the moment at which their value as exchangeable commodities will demand the most interest. Fanny's value is, conversely, confined to the schoolroom: she is deliberately denied passage into the realm of exchange and prevented from becoming as interesting as her cousins. Unfortunately, while he is attending to the economic instability of his colonial holdings in Antigua, Sir Thomas's domestic holdings are exposed to similar forms of misuse, beginning with the way Maria and Julia feel that they are "at their own disposal" (28) in their father's absence. Already noted for their habit of "wasting gold paper" (11) as children, Maria and Julia display a newly burgeoning independence that again taps into the idiom of economic depletion, and although it is their appointed guardian's self-proclaimed duty to prevent waste and to "make the most of things" (128), Aunt Norris will prove a faulty economist when it comes to her nieces.

Interestingly, Aunt Norris's animated turn for domestic economy is attributed to her having married on a small income, and "what had begun as a matter of prudence, soon grew into a matter of choice, as an object of that needful solicitude, which there were no children to supply" (6). Frugality, in other words, is a sublimation of maternal instinct that becomes more insistent and "infatuating" with each "yearly addition to an income which [the Norrises] had never lived up to" (6). In fact, the accumulation of money is further linked with the production of children by the way that Aunt Norris's parsimonious need to "lay by a little at the end of the year" (26), is an idiomatic reminder of her sister Price's nearly annual "lying-in" (3).[41] By the time Fanny is adopted by the Bertrams, Aunt Norris is as skilled at saving her own resources as she is at spending her friends', and her sister's child becomes another unit of value to appropriate and control without any expense to herself. All of her nieces, in fact, become commodities for Aunt Norris to use or exchange in the name of Sir Thomas, and if she has employed Fanny to be an instrument of domestic drudgery, she is just as committed to "promoting gaieties for her (other) nieces, assisting their toilettes, displaying their accomplishments, and looking about for their future husbands" (30).

Aunt Norris's endeavors pay off, of course, in the form of Maria Bertram's engagement to the wealthy but insipid Mr. Rushworth: "a connection exactly of the right sort" (35) for Sir Thomas. Directly following Mr Rushworth's proposal, however, Mary and Henry Crawford arrive at Mansfield parsonage on a visit to their half-sister Mrs. Grant, and the stage is set for Aunt Norris's economic acumen to be severely disgraced. Although "Miss Bertram's engagement made him in equity the property of Julia," Henry Crawford is "the most agreeable young man the sisters had ever known" (39), and Maria does not see the impropriety of allowing his attentions. Identical in their feminine accomplishments, in their dislike of their father, and in their general abuse of Fanny, Maria and Julia are also represented as having identical desires, and their mutual ambition to play Agatha in the Mansfield production of "Lovers Vows" has everything to do with their mutual desire for Henry Crawford. Henry's ongoing flirtation with both sisters enhances the lack of differentiation that early on makes each sister seem like a dim reflection of the other—redundant female figures that problematically diffuse and duplicate each other's social value.

As readers of *Pride and Prejudice* understand, female iteribility is very much an economic problem. Not only does the presence of several marriageable daughters in the family at one time place a heavy burden on the family's financial resources, it introduces a level of competition amongst sisters for husbands that can only be characterized as uneconomical. We may remember Lady Catherine De Borough's shock when she learns from Elizabeth that the five Bennet sisters have had no governess, and that they are all "out" simultaneously: "All!—What, all five at once? Very odd!— And you only the second.—The younger ones out before the elder are married!"[42] Moreover, Lady Catherine's disapproval of the Bennett sisters' redundancy may reflect a more general social concern that the fashionable accomplishments women strove to acquire in order to increase their chances in the marriage market ironically flooded the market with scores of identically educated females. Maria Edgeworth, in fact, is careful to warn parents that while the right combination of female accomplishments may have purchased wealthy husbands in the past,

they forget that everybody now has the same reflections, that parents are, and have been for some years, speculating in the same line; consequently, the market is likely to be overstocked, and, of course, the value of the commodities must fall.[43]

Hannah More, likewise, pointed out that the female pursuit of accomplishments had become so universal that women of the upper classes increasingly found themselves competing for husbands against the well-educated daughters of tradesmen and farmers, producing an "abundant multiplication of superficial wives"[44] to further threaten the already abundant Bennett girls.

Just as these cautionary passages serve to remind us of the

commercial rhetoric that informed descriptions of female education within conduct literature, they should also encourage us to
read Aunt Bertram's busy display of her nieces' accomplishments
as another sign of poor economy, and the perpetual redundancy of
the Bertram sisters in terms of diminishing female value. Even
though Maria is engaged to Mr. Rushworth, she is so habituated to
displaying herself and her accomplishments that she will not easily take on the private utility that should be the end result of the
home consumption of marriage. More confirms that this problem
of female display is so significant that it will eventually reflect
poorly upon the household economy of a young husband:

. . . if a man select a picture for himself from among all its exhibited
competitors, and bring it to his own house, the picture being passive, he
is able to fix it there: while the wife, picked up at a public place, and accustomed to incessant display, will not, it is probable, when brought
home, stick so quietly to the spot where he fixes her; but will escape to
the exhibition room again, and continue to be displayed at every subsequent exhibition, just as if she were not become private property, and had
never been definitively disposed of.[45]

How to encourage young women to properly dispose of themselves
once married, to become private property thoroughly and permanently, was part of the impetus behind the reformed brand of domestic economy put forth by More and Edgeworth. Female accomplishments were bad economy not only because they made
the women who possessed them redundant, they also inhibited
female flexibility as commodities, endangering the whole process
by which women pass from foreign exchange to home consumption, or within the language of *Mansfield Park*, from valuable
daughters to virtuous wives.

Yet the problem of female superfluity in *Mansfield Park* does
not begin and end with the plight of Maria and Julia Bertram; conversely, the novel introduces us to the state of such redundancies
in the opening description of an earlier set of sisters, the three
Ward sisters, and the narrator's famous observation that "there are
not so many men of large fortune in the world, as there are pretty
women to deserve them" (1). Recalling More's previously discussed metaphor of the stage, it is not surprising that this ratio of
men to women announces an economy of female circulation with-

in the text that repeatedly surfaces, especially when the number of aspiring actresses in the Mansfield theater company exceeds the number of significant female roles in "Lover's Vows," and it becomes clear that one woman's talents must inevitably go to waste. The part of Amelia falls "naturally" to Mary Crawford—"Amelia should be a small, light, girlish, skipping figure" in Tom Bertram's opinion (122)—but Maria and Julia's qualities are so identical that Tom carelessly assigns the role of Agatha to "one or other of my sisters" (120).

When Henry chooses Maria to play Agatha to his Frederick, however, he disrupts the redundancy of the sisters so effectively that even Tom is convinced of Julia's unfitness for the part: "She has not the look of it. Her features are not tragic features, and she walks too quick, and speaks too quick, and would not keep her countenance. She had better do the old countrywoman; the Cottager's wife; you had, indeed, Julia"(121). At the moment of taking on the effects of female difference, Julia is offered the role the governess had played at Ecclesford—the substandard part that will eventually, momentarily, fall to Fanny. Female difference can only be articulated in *Mansfield Park* through the ideologically complex figure of the governess, and although the rest of the company denounces Tom's insensitive type-casting, Julia is still stigmatized by her association with Fanny's brand of excess and her assimilation to waste. In this way, it is *Julia* rather than Fanny who at first seems destined to play the figure of perennial redundancy within the Bertram family, as the moment she ceases to double for her sister, she begins to temporarily double for her governess-like cousin. Julia becomes Fanny's fellow "sufferer" (143), a spectator rather than a participant in the rehearsals of "Lovers' Vows," and this similarity remains intact until Maria's marriage to Rushworth, when the sisters are oddly assimilable once again.

More peripheral stories of female circulation and exchange provide a thematic backdrop for Maria and Julia's sisterly redundancies: the two Miss Sneyds, for example, are used by Tom Bertram to illustrate his experiences of female sameness to Mary Crawford.

They looked just the same; both well dressed, with veils and parasols like other girls; but I afterwards found that I had been giving all my attention to the youngest, who was not *out*, and had most excessively offended the eldest. Miss Augusta ought not to have been noticed for the next six months, and Miss Sneyd, I believe, has never forgiven me. (45)

The Sneyds' redundancy is a bad economic strategy in two ways: not only does the value of the unmarried elder sister decrease when a younger, more vivacious version of herself is introduced into the marketplace, female iteribility is also, according to Tom, a waste of male sexual energy. Interestingly, Mary Crawford's remedy for the Sneyd sisters' redundancy throws us once again into the familiar ideological space of female difference: "Miss Augusta should have been with her governess. Such half and half doings never prosper" (45–46). The moral that Mary affixes to the plight of the Sneyd sisters, moreover, repeats itself in Tom's tale of his attentions to an unresponsive Miss Anderson, a girl who failed to register as "in" because "the governess [was] sick or run away" (44). By extending her own social, economic, and sexual liminality to her pupils, the governess italicizes the sexual latency of girls who are "in," enforcing a more prosperous form of sisterly difference along the lines of availability, and circumventing the kind of waste experienced by men like Tom Bertram.[46]

Of course, Tom and Mary's conversation about the "outs and not outs" (43) of female sexual development takes place under the rubric of a discussion of *Fanny's* difference, as Mary cannot initially understand if Fanny is "in" or "out." Edmund's response that Fanny is "grown up" (43) is not particularly helpful to Mary, and she only concludes that "Miss Price is *not* out" when Edmund admits that Fanny does not circulate as an exogamous sexual commodity in the same way that his sisters do: "My mother seldom goes into company herself . . . and Fanny stays at home with *her*" (46). Fanny's adult sexuality hits no social register; like the governess's, her value is supplementary rather than primary, and coded as use rather than exchange.

Even after the sign of the governess has effectively imposed a form of difference between Maria and Julia, the Bertram family continues to have a problem with waste. The Mansfield theatricals prove to be a more expensive undertaking than anyone had foreseen, not only in the cost of constructing a theater and outfitting the players with appropriate costumes, but in the way that playacting rehearses heterosexual desire and prematurely circulates female value within false or faulty economies of exchange. Indeed, Edmund's first objection to the theatrical project is that acting, "real" acting, is a *trade*: a commercial occupation that clearly delineates producers from consumers, performers from audience. Without this commercial logic, the economic component of acting surfaces without boundaries: "we are rehearsing all over the house," (152) Mary is delighted to report to Fanny. In fact, production and consumption become identical in the absence of any audience but the inconspicuous Fanny, not to mention the absence of the green baize curtain (the standard boundary between theatrical production and consumption) that Aunt Norris never manages to hang. Without a process of exchange to regulate supply and demand, without a domestic woman in charge who truly understands More's principles of "order, arrangement, and distribution," the Mansfield theater becomes a place of conspicuous consumption and economic depletion reflective of widespread eighteenth-century suspicions that theaters in general threatened especially the young men of England with both bodily and commercial waste:

England's prosperity, it is argued, depends on its manufactures, particularly its exports, and these, in turn, require a reliable supply of labour, which plays are bound to disturb. For in the first place by painting the matrimonial condition as they do in such ridiculous colours and with such insolent reflections, plays encourage the male members of the audience to gratify their Inclinations in a lewd and unlawful way, and so distract them from their work, as well as hindering their capacity to reproduce their kind . . . It is all very well for fine gentlemen to waste their time and spoil their reproductive powers with profligacy; such fine gentlemen are already useless to the kingdom.[47]

While the theater was liable to corrupt its audience by wasting the productive industry of England as well as the reproductive capacity of British subjects, the labor of the actors and actresses themselves was deemed "unproductive" by political economists like Adam Smith, who felt that "the declamation of the actor, the harangue of the orator, or the tune of the musician . . . perishes in the very instant of its production."[48]

In this way, the British theater is a cultural site of waste long before Maria's overpracticed scenes of affection with Henry Crawford begin to assume (in Fanny's opinion) a disturbing degree of realism, suggesting that Maria, so long used to disposing of herself, has not yet assimilated herself to the wifely condition of private property. Furthermore, Julia's jealousy of her sister's dual role in the Mansfield theatricals inspires an unwise flirtation with a financially undesirable younger son, Mr. Yates. As usual, Aunt Norris is too occupied by the bustle and importance of domestic expenditure to attend to more serious forms of waste:

too busy in contriving and directing the general little matters of the company, superintending their various dresses with economical expedient, for which nobody thanked her, and saving, with delighted integrity, half-a-crown here and there to the absent Sir Thomas, to have leisure for watching the behaviour, or guarding the happiness of his daughters. (146)

By the time "Lovers' Vows" is agreed upon by the players, the theatrical props are already under construction, and Edmund's objection to the impropriety of the choice is dismissed by Aunt Norris on the grounds of potential waste: "the preparations will be all so much money thrown away—and I'm sure *that* would be a discredit to us all" (127). In Aunt Norris's lexicon of value, wasted property takes precedence over squandered propriety, and her nieces are indiscriminately left "at their own disposal." At last even Edmund's discomfort with the "excessive intimacy" (138) of the theatricals is forced to give way to his aunt's discourse of savings, and he agrees to take part in the performance in order to "spare" Mary Crawford the humiliation of acting love scenes with a stranger. Like Aunt Norris, Edmund finally sees his participation in the theatricals as a form of economy, a sacrifice that will secure "material gain" in the long run: "If I can be the means of *restraining* the publicity of the business, of *limiting* the exhibition, of *concentrating* our folly, I shall be well repaid" (139, emphasis added).

Ironically, when the Mansfield rehearsals of "Lovers' Vows" are prematurely canceled due to the unexpected arrival of Sir Thomas from Antigua, the props, the playbooks, and the costumes are immediately scrapped. What appears to be wastefulness in Aunt Norris's understanding is actually a form of savings to Sir Thomas: his destruction of the theater and its accouterments is an attempt to conserve the reputation of his family and the exchange value of his daughters. While Fanny was the only family member who did not take part in the theatricals by choice, she seemingly belies her anti-theatrical stance by "appearing before her uncle" precisely on cue, entering the drawing-room at the very moment Sir Thomas is "looking round him, and saying 'But where is Fanny?—Why do I not see my little Fanny?'" (159). In the words of Henry Crawford, the desire to act is a desire to "be any thing or every thing" (111), and this is precisely the impulse that brings Fanny to the center-stage of the Bertram household by the end of the novel. If theatricality is the dominant metaphor in *Mansfield Park*, then Fanny is the family understudy: her years of existence in the wings of the Bertram household give her the unique ability to learn every part by heart, as she did during the rehearsals of "Lovers Vows."

Yet Fanny's apparent theatricality is the acting of *conduct* rather than the acting of performance, and, as her correct response to her Uncle's cue reveals, her stage is the drawing-room rather than the green-room. As a spare daughter, a figure of family replacement, Fanny clearly represents a unit of value that draws worth from redundancy. By occupying an inherently amorphous role within the household, the niece is the ultimate inconspicuous domestic resource, as she is invested with limitless powers of replication, and can be easily converted, in times of family crisis, from poor relation (a status dangerously close to Gallop's governess) to daughter, sister, or possibly wife. When the Bertram family closes ranks, Fanny is called upon to fill several roles simultaneously, and her status as a stand-in daughter makes her equally useful as a stand-in sister for Edmund ("My Fanny—my only sister—my only comfort now" [405]), and finally, after his disappointment in Mary Crawford, his only resource for a wife. Yet the kind of iteribility that Fanny represents to the Bertram family is markedly different from Julia's brand of imitation: while iteribility between sisters results in the uneconomical duplication of exogamous desire, Fanny's eventual ability to refashion herself in the guise of a daughter while still claiming the status of a niece allows her to have both exogamous *and* endogamous sexual value. Because Fanny is simultaneously inside and outside of the family, Sir Thomas can potentially, inconspicuously, subject her to foreign exchange *or* to home consumption.

It is also the case that the primary role Fanny will be called on to fill has been held in the past by Aunt Norris: the role of the domestic economist. If we miss the fact that Fanny's conduct produces savings for the Bertram family while everyone else's produces waste, we only have to put into economic context the scene in the drawing room on the night of Sir Thomas's return, when his narrative of colonial doings is repeatedly interrupted by Aunt Norris pressuring her brother-in-law to eat.

Mrs. Norris felt herself defrauded of an office on which she had always depended, whether his arrival or his death were to be a thing unfolded; and was now trying to be in a bustle without having any thing to bustle about, and labouring to be important where nothing was wanted but tranquillity and silence. Would Sir Thomas have consented to eat, she might have gone to the house-keeper with troublesome directions, and insulted the footmen with injunctions of dispatch; but Sir Thomas resolutely declined all dinner; he would take nothing, nothing till tea came— he would rather wait for tea. Still Mrs. Norris was at intervals urging something different, and in the most interesting moment of his passage to England, when the alarm of a French privateer was at the height, she burst through his recital with the proposal of soup. 'Sure, my dear Sir Thomas, a basin of soup would be a much better thing for you than tea. Do have a basin of soup.' (162)

While the best kind of domestic economy is supposed to disguise household commerce as family affection, Aunt Norris's crass and disruptive attempts to make her brother-in-law eat only emphasize the processes of a consumption that is anything but inconspicuous. Her derailment of a story about French aggression against British trade routes is contrasted with the way that Fanny loves "to hear my uncle talk of the West Indies," and is the only woman in the household to ask him questions about the slave trade. It becomes clear that Fanny's interest in commerce is appropriate because it is very nearly invisible, revealed not by exhibitions of frugality, nor by an hysterical enforcement of visible consumption, but by the conduct resulting from a "well-regulated mind."[49] By producing the domestic harmony that passes for affect in the best regulated families, domestic economy does indeed become an end in itself, enabling Fanny to pave the way for her own improvement into the best kind of private property: the daughter that Sir Thomas always wanted.

## ≺ IV ≻

### *Home Improvement and Waste Management*

Of course, Austen's invocation of landscape gardener Humphry Repton exemplifies the more material definition of "improvement" in *Mansfield Park*. When Maria's fiancé returns from visiting a friend whose grounds have been recently "laid out by an improver, Mr. Rushworth was returned with his head full of the subject, and very eager to be improving his own place in the same way" (46). According to Maria Bertram, Rushworth's "best friend upon such an occasion" (47) is improver Humphry Repton, whose philosophy of renovation is based upon the primary importance of *appropriation*—otherwise, making one's "property seem larger, more valuable" than it actually is.

The pleasure of appropriation is gratified in viewing a landscape which cannot be injured by the malice or bad taste of a neighboring intruder. . . an ugly barn, a ploughed field, or any obtrusive object which disgraces the scenery of a park, looks as if it belonged to another, and therefore robs the mind of the pleasure derived from appropriation, or the unity and continuity of unmixed property.[50]

Many critics have written about the importance of Repton's presence in *Mansfield Park*, and the subject has been given thorough treatment in Alistair Duckworth's book-length study of the issue, *The Improvement of the Estate*. Here, Duckworth argues that the kinds of improvements represented by Humphry Repton in *Mansfield Park* signal "a radical attitude to cultural heritage"[51]: a disregard for patriarchal inheritance that, Duckworth argues, Edmund Burke "used . . . to illustrate the horrors of revolution" in his 1790 *Reflections on the Revolution in France*.[52] Indeed, Burke likens the violent dissolution of one set of constitutional laws in favor of a wholly different set to "pulling down an edifice which has answered in any tolerable degree for ages the common purposes of society," and "of building it up again, without having models and patterns of approved utility."[53]

This link between wanton estate improvement and disregard for the useful patterns of patriarchal heritage certainly applies to Henry Crawford, who has already subjected his own paternal estate to extensive refurbishments: "I had not been of age three months before Everingham was all that it is now. My plan was laid at Westminster—a little altered perhaps at Cambridge, and at one and twenty executed" (55). Without any sense of the future utility of his improvements, Henry has laid waste to his past, making his conspicuous consumption of Everingham totally visible in his acknowledgment that he has been "a devourer" of his own happiness (55). Moreover, Henry also understands that the perceived value of an estate often increases when its signs of domestic functionality and agricultural utility are thoroughly inconspicuous. Happening accidentally one day upon Thornton Lacey, the parish that is eventually to be Edmund's, Henry begins to plan improvements that will transform a "mere Parsonage House" into "a gentleman's residence" (219), primarily by clearing away the farm-yard, and having it "planted up to shut out the blacksmith's shop" (218). The improvements Dr. and Mrs. Grant have already effected at Mansfield Parsonage are likewise reported to include extending the plantation "to shut out the churchyard" (48): a change that, dubiously, Aunt Norris claims she always wanted to make herself when she lived there. This "shutting out" of the signs of occupation and commerce upon which a country house depends effectively disguises the economic workings of a private residence while blending the social class of its individual inhabitants in a vista of "unmixed property."

Although Duckworth argues that such Reptonian improvements signal a radical "tearing down" of paternal values and institutions, the early nineteenth-century context suggests that Reptonian politics were much more complicated, and tended to reflect conservative rather than radical ideologies. Repton is often seen as the inheritor of Capability Brown's landscape techniques, but he had many problems with the improvements Brown had effected, including the "discommodious" removal of farm-yards, kitchen gardens, and dairies to great distances from the main house.

The intimate connexion between the kitchen and the garden for its produce and between the stables and the garden for its manure, is so obvious, that every one must see the propriety of bringing them as nearly together as possible . . . Yet we find in many large parks, that the fruit and vegetables are brought from the distance of a mile, or more with all the care and trouble of packing for much longer carriage.[54]

In keeping with conservative economic strategies of the early nineteenth-century, Repton's "improvements" were designed to

bring production and consumption more closely together: to reduce the care and trouble of importation and to make the internal
resources and self-sufficiency of the country estate visible in its
very landscape architecture. Tom Williamson and Liz Bellamy
have persuasively argued, in fact, that Repton's designs sought to
impose an organic image of paternalism over estates that were
visually and physically divided from the agricultural labour that
sustained them. Accentuating the "intimate connexion" between
production and consumption would make the healthy state of the
social body seem naturally hierarchical, and allow England to
avoid the more violent reactions to economic inequity represented
by the revolutions in France: "Repton and many other Tory think-
ers believed that social revolution could only be forestalled by the
benevolent paternalism that this landscape idealized."[55]

In this way, Repton's presence in *Mansfield Park* signifies not
radical politics, but a conservative, anti-revolutionary strategy of
paternalistic control. His favored status with Maria Bertram, Mr.
Rushworth, and the Crawfords signals not the rebellious spirit of
the French Revolution, but the attempts of an aristocratic elite to
impose visual unity and an illusion of complete self-sufficiency
over an increasingly unstable social and economic hierarchy.[56]
Other landscape improvers of the time period were actually more
closely associated with the revolutionary spirit Duckworth attributes to Repton; in fact, landscape gardeners like Uvedale Price and
Richard Payne Knight called for a return to more "natural" land-
scapes in keeping with Burkean notions of the picturesque. "Price
and Knight believed that landscape gardens should not merely
imitate nature, but should imitate nature in the raw . . . They
should have a drama and ruggedness that would serve to inspire
awe."[57] Such ideas had more dangerous political implications for
conservative English citizens in the early nineteenth-century than
Repton's subtle renovations. When Anna Seward wrote to Repton
in 1811, she expressed outrage at the uncivilized, anti-paternalistic
philosophy of the Burkean school of improvement as opposed to
his own manicured and healthful vision of the social order:

Mr. Knight would have nature as well as man indulged in that uncurbed
and wild luxuriance, which must soon render our landscape-island rank,
weedy, damp, and unwholesome as the incultivate savannahs of America
. . . save me, good heaven, from living in tangled forests and amongst

men who are unchecked by those guardian laws, which bind the various orders of society in one common interest. May the lawns I tread be smoothed by healthful industry, and the glades opened by the hands of picturesque taste, to admit the pure and salutary breath of heaven!—and may the people, amongst whom I live, be withheld by stronger repellants than their own virtue from invading my property and shedding my blood![58]

For Seward, the inherent unwholesomeness of natural landscape could only encourage a corresponding unwholesomeness in its inhabitants, and this state of "uncurbed and wild luxuriance" would inevitably lead to disrespect for private property and bloody revolution. Her call for Reptonian improvement in order to fend off revolution in England should remind us of Mr. Marshall's similarly reasoned call for the quick enclosure and cultivation of private property, especially in the context of his specific complaints about commonable land:

. . . through uncertainty and expense attending private acts, a great portion of the unstinted common lands remain nearly as Nature left them;—appearing, in the present state of civilization and science, as filthy blotches on the face of the country: especially when seen under the threatening clouds of famine which have now repeatedly overspread it.[59]

This wild and unappropriated land was not only unprofitable, it was an internal state of nature unmolested by civilization or science; a loathsome signifier of England's neglected interior, its "weedy, damp, and unwholesome" wastes.

Just as the idiom of improvement in conduct books represents a safe and permanent passage for women from foreign exchange to domestic utility, improvement functions in political economies to indicate the transition of land from a state of unwholesome, potentially incendiary waste to organic productivity. Although both such transitions are heralded as a return to *amor patria*, the appropriation and enclosure of what Mr. Marshall called "commonable and intermixed" land by the owner enabled such "wastes" to pass from social use to private property precisely by denying peasants and laborers access to arable lands that had been communally farmed under feudalism.[60] As Mr. Marshall explains, communal use of arable land was unprofitable because it was "constantly surcharged, as well as for the want of clearing, draining, inclosing, planting, or cultivation," and could not furnish the necessities of life as well as "what they would in a state of private property."[61] In the name of paternalism, enclosure promised to increase food for the very working-class population it shut out with Humphry Repton's aesthetically pleasing walls and picturesque fences. In both domestic and political economies, the idiom of "improvement" allows an act of economic appropriation to masquerade as paternal benevolence, and the transition from public exchange to private use to disguise itself as *amor patria*.

Perhaps this is the reason Fanny Price so dislikes Reptonian improvements, as we know from her regretful, Romantic contemplation of "fallen avenues" at Sotherton (50). She well understands the false benevolence motivating such paternal acts of appropriation and enclosure. Moreover, Fanny's abiding desire to refrain from acting and to remain behind the scenes of family interaction is implicitly threatened by Repton's own love of theatrical devices, especially his favorite hobby of thinning a "curtain" of trees in order to reveal glimpses of the "infinitely more interesting" scenery behind: in fact, "it is undrawing this curtain at proper places that the utility of what has been called breaking an avenue consists."[62] When Maria's marriage removes her from Mansfield Park, and Julia chooses to accompany her on the honeymoon, a similar thinning of Sir Thomas's family circle finally opens the curtain to reveal Fanny's more inconspicuous points of interest:

Becoming as she then did, the only young woman in the drawing-room, the only occupier of that interesting division of a family in which she had hitherto held so humble a third, it was impossible for her not to be more looked at, more thought of and attended to, than she had ever been before; and 'where is Fanny?' became no uncommon question, even without her being wanted for any one's convenience. (184)

In light of the sudden shortage in marriageable daughters at Mansfield Park, Fanny is finally allowed to leave the schoolroom and take on a displaced form of worth unrelated to her utility. As the "only occupier of that interesting division" of the Bertram family, Fanny must now both bear the interest and attendance of the Bertrams, and *bear interest* as a commodity within the social circuit of the drawing room.

Returning now to Irigaray's description of use value versus social value, it is important to remember that women's "'development' lies in their passage from one to the other."[63] Within the domestic language of *Mansfield Park*, this passage from utility to exchange is referred to as "improvement," and is thereby natural-ized as a form of development that resides in the female body. When Sir Thomas returns from Antigua he surprises his niece by treating her with a loving regard he has never shown in the past, and by joyfully celebrating what he perceives to be Fanny's "equal improvement in health and beauty" (160). Edmund attempts to explain his father's seemingly inexplicable change in behavior to Fanny:

> . . . the truth is, that your uncle never did admire you till now—and now he does. Your complexion is so improved!—and you have gained so much countenance!—and your figure—Nay, Fanny, do not turn away about it—it is but an uncle. If you cannot bear an uncle's admiration what is to be-come of you? (178)

Sir Thomas's interest in Fanny's body and health has often been explained by his prolonged absence in Antigua. As both Avrom Fleishman and Moira Ferguson have pointed out, the serious fi-nancial losses suffered by the Bertram's West Indian plantation would have been historically simultaneous with the 1807 Act for the Abolition of the Slave Trade, and Sir Thomas's journey to An-tigua reflects a measure that many absentee landowners actually undertook at the time.[64] According to Fleishman, "conditions of life and work [in the British West Indies] were so bad that the slaves failed to reproduce and survive in sufficient numbers to provide an adequate, stable labor force"; consequently, "on these sound economic grounds," a plantation owner's task would have been to institute measures of humanitarian reform in order to se-cure the good health and fair treatment of his slaves.[65]

In other words, if Sir Thomas sees Fanny's body differently af-ter his return from Antigua, it is because he has finally learned to view his niece not as a drain on the economic and sexual strength of his family, but as an interior waste that must be nourished, cul-tivated, *improved*. Despite its overdetermined nexus of meaning, the idiom of improvement in *Mansfield Park* always veils an in-ternal architecture of production and consumption, masking the too-conspicuous logic of commercial exchange within aesthetic or affective principles. Just as Repton's project of "improvement" is the task of removing or disguising the intrusive signs of function-ality that ruin "the scenery of a park," Sir Thomas's promotion of

Fanny to the status of a daughter will take an object "that looks like it belonged to another" and create an illusory "continuity of unmixed property." Moreover, in the process of becoming the daughter Sir Thomas always wanted, Fanny will also emerge as the only woman Henry Crawford can really *love*. Without Maria or Julia to occupy his flirtatious attentions, Henry is likewise struck by the miraculous "improvement" in Fanny Price's appearance, as he explains to his sister, Mary.

> You see her every day, and therefore do not notice it, but I assure you, she is quite a different creature from what she was in the autumn. She was then merely a quiet, modest, not plain looking girl, but she is now absolutely pretty . . . her air, her manner, her tout ensemble is so indescribably improved! (20)

Linked by their shared perception of Fanny's "improvement," Sir Thomas and Henry Crawford can be situated along the continuum of male iterability in *Mansfield Park*, a continuum that is as necessary as female iterability in the perpetuation of capitalist patriarchy. Irigaray explains that "in order for a product—a woman?—to have value, two men, at least, have to invest (in) her."[66]

In some ways, Sir Thomas already understands the superior brand of investment that Fanny represents at Mansfield Park. As he watches his niece walk back into the breakfast room after the early morning departure of her beloved brother William to London with Henry Crawford, he takes for granted her seemingly unlimited capacity for savings, attributing to his niece an ability to convert even the waste products of his estate into a species of affect that will extend his patriarchal connections:

> her uncle kindly left her to cry in peace, conceiving perhaps that the deserted chair of each young man might exercise her tender enthusiasm, and that the remaining cold pork bones and mustard in William's plate, might but divide her feelings with the broken egg-shells in Mr. Crawford's. (255)

Just as Fanny herself is a form of family excess that will be reinvested as affect, her ability to work the same kind of transformation with household trash marks her as the kind of inconspicuous consumer and waste manager so valued by turn-of-the-century domestic economies like *Strictures* and *Practical Education*.

Remaining ignorant of his daughters' past flirtations with Henry Crawford, however, Sir Thomas thinks that it is *Fanny* who needs to learn an economic lesson after she refuses to accept Henry's marriage proposals. Sir Thomas decides to send her on an extended visit to Portsmouth:

It was a medicinal project upon his niece's understanding, which he must at present consider diseased. A residence of eight or nine years in the abode of wealth and plenty had a little disordered her powers of comparing and judging. Her Father's house would, in all probability, teach her the value of a good income; and he trusted that she would be the wiser and happier woman all her life, for the experiment he had devised. (335)

Fanny's visit to her father's house certainly does enhance her already strong capacity for judging and comparing the way that different incomes produce vastly different domestic economies. In fact, her stay in Portsmouth gives her ample opportunity for exercising her important knowledge about home trading, as Mrs. Price, Fanny's mother, is as negligent about the process of domestic economy as Aunt Norris is zealous. Just as Aunt Norris's childless state is linked to her frugal hoarding of money, Mrs. Price's excess of children connects unregulated sexual expenditure with her evidently bad domestic management.

Her days were spent in a kind of slow bustle; always busy without getting on, always behindhand and lamenting it, without altering her ways; wishing to be an economist, without contrivance or regularity; dissatisfied with her servants, without skill to make them better, and whether helping, or reprimanding, or indulging them, without any power of engaging their respect. (355)

Fanny begins to make alterations to this scene of "mismanagement and discomfort" (355) not by reorganizing the servants, nor by occupying herself with vulgar, "bustling" domestic tasks, but by inconspicuously resolving "to give occasional hints" to her untrained, but domestically promising sister Susan, and endeavoring "to exercise for her advantage the juster notions of what was due to everybody, and what would be wisest for herself, which her own favored education had fixed in her" (361). First, Fanny successfully intervenes in a loud and longstanding domestic squabble between her two sisters over the ownership of a silver knife by realizing how "a small sum of money" (361) might purchase a second knife. Using her economic skills to promote a regularity and harmony that can pass for affection, Fanny illustrates for Susan's benefit the way that effective domestic economy becomes an end in itself, a system of circulation that ensures household harmony by controlling the behavior of its female inhabitants. To further underscore the pedagogical goals of good domestic economy, Fanny joins a lending library during her stay in Portsmouth in order to better educate Susan:

She became a subscriber—amazed at being anything in propia persona, amazed at her own doings in every way; to be a renter, a chooser of books! And to be having anyone's improvement in view of her choice! But so it was. (363)

Imposing her own definition of improvement over the more hegemonic meanings circulated by her friends and family, Fanny's savvy commercial negotiations purchase increased domestic peace along with Susan's gratitude and affection.

Thematically, however, Sir Thomas's "experiment" realigns more than Fanny's economic appreciations, as her movement from Mansfield to Portsmouth reflects a broader cultural displacement—the ideological deflection of incest from the culturally sanctioned realm of the upper-class family to the expected place of family contamination: the lower classes. Although concern about incest increased throughout the nineteenth century, the primary locus of anxiety was the working-class family. Middle-class philanthropists and social reformers uniformly blamed incestuous behavior upon overcrowded homes, and upon the accidental circumstance of mixed-sex sleeping arrangements.[67] Accordingly, when Fanny re-enters the home of her biological parents and is immediately stunned by the way that "[t]he smallness of the house, and thinness of the walls, brought everything so close to her" (347–48), she is describing the Price household as a culturally recognized place of sexual danger. As opposed to the "propriety, regularity, harmony," of Mansfield Park, Portsmouth is "the abode of noise, disorder, and impropriety. Nobody was in their right place, nothing was done as it ought" (354). Sir Thomas's skill at "keeping everybody in their right place" (145) now appears as an unironic measure of prevention, rather that an insidious form of hierarchism, and his rigid but genteel treatment of his niece can only seem preferable to the way Fanny's drunken father "scarcely ever noticed her, but to make her the object of a coarse joke" (354). In altering his niece's "understanding," Sir Thomas alters narrative understanding as well, and Mansfield Park is steadily cleansed of the family irregularities and sexual idiosyncrasies that are instead projected upon the bad brand of consumption at work in Fanny's "Father's house."

Just as Portsmouth absorbs the stigma of improper sexual circulation, it also takes on the dangers associated with foreign trade that had previously been the province of Sir Thomas's country estate. Portsmouth, a coastal city active in the launching and landing of England's merchant ships, clearly reflects the current crisis caused by of England's past investments in foreign commerce. Mr. Price cannot work due to an old injury, and the only signs of bustle or prosperity in town have been relocated to the Navy yard. For Fanny, the specter of the "natural" family is indeed an unwholesome domestic wilderness, an interior waste long neglected by England's commercial boom. Brought up in the midst of "half-cleaned plates, and not half-cleaned forks and knives" (376), the Price girls have been left at their own disposal in more immediately apparent ways than the Bertram sisters, and we learn for the first time that one daughter is already dead, and that Betsey, the youngest, is a "spoilt child" (356). Moreover, Mrs. Price has taken a page out of Aunt Norris's domestic economy, and considers the death of little Mary in the light of savings. "Well, she was taken away from evil to come" (352), moralizes Mrs. Price, echoing what Fanny will remember as her aunt's domestic "cant": "Three or four Prices might have been swept away," and Aunt Norris would have considered it "a very happy thing, and a great blessing to their poor dear sister Price to have them so well provided for" (390). With death characterized as the best "provision" for the Price children, Fanny's eagerness to return to Mansfield Park is alloyed only by the "material drawback in leaving middle sister Susan behind. That a girl capable of being made, every thing good, should be left in such hands, distressed her more and more" (382). Ironically, when Portsmouth becomes the place of bad domestic economy and female waste, Mansfield Park becomes the site of a thriving home trade: the place where wasted nieces are spared, cultivated, and improved into "every thing good."

Yet *Mansfield Park* insists upon another series of deflections and relocations before the avuncular space can be freely celebrated as a site of female savings and improvement. Even though the father's house has been converted into a place of sexual contamina-

tion and economic waste, the more threatening aspects of female
spoilage must be projected upon an avuncular domicile unvisited
by the events of the narrative: the home of Henry and Mary's uncle, Admiral Crawford. Like Fanny, the Crawfords have been
raised by an aunt and uncle, and all of their adult sins and moral
failures are blamed on the way they have been "spoiled" by the
Admiral's "lessons" (38). Mary's move to Mansfield Parsonage after the death of her aunt is in fact motivated by her uncle's increasingly public licentiousness; as we are told, "Admiral Crawford was a man of vicious conduct, who chose, instead of retaining
his niece, to bring his mistress under his own roof" (36). Although
nieces and *governesses* have had a history of assimilation at Mansfield Park, it is far more insidious that Uncle Crawford finds a degree of equivalence between nieces and *mistresses*. Furthermore,
Mary's unseemly pun on admirals and anal sex suggests, despite
her disclaimer, that her avuncular lessons have not even contained themselves to heterosexuality: "Certainly, my home at my
uncle's brought me acquainted with a circle of admirals. Of *Rears*,
and *Vices*, I saw enough. Now, do not be suspecting me of a pun, I
entreat" (54). In light of Uncle Crawford's apparently bisexual
misconduct, Sir Thomas's crimes against his niece lose resonance,
and Mary replaces Fanny in the novel's metanarrative of avuncular
abuse.

Although Mary Crawford feels that her brother has thrown
Fanny away, it is not Fanny who is finally marked as refuse after
the Bertram family's disastrous clash with foreign exchange. In
order for Fanny to represent savings, another woman must be rescripted as excess, recast as the dangerous interloper who threatens the sanctity of the family with incest. Accordingly, when the
news of Henry and Maria's adultery reaches Portsmouth, Fanny is
quick to rewrite the crime in a different sexual idiom:

The event was so shocking, that there were moments even when her
heart revolted from it as impossible—when she thought it could not be.
A woman married only six months ago, a man professing himself devoted, even *engaged*, to another—that other her near relation—the whole
family, both families connected as they were by tie upon tie, all friends,
all intimate together!—it was too horrible a confusion of guilt, too gross
a complication of evil, for human nature, not in a state of utter barba-
rism, to be capable of!—yet her judgment told her it was so. (402)

If the construction of Portsmouth as incestuous has allowed for the deflection of sexual impropriety from Mansfield Park, the construction of adultery as incest—"too gross a complication of evil, for human nature to be capable of"—will permit endogamy to pass for normative heterosexuality when Fanny finally marries Edmund. The incest potential that has always been in the Bertram family is ultimately naturalized by this conversion of adultery into a *"family-misery* which must envelope all" (403, emphasis added).

Despite the way that incest is steadily transvalued in the course of the novel, it is important to remember that endogamy is a form of family aggrandizement Sir Thomas has always valued. After his disappointment in Rushworth as a future son-in-law, he comforted himself with the thought that "a well-disposed young woman who did not marry for love, was in general but the more attached to her own family" (181). Sir Thomas, in other words, realizes that the ability to exchange Maria while simultaneously reincorporating her within the family would be the most advantageous form of domestic economy after all. It is this economic plan that he finally adopts with Fanny, and her marriage to Edmund is simply the touchstone of a larger effort to enrich his home trade through complete economic self-sufficiency. While Fanny replaces Maria as the emblem of family value, Maria takes Fanny's place as a form of waste that requires management, and it is fitting that Aunt Norris is sent to be perpetual governess to this commodity that will never reenter domestic consumption. Mary Crawford, as well, is cast aside by Edmund's definitive evaluation, "Spoilt, spoilt!" Faring slightly better in the text's economy of waste, Julia's copycat elopement with Mr. Yates is finally made the most of by Sir Thomas, who is happy to discover Yates's "estate rather more, and his debts much less, than he had feared" (421).

≺ V ≻

*Conclusion: Endogamy and Home Trading*

Isolation and foreignness come belatedly in *Mansfield Park*, with Fanny's re-immersion in the natural family providing some semblance of distance between cousins raised together in "brother-and-sister" intimacy. Yet *Mansfield Park* uses the theme of cousin-marriage to exploit similar anxieties about England's over-valued foreign trade and neglected internal economy, forging a final version of the extended family that reflects all the best principles of home trading. When Fanny and Edmund settle at the parsonage, well "within the view and patronage of Mansfield Park" (432), Susan Price, Fanny's younger sister, replaces Fanny as "the stationary niece" (431) enclosed and improved in Sir Thomas's home. More importantly, Sir Thomas congratulates himself on the patronage he has extended to his nieces and nephews, and sees "repeated and for ever repeated reason to rejoice in what he had done for them all" (431–32). By "doing credit to his countenance and his aid" (431), his nieces and nephews extend the perimeters of his avuncular authority, and by collectively "assisting to advance each other" (431), the Bertrams and Prices have become an economic network closely resembling what Leonore Davidoff and Catherine Hall have termed a middle-class familial "labour pool."[68] Fanny's brother William has even extended Sir Thomas's influence into an occupational realm that aristocratic "interest" had been previously unable to reach: the British Navy. And if a nephew increases avuncular power in the political world of England's national defense, a niece proves to be the necessary consolidator and protector of private family interaction, the prerequisite of profitable home trading, and the staple of a new brand of domestic life.

Austen's critics have too often been complicit in Sir Thomas's revisionist finale, and have allowed the affective power of nuclear family terminology to obscure the more radical redistribution of value that is at stake in *Mansfield Park*. Fanny Price is ultimately more economical than a daughter because she is the compromise of exogamy and incest, the domestic commodity that can be retailed in foreign markets or "made the most of" within the home trade. And if endogamy is the prescribed manner of heterosexual coupling in *Mansfield Park*, it also represents the most economical way to reproduce. The fact that Fanny and Edmund's "acquisition of Mansfield living . . . occurred just after they had been married long enough to begin to want an increase of income" (432), implies that the best reproduction of family is coterminous with economic expansion. Rather than linking the rise of industrial capitalism with the rise of the affective nuclear unit, *Mansfield*

*Park* ultimately puts forth a model of family development that sees the transformation and reinvestment of the extended family as a primary source of middle-class empowerment. And, more importantly, *Mansfield Park* turns to the avunculate for a model of family relations that best engages and reflects the social transition to private property under early nineteenth-century capitalism.

# Reproduction and Malthusian Economics

## FAT, FERTILITY, AND FAMILY PLANNING
## IN 'ADAM BEDE'

Daughters are chickens brought up for the tables of other men.
Samuel Richardson, *Clarissa*

MOST CRITICS have tended to read the sexual, social, and moral teleology of George Eliot's *Adam Bede* against the perpetual juxtaposition of Hetty Sorrel and Dinah Morris, the principal female protagonists. As exemplified by the foundational work of Sandra Gilbert and Susan Gubar, the ideological program of *Adam Bede* is saliently "dedicated to dramatizing the discrepancy between the antithetical faces of Eve," by providing "subversive evidence that the fallen murderess is inalterably linked to the angelic Madonna."[1] Moreover, any uncomfortable similarities between Hetty and Dinah are summarily neutralized when the murderess is banished and the Madonna becomes the cynosure of a newly emerging nuclear family, a family framed, significantly, by the historical backdrop of *Adam Bede*—the dawn of industrial capitalism. In this way, Eliot's manipulation of female sameness and difference is not limited to seemingly transhistorical categories of "fallenness" and "purity": if Dinah's "purity" becomes a signifier of a particularly middle-class brand of domesticity, the idiom of female difference in *Adam Bede* is fundamentally economic. It is also the case that differences between and among women in *Adam Bede* are not always played out by the overdetermined pairing of Hetty and Dinah. Within the boundaries of the working-class Poyser family, for example, female difference is an inevitable result of the economic shape of the household, a shape casually exposed by the Poysers' utilitarian motives for adopting their orphaned niece Hetty, and their sanguine views about her potential marriage to Adam Bede:

though she and her husband might have viewed the subject differently if Hetty had been a daughter of their own, it was clear that they would have welcomed the match with Adam for a penniless niece. For what could Hetty have been but a servant elsewhere, if her uncle had not taken her in and brought her up as a domestic help to her aunt, whose health since the birth of Totty had not been equal to more positive labour than the superintendence of servants and children?[2]

While the socially privileged world of *Mansfield Park* couches its concept of female utility within an idiom of inconspicuous consumption, the working-class context of *Adam Bede* more explicitly reveals the affective space of the family to be organized around similarly economic principles of difference between nieces and daughters—a facet of Poyser family life that is easily obscured by the more evident comparisons fostered between Hetty and Dinah. The Poysers' consciousness that Hetty could only have been a "servant elsewhere" lends her position within the family a distinct liminality that resembles Fanny Price's: insofar as Hetty is a "penniless niece," her family title is also her economic title, and if she is not exactly a servant at Hall Farm, the Poysers' home, she is still a "domestic help to her Aunt" rather than one of the children.

While turn-of-the-century debates about agricultural improvement are as important to the economic program of *Adam Bede* as they are to *Mansfield Park*, Eliot's focus on tenant farmers rather than land owners will necessarily point to an alternative understanding of Sir Thomas's celebrated project of home consumption. Renewed interest in England's internal resources also set into motion a series of arguments about the legal and philosophical status of "tenant-right" under an increasingly capitalist social order. The mutual moral obligation of landlord and tenant was anachronistic to agricultural writers like Arthur Young and James Caird, who described the shift from feudalism to capitalism as a transition from metaphoric paternalism to literal paternity: in other words, an economic imperative for the "productive" classes to put the needs of the biological family ahead of any former duties to the social one. In this context, it seems obvious that fictions of family life under burgeoning capitalism would sink the father altogether. When social relations could no longer maintain a guise of affective paternalism, the avunculate rose, in true anthropological style, to lend narrative shape to a variety of stories about the transition to private property in pre-Victorian England. George Eliot's 1859

*Adam Bede* resembles Jane Austen's 1814 *Mansfield Park* in this regard, using a crisis in extended family management to explain and represent an epistemic cultural shift.

This second chapter argues that the controversy over burgeoning middle-class economic autonomy in *Adam Bede* is articulated through the body of Hetty Sorrel, especially its illegitimate and seemingly invisible reproductivity. A thematic preoccupation with female "fat" provides the linchpin between economic concerns and familial tropes in *Adam Bede*, as the bloated, distended, fat female body perpetually insists upon comparisons between not only nieces and daughters, but conspicuous consumption and female sexual transgression, economic production and maternity, private property and bodily integrity. Moreover, a distinctly Malthusian understanding of population, production, and labor interpolates *Adam Bede*, filtering the text's economic discourse through a mathematical (and misogynous) understanding of sex and marriage, and repeated images of fertility that are finally, inevitably barren.[3]

≺ I ≻

## Family Economies

Of course, in privileging what may be called an avuncular model over a paternal paradigm, and in telling a story of nieces rather than a story of daughters, Eliot's novel again disrupts the idiom that Catherine Gallagher has identified as nearly ubiquitous to novels of industrial development: the rhetorical program of social paternalism, and the "tropes of reconciliation" between parent and child that provide the closing tableaux for novels ranging from Gaskell's *Mary Barton* to Disraeli's *Sybil*.[4] Arthur Helps's *The Claims of Labour* was probably the most influential doctrine of paternalist philosophy written in the 1840s, and its thesis that "the parental relation will be found the best model on which to form the duties of the employer to the employed" found a receptive audience among social philanthropists, novelists, and a segment of society that J. S. Mill snidely identified as "the more favored classes."[5] In Mill's opinion, the affective metaphor of paternity obscured the fact that any relationship between employer and employed cannot exist without "a countervailing element, absolute power, or something approaching to it, in those who are bound to afford this support, over those entitled to receive it."[6] Furthermore, Mill pointed out that it would be ultimately impossible for modern industrial society to disguise its economic objectives, and fend off a revolution of the class system with the antiquated "claims of labour": "The age that produces railroads . . . is not an age in which a man can feel loyal and dutiful to another because he has been born on his estate."[7]

In *Adam Bede* class rivalry between owners and workers is neatly rescripted as sexual rivalry between Arthur Donnithorne and Adam, with Hetty Sorrel serving as the index and icon of both brands of exploitation. Rather than reifying the social paternalist project with a hyper-affective tableau of "reconciliation," Eliot brings Arthur and Adam to blows over Hetty in order to diminish the class difference that informs their connection: Adam's patience and subservience only give way because he has decided that "in this thing we're man and man" (354) rather than owner and worker. While Margaret Homans has pointed out that Adam's egalitarian epiphany privileges "shared gender" over "class difference," it is crucial to recognize that gender sameness is only allowed to transcend class rivalry when both Arthur and Adam share a desire for Hetty Sorrel.[8] If the alienation of capital is an intangible, vague concept for Adam and the other precapitalist inhabitants of Hayslope, the alienation of women is the condition under which economic power is visible and recognizable: the site at which the paternalist metaphor begins to erode. Deliberately confusing the linearity of the paternal bond through such devices as the "coming-of-age" party for the young Squire, and Arthur's memories of learning carpentry—the Bede family trade—from working-class Adam, Eliot drives home the fact that paternalism is an inadequate recipe for making sense of social and economic inequities.

Furthermore, by perpetually denying an affective parent-child relationship thematic centrality in *Adam Bede,* and by rescripting the normatively affective space of the family as an economic network regulated by the principles of production and consumption, Eliot problematizes the paternalist notion that bonds of sympathy and understanding should "naturally" transcend both the economic rivalry between classes, and the material conditions of family life. As we will see, tensions between production and consumption, supply and demand, will infect even the expected sanctity of the mother-child bond, in that Hetty's act of infanticide is pointedly described as an assertion of economic autonomy: a choice to nourish her own body at the expense of her child's. Likewise, Adam's perpetual struggle to make up for the loss of income caused by his father's slack work habits and alcoholism makes it impossible for him achieve economic independence or even marry until Thias Bede accidentally drowns on his way home from the pub.

Although Adam's problems with his father are conveniently swept away in the early pages of the novel, it is repeatedly made clear that even the most affective sites of family interaction in *Adam Bede* are rhetorically marked by more material claims of paternity. For example, Adam's adult dealings with his father are painfully contrasted with his happier memories of a vibrant, productive man, and by the way his childhood identity was entirely constituted by being known as "Thias Bede's lad" (92). Given the fact that other families in the Hayslope community are attracted to similar modes of identification, and that two female cousins who share the name of Bess are distinguished from each other by the names of their respective fathers (either "Chad's Bess" or "Timothy's Bess"), it is quite evident that this language of ownership translates the law of the father into a linguistic dominion, one that confers identity as it simultaneously circumscribes individuality. These patronymic chains even extend to Timothy's grandson, who goes by the "notorious" name of "Timothy's Bess's Ben" (65). Such paternal "narcissism," as explained by Luce Irigaray, is the benchmark of patriarchal authority: "Commodities [that] share in the cult of the father . . . never stop striving to resemble, to copy, the one who is his representative."[9]

Yet it is also the case that the idiom of ownership in the working-class community of *Adam Bede* is perpetually deflected from the commercial sphere where possession is impossible, to discursive signs of paternity. Even the more genteel domestic interiors of *Adam Bede*, spaces that are far removed from working-class occupations and concerns, assert the claims of paternity through a discourse of commodification and possession. The "handsome, generous-blooded clergyman, the Rev. Adolphous Irwine" (111), is introduced under the unfortunate status of perpetual bachelor: a man who would have lived a very different sort of life if he had not the heavy financial responsibility of a widowed mother and two spinster sisters, and "would have had tall sons and blooming daughters—such possessions, in short, as men commonly think will repay them for all the labour they take under the sun" (111). With sons and daughters figured as units of value that reward both paternal "labour" and the failure to possess within the commercial sphere, the previously addressed distinction between daughters and nieces will begin to take shape over the discourse of commodification. Avuncular patronage is radically different from paternal possession in *Adam Bede*, and measures female value by the principles of utility rather than the compensatory pride of ownership, or to use Irigaray's term, "accumulation." Recalling the "schism" that Irigaray has recognized in the women-as-commodities system that is the bedrock of capitalist patriarchy, we may also remember that this system determines wealth on the basis of accumulation rather than use-value. Dividing women into the categories of "private use" (the hidden domestic labor of women and their ability to reproduce) and "social use" (exchange value), Irigaray attributes both brands of female utility to the symbolic system represented by the name of the father.[10] The smooth operation of this social order depends upon women's transition from usefulness to exchange, a "passage that never takes place simply" in Irigaray's opinion.[11]

In the case of *Adam Bede*, the circulation of women is threatened by the fact that nieces are not authorized by the name of the father—not appropriated by the idiom of paternal possession—and cannot be seamlessly accumulated for circulation within the social order. While it is evident that the set of cousins who share the same name are meant to mirror a more central pair of female cousins (the modest maternity of one "Bess" significantly contrasted with the easy virtue, gaudy dress, and large earrings of the other), it is also clear that the name of the father is the immediate factor separating Dinah and Hetty from their counterparts. While we know very little about Dinah's parentage, we do learn that Hetty's father, "that good-for-naught" Sorrel, married Hetty's mother against the wishes of her family, the Poyser clan, and soon brought his own household to financial ruin (383). Hetty's paternal heritage is a history of economic distress, of failed accumulation, and her body itself is tainted by the fact that she has "Sorrel's blood in her veins" (383). Given that Hetty's body circulates the faulty authority of the father, it seems inevitable that it should eventually become—as it does—both an icon of paternal failures and an index of paternalistic exploitations. Uncle Poyser's attempt to use his niece and accumulate her too—to retain the utility of Hetty's private labor while placing her within the social economy of exchange—will fail because Hetty's "labor" is, in fact, like his own: always already possessed by the Donnithornes.

Just as Hetty's paternal heritage is economic failure, her maternal heritage is a form of bodily crisis associated with *reproductive* failure. Old Mr. Poyser complains that Hetty's mother married "a feller wi' on'y two head o' stock when there should ha' been ten on's farm," and died "o' th' inflammation afore she war thirty" (383). As I will be taking up the issue of Malthusian economics later in this chapter, it is important to note here that the undoing of the Sorrels is blamed not only on a failure to economize, but on a disregard of arithmetic: a failure to recognize the material difference between two and ten. Yet as the subject will soon turn toward the place of reproduction within a labor theory of value, I want to point out that the effects of the Sorrels' economic crisis descend to Hetty paternally through a diseased circulatory system, and maternally through "inflammation." The mysterious "inflammation" which killed Hetty's mother is the same illness that now inhibits Mrs. Poyser's ability to labor (120), and although the precise nature of the disease is vague, Mr. Poyser localizes his wife's discomfort by referring to the habitual "pain in thy side" (192). In this way, "inflammation" is coded as a trauma to the reproductive capacity of the female body: a malignant swelling that displaces other, procreative outgrowths. This illness not only links Mrs. Poyser's nonproductive body with her deceased sister-in-law's, it identifies "inflammation" as part of Hetty's maternal heritage. Hetty's circulation may be tainted by her father's bad blood, but as old Mr. Poyser ominously notes, she also "takes arter her mother" (383).

< II >

*Farming Economies*

The way that Hetty's problematic body becomes a resonant metaphor for the circulatory difficulties endemic to the Poysers' tenure
on the bountiful Hall Farm can be clarified by an interrogation of
the socioeconomic status of tenant farmers in the late-eighteenth
and early nineteenth-century. F. M. L. Thompson's analysis of
land ownership and economic growth in eighteenth-century England, for example, identifies most turn-of-the-century tenant
farmers as "middling consumers—exactly on a par in income
terms with the lesser clergy and dissenting ministers, slightly
more affluent than innkeepers, slightly less well off than naval
and military officers, or shopkeepers."[12] This carefully qualified
economic scale allows Thompson to suggest that "without committing ourselves to the view that the farmers did form one-third
of the middle class, we may still hold that very many farmers were
indeed in that social and economic category."[13] As tentative as
Thompson's definition of "middle class" may seem, it does seem
to reflect certain aspects of *Adam Bede*'s pre-industrial world.
While the class system in Hayslope is flexible enough to dispense
with any "rigid demarcation of rank between the farmer and the
respectable artisan" (142), Mr. Poyser's "latent sense of capital and
of weight in parish affairs" (142) is associated with a newly developing but still dormant middle-class identity; a feeling of self-
importance conferred by economic accumulation that effectively
separates penniless nieces from portioned daughters within the
boundaries of his own family.

Yet while the socioeconomic position of farmers such as Mr.
Poyser may be loosely termed middle class, it is important to recognize that "there was no statutory control of the relations between tenant and landlord" until the Agricultural Holdings Act
was passed in 1875.[14] Throughout the eighteenth and for most of
the nineteenth century, therefore, relations between landowner
and tenant were governed by a vague set of customary laws that
presumed landlords would be motivated by a paternalistic sense of
social duty in all dealings with their tenantry. According to J. V.
Beckett,

by 1750, a rough division already existed whereby the owner undertook to provide fixed capital, and the tenant the working capital . . . the landlord's capital consisted of the land, the farm buildings, fences, hedges, gates, access roads, drainage works and river and sea defences, all of which required an annual outlay on the maintenance.[15]

An 1880 pamphlet directed "To the Tenant Farmers of Great Britain" thus describes the "ideal" landlord/tenant relationship as depending entirely upon the landlord's good will:

The ideal of the English system of large proprietors and of tenants hiring the land they farm instead of owning it, is where the landlord, being a capitalist, is able to relieve the tenant of all expenditure of a permanent character, and to leave him the full employment of his capital in his trade of farming, in stocking and cultivating the land . . . if these functions are performed by the landlord; if he has the capital and does what is recognized as a duty, nothing can be better from an economic point of view than the . . . relationship of Landlord, Tenant, and Labourer.[16]

Understandably, by the time Eliot published *Adam Bede* in 1859, the question of "tenant right" had a long and contentious history, and the difference between an improving and unimproving landowner was tantamount to a farmer's economic prosperity. Despite some middle-class pretensions, tenant farmers had little ready capital at any given time to enact their own improvements, and as nineteenth-century agriculturist James Caird explained, "unlike that of the landowners, much of it is in daily use, circulating among tradesmen and labourers."[17] As we know from Mrs. Poyser, Squire Donnithorne is no improver, and his tenant's requests for repairs and innovations have been perpetually ignored: "my husband's been asking and asking till he's tired, and to think o' what he's done for the farm, and he's never had a penny allowed him, be the times bad or good" (126). Not only has the Squire denied the Poysers their customary tenant rights, he has forced Mr. Poyser to put his relatively scarce capital into the enrichment of land that he doesn't actually own, without any legal right to compensation for the long-term improvements he may effect.

Tenant's compensation was at the crux of nineteenth-century agricultural controversy, especially in cases where short-term leases were insisted upon by landlords. In his 1850–51 analysis of English farming systems, Caird observed that since "the investment of a tenant's capital in land seldom contemplates an immediate return . . . an improving tenant has no legal security for the capital he invests in the cultivation of another's land."[18] Similarly, in 1848 tenant-farmer Charles Higby Lattimore claimed he had been evicted from his farm because he voted against his landlord's interests in a local election, and consequently appealed to the law for compensation for the "unexhausted" improvements he had effected at the coincidentally named Bride Hall Farm. Lattimore writes:

. . . with extreme reluctance, but animated by the conviction of public duty to my brother farmers, I was compelled to test the law in order to ascertain (what I had ever doubted) whether there is any *legal recognition* of the floating capital of a tenant-farmer sunk in the soil, or expended upon the premises of another person . . . the result proved to be that an agreement—good in law, if applied to commercial or trading matters— was not available to a tenant-farmer against a landlord . . . no such phrase legally exists as *tenant-farmer's capital*.[19]

Under Caird and Lattimore's analysis of "Tenant Right," the ambiguous "latency" of Martin Poyser's capital takes on a very tangible nineteenth-century commercial significance. Without any legally recognized capital, Mr. Poyser isn't really a capitalist, and his apparent wealth in property is as illusory as his blooming abundance of nieces. Although the Poysers have cultivated the Hall Farm for generations, it seems that they renew their lease with Squire Donnithorne every three years (393): a period of time too short for a tenant to reap the benefits of long-term improvements, especially in light of the perpetual threat that the Squire will choose to terminate their occupancy.[20] Moreover, as Mrs. Poyser will declare when Squire Donnithorne actually does menace them with imminent eviction,

I should like to see if there's another tenant besides Poyser as 'ud put up wi' never having a bit o' repairs done till a place tumbles down—and not then, on'y wi' begging and praying and having to pay half—and being strung upwi' the rent as it's much if he gets enough out of the land to pay, for all he's put his own money into the ground beforehand. (394)

If the Poysers' capital is figuratively latent because it is unrecognized by law, it is also literally latent because it is always either buried in the soil, or perpetually circulating in the form of seed money, stock, and laborer's wages.

Interestingly, Mrs. Poyser's understanding of farming is actually more canny than her husband's, and reveals the false prosperity and hand-to-mouth nature of tenantry: "As fur farming, it's putting money into your pocket wi' your right hand and fetching it out wi' your left. As fur as I can see, it's raising victuals for other folks, and just getting a mouthful for yourself and your children as you go along" (125). While Lattimore's plea for legal compensation aligned him with his "brother" tenant farmers over his paternalist landlord, Mrs. Poyser's economic perspective on tenantry is articulated in the familial idiom of parents and children. Tenant farming, in Mrs. Poyser's representation, is a process by which parents are forced to privilege the economic imperative to feed other people over the affective responsibility of nourishing their own family. Many agricultural writers throughout the nineteenth century similarly viewed the controversy over tenant right as a social conflict between the metaphoric family and the "real" family: a choice between a paternalist's duty to his workers and a father's responsibility to his children. I. S. Leadam, for example, insisted that the English custom of primogeniture prevented any landowner from being as financially supportive of his tenantry as he might have been under different circumstances:

. . . the landlords of this country cannot provide the needful capital because they are not the real owners, they enjoy a life-interest on the estate which with or without their will, goes upon their death to their eldest sons. The less capital, therefore, that they expend upon the land the more they have for their younger children, who are also provided for by charges out of the estate.[21]

Likewise, Caird insists that the customary rights accorded to tenants will not protect a farmer from the fact that an eldest "son does not always inherit the virtues of his father."[22] A breakdown in the affective connection between a landowning father and son, in other words, could produce subsequent breakdowns in the affective philosophy of social paternalism. On the tenant side of the family spectrum, moreover, a farmer who failed to stand up for tenant right was a bad father, who allowed the economic future of his own children to be sacrificed for the prosperity of his landlord's heirs. Lattimore, for example, hopes that the moral of own his story will direct tenant farmers to consider

the insecure position in which they must leave their children under the present law,—a circumstance of peculiar interest to every good man at the close of his life. I can never forget that my father assured me upon his deathbed, in 1834, the last time I ever conversed with him, that the only earthly anxiety he felt at that time was his regret for my exposure to the possible consequences of my occupation of this farm, under the thralls of the owner and his agents.[23]

According to mid-century agriculturists, the economic tensions between the "real" family and the social family finally could not be elided by the affective rhetoric of paternalism: in a world mediated by supply and demand rather than by custom or tradition, "the relation is and must become one of business, and not merely of mutual confidence."[24]

Mrs. Poyser is certainly able to detect the incompatible economic claims of the literal family and the social family, and she recognizes that tenantry puts too much Poyser labor into circulation outside of the family, feeding bodies other than Poyser bodies, and nourishing children other than Poyser children. Unfortunately, however, she cannot notice her niece's body as the weakest link in the family cycle of labor and nourishment, the site at which Poyser "victuals" are most egregiously appropriated to nourish non-Poyser bodies. The question of who is producing and who is consuming is central to an economic understanding of the working-class household, as Wally Seccombe's *A Millennium of Family Change* makes clear. By viewing maternity as a form of economic production (as the *literal* reproduction of labor power), Seccombe is able to envision the household not as an affective space but as a tenuously balanced network of producers and consumers: adults capable of productive labor, and members such as children and aged people unable to contribute to their own subsistence.[25] Seccombe explains:

The lifespan pattern of productive capacity is roughly in symmetry with the maturation of procreative capacity as well. The middle generation commands both elements of labour-power, while children and the aged are incapable of sustaining either of the two basic conditions of life. It is therefore necessary for every class of adult producers to generate continuously a "subsistence surplus" (in addition to any surplus which may be extracted from non-productive classes) in order to reproduce itself from one generation to the next.[26]

In this Malthusian understanding of the history of family development, the "middle generation" of productive adults is the linchpin of economic stability in the laboring household, and must be periodically stabilized either through the limitation of births or the inclusion of extra adult members to bridge the gap between familial consumption and production. For Seccombe, this horizontal expansion of the working-class family is indicative of new and powerful ideologies of work, production, and especially of reproduction.

In the context of *Adam Bede*, of course, it is this last term that is the most provocative, as Hetty Sorrel's illegitimate pregnancy is arguably the focus of the novel. Yet even before Hetty's seduction, the production of children as a form of economic production is suggested by the figure of Mrs. Poyser, whose last experience of childbirth, as we remember from the opening quotation, has rendered her permanently unfit for "more positive labour." Registering in the idiom of both domestic work and childbirth, Mrs. Poyser's inability to "labour" must be compensated by the addition of what Seccombe terms "middle-generation" family members: productive bodies to make up for the "subsistence goods" Mrs. Poyser is now unable to supply, as well as for the absence of future sons and daughters that she will never possess. This ratio of consumers to producers in the Poyser family is repeatedly thematized by the parodies of labor enacted by Mr. Poyser's elderly father: for example, his "job" of holding the farmyard gate open for his family as they set off for church, "pleased to do his bit of work; for, like all old men whose life has been spent in labour, he liked to feel that he was still useful" (233).

At the other end of the generational spectrum are the mischievous and sometimes destructive antics of the Poysers' young children, especially three year-old Totty. In her quieter moments, Totty parodies the domestic labor of the busy household by "arduously clutching the handle of a miniature iron with her tiny fat fist" (120) and demanding that her harried mother participate in the farce by warming the toy in the fire. Yet Totty's playful mimicry soon erodes the positive effects of her mother's labor, as she takes advantage of "her momentary leisure, to put her fingers into a bowl of starch, and drag it down, so as to empty the contents with tolerable completeness on to the ironing sheet"(120). In light of Totty's unhelpful participation in the rites of domestic work, it is clear that adult nieces are actually more *economical* family additions than daughters. Dinah and Hetty, with their contributions of real work, are necessary components of productivity at Hall Farm; this is especially true of Hetty, who resides with the Poysers on a full-time basis and is solely responsible for the making of butter in Mrs. Poyser's large and well-respected dairy. Nevertheless, the Poysers' narcissistic investment in their own daughter "blurs the seriousness of utility," making labor less valuable than exchange, and nieces less valuable than daughters.[27] Under a capitalist regime, in other words, "wealth amounts to a subordination of the use of things to their accumulation" (174). Uneconomical accumulation, furthermore, is like "inflammation," and will register directly upon Hetty's body.

≺ III ≻

*Bodily Economies*

Although I earlier introduced the problem of economic autonomy as an important factor in the social organization of the family, it is also clear that the economic awkwardness of tenantry within *Adam Bede*—a text that negotiates identity through the trope of possession—is first encountered as a bodily awkwardness. In the opening paragraphs of the second chapter the reader is confronted with the oddly bifurcated body of Mr. Casson, caretaker of the Donnithorne Arms Inn:

On a front view it appeared to consist principally of two spheres, bearing about the same relation to each other as the earth and the moon: that is to say, the lower sphere might be said, at a rough guess, to be about thirteen times larger than the upper, which naturally performed the function of a mere satellite and tributary. But here the resemblance ceased, for Mr. Casson's head was not at all a melancholy-looking satellite, nor was it a 'spotty globe,' as Milton has irreverently called the moon; on the contrary, no head and face could look more sleek and healthy, and its expression . . . was one of jolly contentment, only tempered by that sense of personal dignity which usually made itself felt in his attitude and bearing. This sense of dignity could hardly be considered excessive in a man who had been butler to the family for fifteen years, and who, in his present high position, was necessarily very much in contact with his inferiors. (59)

Mr. Casson is the reader's first perspective on the Hayslope commercial community and on the socioeconomic conditions that divide farmers from artisans and pub owners from the gentry. If Mr. Casson's past occupation as "butler to the family," the Donnithorne family, has given him an air of social superiority, his present occupation as innkeeper to the family now separates him from his customers, places him in a liminal economic position linked to Mr. Poyser's through the idiom of tenantry. As a tenant, Mr. Casson can participate in the enterprise of capitalism, leasing the Donnithorne Arms and the "pretty take" of land attached to it (58). His capital itself, however, is like Mr. Poyser's "latent" capital: unable to circulate within the larger economy because it is always already possessed by the Donnithornes. The two engorged "spheres" that constitute the innkeeper's physical person are part of the thematic representation of this economic latency, as they suggest an innate failure of the whole to possess its disparate parts. Furthermore, as Eve Sedgwick has recognized in her work on *Our Mutual Friend*, this kind of bodily disruption is a metaphor for economic crisis: "the illusion of economic individualism."[28]

Sedgwick's argument implies that the generic bodily icon of struggling bourgeois independence is male, and posits corporeal metaphors of digestion and anality as signifiers of the failure to "possess." However, Mr. Casson's disembodied head and swollen gut merely introduce an economy of the body into *Adam Bede* that will eventually be grafted upon its representation of Hetty Sorrel, a reinscription that ultimately suggests that the female body enacts a similar crisis of ownership when it is unable to register the signs of its own pregnancy. The novel's two famous mirror scenes provide a telling map of Hetty's body, both before and after she is pregnant, as her disfigured and disfiguring bedroom mirror is "fixed in an upright position, so that she could get only one good view of her neck and arms" (194). Likewise, the small, hanging mirror she removes from Dinah's room "would show her nothing beneath her little chin, and that beautiful bit of neck where the roundness of her cheek melted into another roundness shadowed by dark delicate curls" (294). Just as neither of Hetty's mirrors will reflect her lower body, neither the Poyser family nor the Hayslope community are able to see Hetty in relation to her corporeality; like the broken mirror, they are "fixed in an upright position," and refuse to reconcile the much-admired "roundness" of Hetty's head, neck, and arms with the other, more disturbing "roundness" of her emerging middle.

Hetty's invisible pregnancy has been widely commented upon by scholars of the Victorian novel: for example, Helena Michie suggests that Hetty's "fleshy" body is unreadable because it belies physiognomy, and is finally unassimilable with her kittenish looks and flower-like delicacy.[29] However, it is also the case that Hetty's distended middle belies the economic autonomy of her class status, as her very "fleshiness" is a mark of the economic exploitation that infects the Poyser family's commercial position within the Hayslope community, and especially in relation to the Donnithornes. Other critics have allowed Hetty's extreme egoism and vanity to deflect from the strangeness of the mirror scenes in *Adam Bede*: John Kucich, in fact, describes Hetty as psychically "driven to imagine herself as she wants others to see her."[30] Yet Hetty's lack of bodily integrity is not a simple inscription of her vanity, but rather a portrait of an already vague sense of subjectivity unraveling under the mutually reinforcing ideologies of class and gender that began to shape social identity in the late eighteenth century. As noted by Leonore Davidoff,

. . . the same forces which produced a world view dividing the society between masculine and feminine, working class and middle (upper) class, urban and rural, also separated physicality, e.g., bodily functions in general and sexuality in particular, from the public gaze. This is an example of the privatization we have come to associate with the development of industrial capitalism and was part of a changing view of men's and women's positions in the cosmos and of their relation to Nature.[31]

Although Davidoff's argument has been criticized for suggesting that pre-capitalist notions of the body were uninformed by any distinction between public and private, it is important to register the way that the social body was organicized, naturalized by an image of the literal body: "The adult middle class (or aristocratic) man, representing the governing or ruling group, was seen as the Head . . . The Hands were unthinking, unfeeling 'doers' without characteristics of sex, age, or other identity . . . Middle-class women represented the emotions, the Heart, or sometimes the Soul, seat of morality and tenderness."[32] The unmentionable re-

gions of the body were, of course, rounded out by the social out-
casts: prostitutes, criminals and other brands of poor who were finally as unarratable or invisible as those body functions normatively concealed from the "public gaze."

With this social mapping of the body in mind, Hetty's bisected
form becomes an assortment of gendered, class-inflected parts organized around the principles of private and public. If her buttermaking links her literal hands with the "doers" of the social body,
and her beautiful head and neck function as false barometers of
her "Soul," her unrepresentable lower body, with its mysteriously
developing roundness, marks her as a social criminal by betraying
her sexual capacities. Read along the axis of gender, Hetty's body
literalizes the popular Victorian myth of women's lack of con-
scious sexual desire or bodily curiosity, and serves as a corporeal
emblem of the stereotypical female failure to integrate the various
uses of the body into an organic whole. If the potential for male
exploitation of women's schooled ignorance is not made abundantly clear by Hetty's seduction, it brutally reverberates at the
end of the novel when Tommy Poyser is seen "amusing himself"
with his sister's legless doll, "turning Dolly's skirt over her bald
head, and exhibiting her truncated body to the general scorn"
(522). Read along class lines, however, Hetty's failure to integrate
her body links her with Mr. Casson's tenantry, and translates her
bodily failure into a problem of ownership: a failure to possess the
fruits of labor. Similarly, because Hetty is seduced by Arthur
Donnithorne, her sexual exploitation is rewritten as an economic
exploitation: just as the baby that no one is willing to "see" is Arthur's illegitimate child, the unacknowledged Donnithorne heir,
the bountiful farm that the Poysers' work is owned and controlled
by Arthur's grandfather the Squire.

Although the problems with metaphorizing political economy
have been widely discussed, reading Hetty's bodily metamor-
phoses in terms of commercial oscillation is imperative in light of
a specifically late eighteenth-century through Victorian tendency
to use the human body as an economic icon. In 1776, for example,
Adam Smith criticized England's "unhealthful" concentration on
the colonies as the one "great channel" of industry and commerce,
by likening the economic constitution of the British empire to a
potentially "apoplectic" human body:

In her present condition, Great Britain resembles one of those unwholesome bodies in which some of the vital parts are overgrown, and which, upon that account, are liable to many dangerous disorders scarce incident to those in which all the parts are more properly proportioned. A small stop in that great blood-vessel, which has been artificially swelled beyond its natural dimensions, and through which an unnatural proportion of the industry and commerce of the country has been forced to circulate, is very likely to bring on the most dangerous disorders upon the whole body politick.[33]

Moreover, contemporary critic Susan Walsh believes that a specifically female body was used increasingly in the Victorian period to provide a metaphor for commercial disorders. Dubbing this gender-specific representation of financial crisis "climacteric economy," Walsh explains that "women's bodies, as advertisements, medical handbooks, and health manuals made clear, were the human bodies most agitated by cyclical 'crises.'"[34] Although Walsh's argument primarily focuses on the way that an image of the elderly female body was used textually and pictorially "as a potent analogue for economic as well as reproductive 'bankruptcy,'" she insists that medical discourse surrounding the health and well-being of the female body at any stage of development provided a plethora of metaphors for representing economic instability.[35]

In nineteenth-century parlance . . . the "obstruction," "constriction," or "depression" of an "ill-regulated circulation" in women meant more than digestive or circulatory arrest: these terms were code words for stopped menses, whether the result of delayed menarche, pregnancy, menopause, or a general overine-uterine "derangement."[36]

Walsh uses a series of *Punch* cartoons featuring the Old Lady of Threadneedle Street in order to drive home this point: they uniformly depict an ancient woman with a ballooning bottom-half as a comic metaphor for the Bank of England. If these bifurcated female images remind us immediately of Mr. Casson and his engorged lower sphere, they should remind us eventually of Hetty, and of the way Hetty's own "stopped menses" provide a resonant metaphor for the "ill-regulated circulation" of her uncle's tenant-capital.[37]

≺ IV ≻

*Fertility, Fatness, and the Family:*
*Malthusian Perspectives*

At first glance, Hall Farm seems to be a place of infinite productivity and fertile richness; in fact, many critics have pointed out the edenic nature of this garden where Adam will find first the wrong, and finally the right Eve.[38] Yet closer inspection of the metaphors of plentitude and fecundity reveal the seeds of degeneration and decay: not only was the Hall Farm once the Hall, the place where the local gentry lived, but "one might fancy the house in the early stages of a chancery suit, and that the fruit from the grand double row of walnut trees on the right hand of the enclosure would fall and rot among the grass" (115). Although Hall Farm is filled to capacity with milch cows and hens, and Mrs. Poyser's dairy makes the finest butter and cheese in Hayslope, the once "well-tended kitchen-garden of a manor house" is now littered with "unpruned fruit trees, and kitchen vegetables growing together in careless, half-neglected abundance," flowers that are "large and disorderly for want of trimming," and "a huge apple tree making a barren circle under its low-spreading boughs" (263–64). This ominous "barren circle" seems to plant potential scarcity at the root of economic plentitude, despite the narrator's disarming, disingenuous dismissal: "what signified a barren patch or two? The garden was so large" (264).

Thomas Robert Malthus's *First Essay on Population* was published in 1798, a year before Hetty Sorrel's crisis in family planning is played out against the historical backdrop of *Adam Bede*. Written in the wake of the French Revolution, at a time when the issue of society's "perfectibility" was a central economic and philosophical concern, Malthus's essay dispels the more utopian scenarios of social improvement put forth by such theorists as Condorcet and William Godwin by insisting that certain laws of necessity inevitably regulate the progress of mankind.[39] The most famous of Malthus's "laws" is the one that reflects the codes of production and consumption in *Adam Bede* and explains the inevitable decay that is shrouded within the deceptive richness and ripeness of Hall Farm:

Population, when unchecked, increases in a geometrical ratio. Subsistence increases only in an arithmetical ratio. A slight acquaintance with the numbers will shew the immensity of the first power in comparison with the second.

By that law of nature which makes food necessary to the life of man, the effects of these two unequal powers must be kept equal.

This implies a strong and constantly operating check on population from the difficulty of subsistence. This difficulty must fall some where; and must necessarily by severely felt by a large portion of mankind.

Through the animal and vegetable kingdoms, nature has scattered the seeds of life abroad with the most profuse and liberal hand. She has been comparatively sparing in the room, and the nourishment necessary to rear them. The germs of existence contained in this spot of earth, with ample food, and ample room to expand in, would fill millions of worlds in the course of a few thousand years. Necessity, that imperious all-pervading law of nature, restrains them within the prescribed bounds. The race of plants, and the race of animals shrink under this great restrictive law. And the race of man cannot, by any efforts of reason, escape from it. Among plants and animals its effects are waste of seed, sickness and premature death. Among mankind, misery and vice.[40]

In Malthusian rhetoric, therefore, the barrenness implicit in fertility is an economic and mathematical given, as an economy of plenitude, a period of uninterrupted production and uncircumscribed reproduction, will eventually give way to an economy of scarcity: a time when the production of food cannot keep up with the increase in population.[41] By associating fertility with social distress instead of prosperity, Malthus's brand of political economy, according to Catherine Gallagher, "occluded the possibility of using the healthy body to signify the healthy society."[42] Instead, the healthy reproductive body loses,

in the very power of its fecundity, the integrity of its boundaries, and hence comes to be a sign of its opposite. The blooming body is only a body about to divide into two feebler bodies that are always on the verge of becoming starving bodies. Hence, no state of health can be socially reassuring.[43]

Within the context of *Adam Bede*, the blooming body that becomes a Malthusian precursor of social decay is of course Hetty Sorrel's: the health of Hetty's body measures not economic prosperity but the potential enfeeblement of uncontrolled reproduction. But Eliot's economic metaphors also allow us to interpret the *family* body as an index of commercial distress, and to read the

hyperbolic prosperity of the Poysers as the harbinger of future at-
rophy. If the flexibility and amorphousness of the Poyser family,
its seemingly benevolent ability to incorporate two orphaned
nieces, registers at one time as a sign of affective health, its lack of
integrity as a unit will eventually become "a sign of its opposite."
While paying lip service to the affective ideologies of the paternal
family, the avuncular family mistakes fat for fertility, fertility for
prosperity, and economic expediency for family sentiment. Obsessed with one side of the Malthusian drama—the production and
consumption of food—the Poysers finally cannot keep up with the
mathematical teleology of the population principle.

Food is increasing at such a rate at Hall Farm that it becomes
more and more difficult for the Poyser family to monitor its various sites of productivity, and Malthus's image of the "profuse and
liberal hand" of nature resurfaces in the way that the corn itself is
"ripe enough to be blown out of the husk and scattered as untimely seed" (337). Moreover, the corn is not the only bearer of
"untimely seed" in Hayslope, and the empty circle concealed by
the apple tree's profusion of leaves, blossoms, and fruit is not the
only source of potential barrenness within the fecundity and ver-
dure of Hall Farm. The narrator reminds us of what exaggerated
sites of fertility so often conceal, "an image of great agony—the
agony of the cross" (409):

if there came a traveler to this world who knew nothing of the story of
man's life upon it, this image of agony would seem to him strangely out
of place in the midst of this joyous nature. He would not know that hidden behind the apple blossoms, or among the golden corn, or under the
shrouding boughs of the wood, there might be a human heart beating
heavily with anguish: perhaps a young blooming girl, not knowing where
to turn for refuge from swift-advancing shame . . . such things are sometimes hidden among the sunny fields and behind the blossoming or-
chards; and the sound of the gurgling brook, if you came close to one spot
behind a small bush, would be mingled for your ear with a despairing
human sob. (409–10)

This image of illegitimate reproduction at the mainsprings of economic plenty links the blooming Hetty with the rapid overgrowth
at Hall Farm and with the Malthusian laws that circumscribe both
brands of production. From the overripe cornfields, to the "half-
neglected" kitchen garden, to their niece's unregulated sexuality,
the Poyser family, for all its adherence to the principles of domes-

tic economy, is finally unable to police its own fertility, to control the productivity of its various parts.

On the one hand, it seems uncharacteristic for Mrs. Poyser to be negligent about the state of overripeness on the farm and in her dairy: if she is aware of the exact moment that the currants in the garden need to be picked, she is also perpetually poised to nip her servants' burgeoning sexuality in the bud. All expressions of desire on the part of her housemaid, for example, are immediately translated into sexual desire, as Molly's seemingly innocent request to sit down to her spinning, "according to Mrs. Poyser, shrouded a secret indulgence of unbecoming wishes which she now dragged forth and held up to Molly's view with cutting eloquence":

Spinning, indeed! It isn't spinning as you'd be at, I'll be bound, and let you have your own way. I never knew your equal for gallowsness. To think of a gell o' your age wanting to go and sit with half-a-dozen men! . . . That's the way with you—that's the road you'd all like to go, headlong to ruin. You're never easy till you've got some swetheart as is as big a fool as yourself; and you'll be finely off when you're married, I daresay, and have got a three-legged stool to sit on, and never a blanket to cover you, and a bit o' oatcake for your dinner, as three children are a-snatching at. (118–19)

Yet while Mrs. Poyser vigilantly polices her servants' bodies and their sexuality, she fails to discern that her niece also participates in the sexual economy of Hall Farm and shares the capacity for "labour" with the housemaid. What is more, Arthur Donnithorne does not constitute a sexual threat that Mrs. Poyser can recognize. To the Poysers, their future landlord signifies the potential for economic improvement rather than exploitation, and while they fiercely guard their farmyard from the "loiterers" and transient laborers who may lead their young female servants astray, Arthur, in the role of benevolent paternalist, is allowed to enter at will.

Ironically, the tenants of Hayslope are not the only people convinced of Arthur Donnithorne's potential largesse as a landlord. Arthur views himself as the antithesis of his grandfather, a potential improver of property who busily studies contemporary agricultural writers in preparation for his succession to the estate. In conversation with Reverend Irwine, Arthur eagerly describes his future plans:

I've been reading your friend Arthur Young's books lately, and there's nothing I should like better than to carry out some of his ideas in putting the farmers on a better management of their land; and, as he says, making what was a wild country, all of the same dark hue, bright and variegated with corn and cattle. My grandfather will never let me have any power while he lives; but there's nothing I should like better to do than to undertake the Stonyshire side of the estate—it's in a dismal condition—and set improvements on foot, and gallop about from one place to another and overlook them. I should like to know all the labourers, and see them touching their hats to me with a look of good will. (214–15)

As we know from Chapter One, Young's agricultural theories have conservative political implications, and the "improvement" of internal wastes is motivated by a desire to restore feudal values for the benefit of an aristocracy in decline. Young Donnithorne wants his estate to produce more food, but only, it seems, to revel in the deferential "good will" of his laborers and tenants. The Reverend approves of Arthur's enthusiasm, but tries to temper it with a warning: although "increasing the quantity of food" is a noble endeavor, "You must make it quite clear to your mind which you are most bent upon, old boy—popularity or usefulness—else you may happen to miss both" (215). Irwine's advice penetrates to the heart of what will be Arthur's premature failure as an improver. By confusing affection for Hetty with economic interest in the Poysers, Arthur brings fertility to the wrong side of the estate, and instead of increasing the quantity of food, only ends up increasing the population. For all his benevolent impulses, the young improver ends up being just as appropriative of tenant capital as his unpaternalistic grandfather the Squire.

In fact, Arthur's initial contact with Hetty is actually enabled by Mrs. Poyser, as her pride in her dairy leads her to believe that Arthur is "really interested in her milkpans" (126), rather than in her beautiful buttermaker. Hetty's liminality—of body, of class, and of family—allows her to evade the perimeters of her aunt's normally rigid supervision; furthermore, in the context of the dairy, Hetty is merely another implement of labor to her aunt, a set of "hands" that makes the butter, and her actions can only seduce Arthur's regard for economic efficiency. Yet it is the sensuality of Hetty's "attitudes and movements" that is of primary interest to Arthur while he watches her work, and her "hands" register in an entirely different nexus of meaning: the "tossing movements that give a charming curve to the arm, and a sideward inclination of the round, white neck . . . little patting and rolling movements with the palm of the hand, and nice adaptations and finishings which cannot at all be effected without a great play of the pouting mouth and the dark eyes" (129). While Mrs. Poyser quickly transforms the domestic productivity of her housemaid into a tale of potential *re*productivity, her niece's labors remain in the economic realm, and at the end of Hetty's performance she is merely pleased by the material fact that Hetty "is particularly clever at making the butter" (129).

Even Arthur's solicitation of Hetty to partner him in two dances at his upcoming birthday feast is carried out with Mrs. Poyser's unthinking approbation: "Indeed sir, you're very kind to take notice of her. And I'm sure, whenever you're pleased to dance with her, she'll be proud and thankful, if she stood still the rest o' the evening" (129). Mrs. Poyser is finally unable to see the workplace as the scene of her niece's initial seduction because it is a cross-class seduction: an exchange that has only economic significance at Hall Farm. Although Mrs. Poyser's natural sagacity is renowned throughout Hayslope, and Mr. Poyser is "secretly proud of his wife's manner of putting two and two together" (235), it is a shame that Bartle Massey, the Hayslope schoolteacher, has never taken the time to teach the couple his brand of Malthusian mathematics. Following Malthus's assertion that sexual passion "may always be considered in algebraic language, as a given quantity," Bartle calculates that the principles of "simple addition" clearly indicate that if you "add one fool to another . . . in six years time six fools more—they're all of the same denomination, big and little's nothing to do with the sum" (291).[44] Bartle even comments upon the issue of human perfectibility that inspires Malthus's first *Essay*, as he blames Adam's mistaken faith in Hetty's fidelity and innocence on his lack of mathematical knowledge: "If he hadn't had such hard work to do, poor fellow, he might have gone on to the higher branches, and then this might never have happened— might never have happened" (463). Like Malthus, Bartle realizes that the daily realities of work keep the lower classes from the "higher branches" of intellectual development, and prevent them from understanding—what the Reverend Irwine also knows—that human affections can interfere with economic prosperity. This crucial lesson is the one with which the Poysers and others in their economic situation are grappling; it is the inaugural factor of middle-class identity, and the reason Malthus rests all hopes for human improvement on the rise and empowerment of the middle classes through the "established administration of property" (Malthus, 286).

Like Arthur Donnithorne, the Poysers have confused "the established administration of property" with family sentiment, and have allowed rhetorical assessments of what "a good father" to Hetty Uncle Poyser has been to elide the fact that Hetty's place in the family registers economically rather than affectively. The mistaken impulses of paternalism have been inadvertently replicated by the Poysers, and despite the sentimental idiom that allows them to understand themselves as a family, the economic and affective claims of their own children perpetually obscure what is due to their metaphoric daughter. Uncle Poyser's proprietorship of Hetty is finally like his tenant-farming: a secondary form of appropriation that has nothing to do with ownership. Although he expects to channel Hetty's fertility into a mutually empowering marriage with the innovative, upwardly mobile Adam Bede, Uncle Poyser's interest in his niece will prove to be as latent as his "stuck in the soil" capital: cultivated by the Poysers, but devoured by the Donnithornes.

Furthermore, when Hetty's economic productivity becomes reproductivity, it signals that another of Bartle Massey's ominous predictions has come true, and that sooner or later, a woman's food "all runs either to fat or to brats" (285). Bartle's misogynous words return us finally to the problem of fatness, a problem that has been previously addressed both under the delicate euphemism of "fleshiness" and under the sign of Mr. Casson's distended frame. Although Hetty's brand of fleshiness, her uneconomical form of productivity, is unnoticed by her family, other kinds of fat are hysterically and repetitiously recognized and celebrated by the Poysers.[45] As much as Hetty's uneconomical fatness belies the Poysers' financial independence, Totty Poyser's "fat" body is a sign of the idealized economy of plentitude at Hall Farm. The difference between daughters and nieces in *Adam Bede* finally materializes over the discourse of fat, marking the bodily excess of daughters as an illusory sign of accumulation, a displaced embodiment of wealth. Conversely, the fleshiness of Hetty's body is an ignored site of exploitation, and the true measure of Poyser economic status. From the time we first glimpse four year-old Totty "in retreat towards the dairy, with a sort of waddling run, and an amount of fat on the nape of her neck, which made her look like the metamorphosis of a white sucking pig" (120), it is clear that Totty functions within *Adam Bede* as a hyperbolic image of Hetty, her fat body standing in for the unarticulated "metamorphosis" of her cousin.

Even Hetty's first rendezvous with Arthur in the Fir-tree Grove is symbolically illustrated by the way that she returns home to find, despite the lateness of the hour, that her aunt is still awake "trying to soothe Totty to sleep" (189). As Hetty enters the room, Totty "raised herself up, and showed a pair of flushed cheeks, which looked even fatter than ever now that they were defined by the edge of her linen night-cap" (189). Although Mrs. Poyser initially begins to scold her niece for her tardiness, she soon digresses into a description of her daughter's unusual "fever for what I know . . . and nobody to give her the physic but your uncle, and fine work there's been, and half of it spilt on her nightgown" (190). Paradoxically, Totty's restlessness and "fever" both supply the otherwise absent symptoms of Hetty's late-night tryst with Arthur, and finally draw Mrs. Poyser's attention completely away from her wayward niece, as a new bout of crying from her daughter erupts just as Mrs. Poyser complains that Hetty would like her clock to be "set by gentlefolks time" (190), rather than the time at Hall Farm. Yet another stain (this one, significantly, on Totty's nightgown) literalizes Hetty's sexual stain, fixing Totty's "fat" body as a hyperbolic emblem of concealed sexuality: an exaggerated narrative record of Hetty's bodily transgressiveness.

Returning now to Malthusian logic, "fatness" takes on even greater significance, as the habit of turning rich agricultural land over to the "fatting" of high-grade cattle is one of Malthus's pet peeves: "A fatted beast may in some respects be considered, in the language of the French economists, as an unproductive labourer: he has added nothing to the value of the produce consumed."[46] As Catherine Gallagher points out, this fatted beast is an "immediate threat to society's well being . . . a distention, an overgrowth of its own circulatory system."[47] Similarly, Totty Poyser is the very embodiment of nonproductive value, a healthy sign of economic plenty that is simultaneously a swollen marker of unregulated consumption. We frequently catch glimpses of Totty in the garden of Hall Farm, undoing the picking, gathering, and unearthing of harvest-work by stuffing everything she takes from tree or soil directly into her mouth. Adam Bede is looking for Hetty in the garden one evening when he instead encounters Totty,

Yes—with a bonnet down her back, and her fat face dreadfully smeared with red juice, turned up towards the cherry-tree, while she held her little round hole of a mouth and red-stained pinafore to receive the promised downfall. I am sorry to say, more than half the cherries that fell were hard and yellow instead of juicy and red; but Totty spent no time in useless regrets, and she was already sucking the third juiciest when Adam said, "There now, Totty, you've got your cherries. Run into the house with 'em to mother." (264)

Totty's red-stained face will soon be reflected by the "deep red" blush that spreads over Hetty's face when Adam finally finds her—an appropriately metaphorical "stain" because Adam has interrupted her fantasies about Arthur Donnithorne. What is more, the dangerous sexual imagery of this passage is matched by an equally problematic economic message, and the two lines of signification collide in the slippery "hole" of Totty's open mouth. If the sexual signs are self-explanatory, the economic signs should perhaps be qualified by a term that Malthus recognizes as a "vulgar" but accurate expression: "hand to mouth" subsistence.[48] Malthus's complaint that the labouring classes are prevented from planning for the future by the "hand to mouth" manner in which they must live echoes both Bartle Massey's feeling that Adam's daily labors keep him from important economic knowledge, and Martin Poyser's sense that his capital is latent, unable to circulate properly within the larger social economy. In this way, Totty's fat body and stained mouth not only stand in for Hetty's concealed sexual identity, but for the "fatted beast" in her father's failed circulation of capital, the fleshy middle that is grossly out of proportion with the rest of the economic body.[49]

What is more, Arthur Donnithorne's admiration for Totty, or as he calls her, that "funny little fatty" (130), is represented in a manner that clearly exposes the economic effects of his seduction of Hetty. While on one of his infamous visits to the dairy, he pleases Mrs. Poyser enormously by his benevolent attentions to the child:

"Totty's a capital name. Why she looks like a Totty. Has she got a pocket on?" said the Captain, feeling in his own waistcoat pockets.

Totty immediately with great gravity lifted up her frock, and showed a tiny pink pocket at present in a state of collapse.

"It dot notin' in it," she said, as she looked down at it very earnestly.

"No! What a pity! Such a pretty pocket. Well, I think I've got some things of mine that will make a pretty jingle in it. Yes; I declare I've got five round silver things, and hear what a pretty noise they make in Totty's pink pocket." (131)

If the exchange of money for the lifting of a frock resembles prostitution in this scenario, the metaphor will retain the same valence when a pregnant and abandoned Hetty is finally forced by economic necessity to convert the expensive jewelry Arthur has given her into cash and run away from Hayslope. Capitalism, or as it is glossed by Malthusian language, "the established administration of property," will become Hetty's last hope for survival, as we painfully watch her apply "her small arithmetic and knowledge of prices to calculate how many meals and how many rides were contained" (418) in her small stock of funds. When she realizes, perhaps too late, that "There's nothin you can't turn into a sum, for there's nothin but what's got a number in it" (282), Hetty's fears take on a distinctly economic bent:

Now, in her faintness of heart at the length and difficulty of her journey, she was most of all afraid of spending her money, and becoming so destitute that she would have to ask for people's charity; for Hetty had the pride not only of a proud nature but of a proud class—the class that pays the most poor-rates, and most shudders at the idea of profiting by a poor-rate. (418)

Hetty's intuitive economic sense becomes an instinct for self-preservation that even prevents her from committing suicide: "It was no use to think of drowning herself—she could not do it, at least while she had money left to buy food, and strength to journey on" (434). Not only food, but the bodily strength derived from nourishment is a commodity that can be given numerical value, or "turn[ed] into a sum." Although her mother died under the dual oppressions of "inflammation" and Mr. Sorrel's economic incapacities, Hetty's emerging fatness brings out the latent economic characteristics of her "proud class" as she confronts the principles of "simple addition" that shape middle-class identity.[50]

While Hetty's education in the ways and means of capital is no doubt abrupt, her earlier insights into the economic realities of her pregnancy are primarily marked by her vague desires to move away from Hall Farm before her secret is revealed. Before she finally settles on a marriage to Adam as the only feasible way of altering her living conditions, she first asks the Poysers for permission to enter domestic service in the capacity of a lady's maid. Mr. Poyser is quick to assert the sufficiency, and more importantly, the autonomy of economic production at Hall Farm as the primary reason Hetty's request is ridiculous, appealing to his aged father for corroboration: "my family's ate their own bread and cheese as fur back as anybody knows, hanna they father?" (383). Similarly relying on the principles of supply and demand, Mrs. Poyser's scornful response throws us once again into the vernacular of "fatness," this time with an interesting twist:

I'll never gi' my consent to her going for a lady's-maid, while she's got good friends to take care on her till she's married to somebody better nor one o' them valets, as is neither a common man nor a gentleman, an' *must live on the fat o' the land*, an's like enough to stick his hands under his coat tails and expect his wife to work for him. (384, emphasis mine)

In this invocation, "fat" is not the illusory emblem of capital, an emblem that is—within fledgling middle-class culture—symbolic, metaphorical, and finally, unproductive; rather, "fat" is *capital itself*, a general synecdoche for the rich upper classes, and an immediate sign of the Donnithornes.

It is in this context that Squire Donnithorne's late-breaking desire to negotiate a business deal with the Poysers resonates within the larger nexus of *Adam Bede*, and particularly Hetty's story. Delicately indicating that the Poysers' perpetual dread of eviction may become reality if their compliance is not received, the Squire proposes that they turn over a sizeable portion of their corn land to the potential tenant of Chase Farm in return for an increase in their dairy land—an exchange that will nominally give the Poysers the privilege of supplying the manor house with "milk, cream and butter at the market prices" (391).[51] Like Sir Thomas Bertram, Squire Donnithorne is attempting to convert to a home trade, trying to harness the productivity of his estate for his own exclusive consumption. Mrs. Poyser penetrates the Squire's objectives as easily as she discerned her housemaid's, however, and she refuses his offer in an explosive moment of class consciousness: "I'll not consent to take more dairy work into my hands, either for love or money; and there's nayther love nor money here, as I can see, on'y other folks love o' theirselves, and the money as is to go into other folks's pockets. I know there's them as is born't own the land, and them as is born to sweat on't" (392). When the Poysers are confronted with this exemplary tableau of business-as-usual at Hall Farm, the local mechanisms of economic exploitation become apparent to them, and their pretense of autonomy crumbles under the actualities of tenantry. The plentiful "bread and cheese" that the Poysers have eaten for generations is simply another manifestation of Donnithorne fat: like the domestic servants that Mrs. Poyser criticizes, the Poysers are neither "common" nor "gentle," and the unpossessed richness of Hall Farm places them in a similar socioeconomic position to those who must "live on the fat o' the land."

This exchange with Squire Donnithorne represents a major economic triumph to the Poysers, as they manage to circumvent eviction while forcing the Squire to abandon his scheme of monopolizing dairy production at Hall Farm. Apparently, the prospective tenant of Chase Farm refused to negotiate a lease without the promised corn land, and "it was known throughout the two parishes that the Squire's plan had been frustrated because the Poysers had refused to be 'put upon'" (396). Yet if Mrs. Poyser believes that she has also circumvented Bartle Massey's econometric on female nourishment and has literally prevented her dairy goods from running to Donnithorne fat, she will eventually realize that it is too late: her food has already run to fat in the form of the emerging fleshiness on her niece's body and in the illegitimate Donnithorne child that has been indirectly nourished by Poyser labor. Ironically, it will be Hetty's own belated understanding of the operations of capital that finally, permanently, prevents Poyser goods from running to fat, as her act of infanticide, her refusal to nourish another body at the expense of her own, is an assertion of individualism that replicates Mrs. Poyser's refusal to give her milk to the Donnithornes instead of retaining it for her own family or retailing it for personal profit on the open market.[52] While this seemingly smooth equation of infanticide with economic individualism is politically unpalatable, it is impossible not to identify the redundancy of the two incidents, especially when we are confronted with the gruesome fact that Hetty is arrested at the site of the baby's grave with "a big piece of bread in her lap" (481), literally putting her own need for nourishment before her child's. It is also telling that the baby's death is coterminous with the death of his unknowing grandfather, Squire Donnithorne, as if Hetty's refusal to nurse her child and Mrs. Poyser's refusal to provide milk products for the Manor House have, at either end of the generational spectrum, the same effects.

≺ V ≻

*Economies of Replacement: The Redistribution of*
*Fat and Middle-Class Empowerment*

With this pair of Donnithorne deaths, fat begins to redistribute itself throughout the body of the novel, and the economics of replacement take over the management of both the family plot and the marriage plot. If at one point in the text Arthur Donnithorne's birthday feast for his tenants and laborers underscored the feudal organization of Hayslope, by the end of *Adam Bede*, the Poysers' boisterous Harvest supper has disrupted and rewritten the brand of class-consciousness that informed Arthur's party. Martin Poyser enjoys the role of the "young master" (562) during these latter festivities, but unlike Arthur, Mr. Poyser sits at the head of one large table "helping his servants to the fragrant roast beef, and pleased when their empty plates came in again" (560). With this celebration of economic plenty replacing the paternalistic significance of the local gentry's "coming-of-age," middle-class power emerges in the guise of collectivism to foster more harmonious relations between the "head" of the social body and its "hands." Yet if the philosophy of social paternalism has been overthrown by the end of *Adam Bede*, another ideological program has taken its place: as Margaret Homans notes, Mr. Poyser's feast is only for men.[53] By literally segregating the women from the "fat," the Victorian doctrine of separate spheres begins to shape the social economy of *Adam Bede* in time to neutralize the sexual dangers inherent in representations of capitalist excess.

Although the socioeconomic privileges attached to ownership and autonomy are finally awarded to the Poysers, they still must be disciplined for mistaking economic expediency for affection in their early confusion about the differences among nieces, daughters, and servants. When the Poysers attempt to replace one niece with the other—to make Dinah compensate the loss of Hetty's labor at Hall Farm—and fail, it is apparent that some brands of accumulation are unwelcome in the new social order. Despite her aunt's wheedling, Dinah realizes that the position of the perennial niece in the Poyser household is a service-oriented rather than family-oriented role:

". . . an' now I can trust you wi' the butter, an' have had all the trouble o' teaching you, an' there's all the sewing to be done, an' I must have a strange gell out of Treddles'on to do it—an' all because you must go back to that bare heap o' stones as the very crows fly over an' won't stop at."

"Dear aunt Rachel," said Dinah, looking up in Mrs. Poyser's face, "it's your kindness makes you say I'm useful to you. You don't really want me now; for Nancy and Molly are clever at work, and you're in good health now, by the blessing of God." (518–19)

By quietly pointing out that Nancy and Molly, the servants, are what Mrs. Poyser "really wants" instead of a niece, Dinah refuses to be absorbed into Hall Farm's economic grid and reduced to a redundant pair of hands in the Poyser family dairy. After all, once the dangerous collusions of fat and femininity are eliminated from *Adam Bede*, buttermaking is the last occupation that the newly domesticated Dinah can undertake. This kind of productivity, as Hetty has made abundantly clear, is both uneconomical and antithetical to middle-class empowerment.[54]

Although Dinah refuses to replace her cousin at Hall Farm, Hetty's enforced emigration allows Dinah to marry Adam, her thin body gaining in "fullness" and health (581) as she adapts herself to new conventions of domesticity and maternity. The metaphors of dilation and distention proliferate as this exchange is explored, describing Adam's love for Dinah as "the outgrowth of that fuller life which had come to him from his acquaintance with deep sorrow" (574). Within *Adam Bede*'s vernacular of fatness, Dinah is an "outgrowth," a product of Hetty's "fullness" that will clean up after sexual misconduct, renaturalize maternity, and restore the integrity of the social body through a rapid deployment of domestic ideology. Accordingly, within the seven-year gap between the end of the novel proper and its epilogue, just as Dinah's thin, "starved" body has begun to bloom and reproduce, Adam has come into some capital and owns the timber-yard where he used to work. As new "outgrowths" replace more deviant forms of fatness, it becomes increasingly clear that successful "possession" and the rise of the middle class are simultaneous socioeconomic events. In good Malthusian form, *Adam Bede*'s economic philosophy is cyclical: Hetty gives way to Dinah, barrenness gives way to plenty, and the accumulated wealth of the upper classes begins to circulate and finally settle around the "middle" regions of the social body.

# In Loco Parentis

## DICKENSIAN UNCLES AND THE
## VICTORIAN PAWNSHOP

The circulation of wealth in a nation resembles that of the blood in the natural body. There is one quickness of the current which comes of cheerful emotions or wholesome exercise; and another which comes of shame and or fever. There is a flush of the body which is full of warmth and life; and another which will pass into putrefaction.

John Ruskin, *Unto This Last*

EVEN WITHIN THE radically urban novels of Charles Dickens we can find a version of George Eliot's rural buttermaker: in *Bleak House*, for example, we see rising law clerk and amateur detective, Mr. Guppy, taking the impoverished, illiterate, orphaned street-sweeper Jo "in hand as a witness, patting him into this shape, that shape, and the other shape, like a butterman dealing with so much butter, and worrying him according to the best models."[1] Although buttermaking becomes a figurative scene of production in the thoroughly mid-Victorian *Bleak House*, Jo's conversion into fat at the hands of a legal system that fails to define him as a legitimate citizen can only underscore his textual function as a living emblem of sexual, economic, and social excess. In *Bleak House*, the machinations of the law assume the proportions of a diabolical dairy, metabolizing vulnerable "witnesses" and clients into a kind of fat that throws us back upon *Adam Bede*'s idiom of failed ownership and blocked circulation. By knowing "nothink," by possessing nothing, by connecting nothing, Jo spreads only the bewilderment of fever and the confusion of misinformation; he is one of the many weak links in the circulation of knowledge in *Bleak House*, one of the most egregious reasons that information is perennially posthumous and potentially disfiguring. From the blocked drainage in the slum where Jo lives, to the blocked chancery suit that keeps the slum stagnant, from Sir Leicester Dedlock's hereditary gout and Grandfather Small-weed's lower-body paralysis, to the self-consuming costs of Chancery and the self-combusting "Chancellor" of the Rag and Bottle shop, the thematics of *Bleak House* are like the thematics of *Adam Bede* in that they are punctuated by a medley of bodily and economic obstructions.

Yet if the dairy provides the first image of fat-production in *Bleak House*, the tannery will perhaps provide the most thematically significant, as the constantly copied and unproductively circulated parchments in the perennial Jarndyce case are the greasy end-products of dumb animals much like Jo—animals herded through the streets of London on market days as regularly in *Bleak House* as Jo is "moved on." Entering the law offices of the vampiristic Mr. Vholes, we are struck by "a smell as of unwholesome sheep, blending with the smell of must and dust . . . referable to the nightly (and often daily) consumption of mutton fat in candles, and to the fretting of parchment forms and skins in greasy drawers" (415). As the representative of Richard Carstone's legal interests in the Jarndyce suit, the perpetual greasiness of Mr. Vholes's office, and indeed, of all legal portals in *Bleak House*, seems to be the direct result of lawerly habits of consumption: not only do Vholes's eyes make "a lingering meal" (418) of Richard's ever-wasting body, but we are assured that Vholes is a "minor cannibal" (417) of the legal professions whose digestion is, predictably, "much impaired" (405). We hardly need Esther's suspicion that that the money Ada Clare brings to Richard upon their marriage "was melting away with the candles I used to see burning after dark in Mr. Vholes's office" (619) to realize that Richard Carstone's body is becoming his lawyer's grease in *Bleak House*, or that an inscription of bodily consumption has provided us with yet another narrative of economic depletion and waste. Indeed, the metabolic process that threatens to worry and fret the human body into grease is so widespread in *Bleak House* that it extends even to the insignificant Peepy, neglected and uncivilized child of philanthropist Mrs. Jellyby, who habitually follows the sheep "quite out of town" on market days, and returns "in such a state as never was!" (139)

But the most hideous representation of fat in *Bleak House* is also the novel's most hyperbolic scene of failed digestion, as the spontaneous combustion of Krook, the owner of the rag and bottle shop, randomly splatters a greasy combination of black fat and yellow oil upon his neighbors and tenants in Chancery Lane. Krook's shop, where "everything seemed to be bought and nothing to be sold" (38), serves as the epitome of blocked circulation in the novel, its relation to the constipations of the law italicized by the fact that the shop is nicknamed the Court of Chancery, and Krook himself stands in as Lord Chancellor. Whether Krook is "a smuggler, a receiver, or an unlicensed pawnbroker, or a money-lender" (214), confuses curious individuals like Mr. Guppy as much as the manner of his death. While it is true that rag and bottle stores often functioned as illicit pawnshops in the Victorian period,[2] Krook's habitual retention of all incoming merchandise, his uneconomical hoarding of all brands of waste and excess, is a marked stoppage of the capitalist system that the social body cannot long withstand. It could easily be the coroner's judgment that Krook's death is the result of too much grease in his diet: among his favorite articles of purchase have been the oily waste papers of the legal profession, piles of bones picked clean, and numerous "sacks of ladies' hair" (39). Moreover, the kind of commercial obstruction represented by Krook's shop was believed to be endemic to the poor circulation of Chancery; for example, George Cochrane's 1855 dissertation *On the Economy of the Law* called delays in Chancery "the bane of commerce," likening the enforced withholding of revenue from clients to "keep[ing] money in a closet without using it."[3] The death of the Lord Chancellor of the rag and bottle shop, in other words, is particularly appropriate to the rank, title, and bodily incapacities of his namesake:

The Lord Chancellor of that Court, has died the death of all Lord Chancellors in all Courts, and of all authorities in all places under all names soever, where false pretenses are made, and where injustice is done. Call the death by any name Your Highness will, attribute it to whom you will, or say it might have been prevented how you will, it is the same death eternally—inborn, inbred, engendered in the corrupted humours of the vicious body itself, and that only—Spontaneous Combustion, and none other of all the deaths that can be died. (346)

Yet before the destructive accumulations of both the Court of Chancery and Krook's dysfunctional pawnshop distract us entirely from our broader focus on the Victorian family, I should say that *Bleak House* resembles *Adam Bede* not only in its idiom of fat, but in its economy of the avunculate: as early as 1756, for reasons unspecified by the OED, "uncle" was a common euphemism for pawnbroker. As I've already indicated in the introduction, Dickens cheerfully exploited the avuncular euphemism in a variety of writings throughout his career, and is perhaps the best barometer of the extent to which the nickname remained in popular circulation during the Victorian period. Putting the avunculate of *Bleak House* aside for a moment in favor of the earlier *Martin Chuzzlewit*, we see Dickens introducing the reader to the complicated genealogy of the Chuzzlewit family by satirically citing "documentary evidence" that at least one member of the historically hapless clan achieved some degree of commercial eminence:

Throughout such fragments of his correspondence as have escaped the ravages of the moths . . . we find him [Diggory Chuzzlewit] making constant reference to an uncle, in respect of whom he would seem to have entertained great expectations, as he was in the habit of seeking to propitiate his favor by presents of plate, jewels, books, watches, and other valuable articles. Thus, he writes on one occasion to his brother in reference to a gravy-spoon, the brother's property, which he (Diggory) would appeared to have borrowed or otherwise possessed himself of: "Do not be angry. I have parted with it—to my uncle." . . . Still it does not appear (which is strange) to have procured for him any lucrative post at court or elsewhere, or to have conferred upon him any distinction than that which was necessarily included in the countenance of so great a man, and the being invited by him to certain entertainments, so splendid and costly in their nature that he emphatically calls them "Golden Balls."[4]

If in *Martin Chuzzlewit* Dickens manufactures humor by pretending to mistake avuncular mercantilism for affective manifestations of kinship, in *Bleak House* he exploits the connection between pawnbrokers and uncles in order to launch a more serious attack on an ethic of economic individualism that located the doctrine of usury at the cornerstone of the nineteenth-century commercial system. Despite the ironic treatment "Uncle" sometimes receives from the pen of Charles Dickens, a glance at Victorian tracts and pamphlets on pawnbroking is enough to indicate that the avunculate epitomized a new kind of commercial patriarchy that had been steadily replacing the feudal, paternalistic culture of pre-industrial England. Because the brand of social paternalism advocated by writers such as John Ruskin and Arthur Helps insisted that business relationships be modeled after parent-child relationships, the pawnbroker's usurious commercial pursuits made him an unfit parent, incapable of affective family attachments. Moreover, as the pawnshop was the lowest common denominator of the banking industry, it was a useful red herring for middle-class moralists who sought to project this ostensible erosion of the affective family upon the laziness and thriftlessness of the poorer classes.

In this context, Chapter Three explores the debate over pawn-broking as one manifestation of an ongoing philosophical crisis over the paternal metaphor. Proving once again that all politics is local, a variety of literary texts—from economic essays and temperance tracts to short stories and novels—appropriated the avuncular trope with zest, rewriting cultural anxieties about the disintegration of paternalistically ordered Victorian society as tales of literal family decay or corruption. Yet these tales of the avunculate by no means functioned as a uniform condemnation of his powers; in fact, two competing images of "uncle" emerge from Victorian sources, reflecting and personifying a widespread debate over the effects of capitalism upon social benevolence and familial affection. Was the pawnbroker a commercial cannibal who fattened himself upon the poverty and desperation of his poor nephews and nieces, or was he, as his avuncular title seemed to suggest, a benevolent agent of economic autonomy who transformed washerwomen into capitalists for the price of a flatiron?

Of course, it is hardly necessary to focus on Krook and his greasy pawnshop to find the avunculate in *Bleak House*, nor to begin theorizing the anti-paternalism that runs rampant through Dickensian houses in general: *Bleak House* is a novel "crowded with orphans" in the words of Christine van Boheemen; a novel that represents "illegitimacy as non-existence within patriarchal culture" according to Richard T. Gaughan; a novel that resorts to the thematics of "carceral institutions" to rectify "laspses in the proper management of the family" for D. A. Miller.[5] In fact, John Jarndyce's objectives in becoming Guardian to Richard Carstone and Ada Clare, orphaned wards in the obstructed Chancery suit, are similar to Sir Thomas Bertram's objectives at the end of *Mansfield Park*: that is, Jarndyce also hopes that a marriage between cousins will begin to conserve the economic and affective integrity of his family, a family that in *Bleak House* is perpetually at war over the conflicting wills of a long-dead ancestor.

Entering *Bleak House* by way of the family rather than by way of the fat, we see that the economic obstructions engendered by the falsely paternalistic Lord Chancellor erode real kinship ties and undermine family sentiment, causing even the legal receiver in the case to acquire a "distrust of his own mother, and a contempt for his own kind" (4). In *Bleak House*, an unusual likeness between the pawnbroker and the Lord Chancellor finally forces the avunculate to the center of narrative, as the social institution that should stand *in loco parentis* to its infants, orphans, and wards is actually responsible for hoarding paternal inheritances and consuming family affections. Many years of expecting a judgment have decimated the family of the mad Miss Flite, who resides with the other human remains and legal "skins" above Krook's shop. Likewise, the suit of Mr. Gridley, while still pending, no longer has commercial or sentimental impetus: "My whole estate left to me in that will of my father's, has gone in costs. The suit, still undecided, has fallen into rack, and ruin, and despair, with everything else" (163). When Richard Carstone proves unable to resist the hereditary temptation of Jarndyce v. Jarndyce, he is convinced by his greasy lawyer that he has "conflicting interests" with his Guardian, and eventually decides that "natural relations are incompatible" with the business of Chancery (400). What is more, the prematurely wizened young Smallweed has been "so nursed by Law and Equity that . . . it is reported at the public offices that his father was John Doe, and his mother the only female member of the Roe family" (210). While Smallweed's parents are anonymous, his uncle is not: young Smallweed is the nephew of the quasi-pawnbroker Krook, and the inheritance he shares with his avaricious family upon his uncle's combustion is the greasy Rag and Bottle shop.

Like the Lord Chancellor, Krook hoards the fragments of paternal heritage, the last remnants of economic and bodily decline; whether it be the hair shorn from the heads of ladies in the last stages of genteel poverty, or the most crucial parchment in the gargantuan family battle called Jarndyce v. Jarndyce, Krook's shop is a greasy tomb for the buried remains of both the private family and the social family. The most significant paternal remnant to be found in Krook's shop is, of course, his tenant Nemo: an anonymous and solitary copywriter who considers the pawnbroker to be his "nearest relation" (106), but is eventually revealed to have nearer kin in the shape of his illegitimate daughter, Esther Summerson. Yet by the time the greasy bowels of the pawnshop give up this paternal relict, Nemo is little more than another pile of bones, skin and grease, possessing only "some worthless articles of clothing in the old portmanteau" and "a bundle of pawnbroker's duplicates, those turnpike tickets on the road of Poverty" (109). No record of identity clings to Nemo's body as it lies there "with no more track behind him, that anyone can trace, than a deserted infant" (110), and even his name, as lawyer Tulkinghorn reminds us, is "Latin for no one" (102).

Although many Victorian annalists and satirists of the pawnshop used the avuncular euphemism frequently throughout the century, modern historians of pawnbroking have been uniformly uninterested in Dickens's Uncle and in the mutually constituitive ideologies of kinship and commerce that are embodied by his nickname. For example, in an otherwise careful and historically scrupulous study of the nineteenth-century pawnshop, Melanie Tebbutt casually mentions that pawntickets were called "uncle's cards" without so much as a discursive footnote to explain the slang term.[6] Apparently many pawnshop historians rely upon an ahistorical ideology of the family as a sympathetic social entity in order to make sense of the euphemism, presuming the term "uncle" to be an indisputable, inviolable benchmark of the benevolent effects pawnbrokers had upon the lives of the Victorian poor. Kenneth Hudson's whimsical description of the pawnbroker as "the friendly neighborhood figure to whom his hard-up nieces and nephews could always turn for advice and a loan, the solid leaning-post in times of weakness and trouble,"[7] reflects certain standard twentieth-century assumptions about affective kinship. These cultural givens provide the bedrock for Hudson's primary thesis that a century of silence about the cultural importance of the pawnbroker in nineteenth- and early twentieth-century England can be blamed on the fact that "pawning, like sex," was a familial concern. "Strangers would not understand. They would be unable to see pawnbroking in its proper context, to grasp how it fitted into family life."[8] Repeatedly, the avuncular euphemism provides inherent justification for prematurely situating the pawnbroker in this "proper context" of the affective family; in fact, John Caskey's most recent book, *Fringe Banking*, goes no further than an "amusing" and "probably inaccurate" 1826 anecdote about a pawnbroker named Simpson and the three nephews who worked for him.[9] For Caskey, as for Hudson and Tebbutt, the correct etymology of the nickname is beside the point; because the familial connotations of the term "uncle" immediately establish the pawnbroker within an affective genre, more complicated connections between the shadiest inhabitant of the nineteenth-century commercial world and the much-contested sphere of the Victorian family do not have to be theorized.

While the impulse to understand pawnbroking within the context of kinship is as central to this chapter as it is to the work of Caskey, Hudson, and Tebbutt, it is the contention of my larger project that our collective cultural investment in a concept of the affective family can sometimes elide the sociohistorical specificity that a term like "Uncle" assumes in the context of nineteenth-century debates over self-help and paternalism, free-will and social determinism, economic individualism and feudal dependence. Although the exact etymology of "Uncle" is unclear, in the Victorian period the economic shape of pawnbrokers and the familial shape of uncles became a bilateral repository for a range of anxieties about what capitalism was doing to both the private family and the social family. In order to measure the extent to which thematic representations of pawnbroking engage with an avuncular discourse, and in turn to approximate the pervasiveness of "uncle" as an anti-paternalistic metaphor, Chapter Three situates the pawnshop within Victorian debates over economic and personal autonomy, foregrounding the way conflicting images of family life were deployed by both detractors and advocates of pawnbroking. From these broader speculations about how the avunculate became a specific familial ideology in the Victorian period, I will argue that texts like *Bleak House, Our Mutual Friend, Nicholas Nickleby,* and *Oliver Twist* exploit the rhetorical equation between uncles and pawnbrokers in order to foreground the effects of capitalism on affective relationships.

≺ I ≻

*Pawnshop Controversies, Political Economy, and*
*the Dickensian Avunculate*

Of course, Dickens's apparently contradictory view of uncles would seem to make him a bad candidate for any uniform argument about the status of pawnbroking within Victorian culture. By characterizing the pawnshop in *Household Words* as an important, even necessary, aspect of working-class life, and the only possible means by which the poor could emulate the economic standards set by middle-class existence, Dickens seems to belie his own more prevalent image of the pawnbroker who, like Diggory Chuzzlewit's Uncle, was a catalyst of insolvency, an enabler of debt, and an extortionist, or like Krook, was a voracious consumer of his client's hair, skin, and bones. Moreover, this apparent discordancy in the Dickensian avunculate has been addressed before, most notably by Harry Levin in a 1975 article succinctly entitled "The Uncles of Dickens." Levin notes that two archetypal figures emerge from Dickensian plots: "the orphan child . . . and the surrogate father, who is often quite literally the uncle, and who always mediates between the protagonist and the world, whether as sponsor or adversary."[10] For Levin, Dickens's frequent use of the pawnbroking alias merely extends the potential duplicity of the avuncular function, disguising the "avaricious loanshark" as the "friend in need."[11] Using Lévi-Strauss to position the avunculate as a passageway from the private sphere of the family to public transactions with society, Levin points out that the function of Uncles is necessarily binarized:

Since Uncle is well established in the community, it seems natural that he should be expected to show himself a generous protector, a tutelary spirit looking after the lives of his younger connections. If he disappoints such an expectation, he would seem to be unnatural, hostile and malicious, a proponent of those negative forces which he should be tempering.[12]

Summarily concluding his argument with Dostoevsky's maxim that "God and the Devil are always fighting,"[13] Levin's focus on archetype eventually draws our attention away from the specifically historical conditions that may have made the avunculate a particularly appropriate signifier of the nineteenth-century pawn-

shop. Yet by concentrating on the bipartite shape of uncles in the
Dickens canon, Levin inadvertently identifies a schism in the Victorian concept of the social family, a family that was governed in
the nineteenth-century not by the paternalist philosophies of feudalism, but by the morally ambivalent forces of capitalism.

In fact, the tension Levin detects between good and bad uncles
in Dickens is as endemic to Victorian debates over usury as it is to
more general controversies about political economy. Writing about
the 1865 *Our Mutual Friend*, for example, Mary Poovey addresses
a philosophical contest between a mechanized interpretation of
economic transactions that came to life with David Ricardo's 1818
*On the Principles of Political Economy*, and a desire on the part of
novelists like Dickens to simultaneously "defend a moral interpretation of business practices"[14] that would allow for the possibility of moral agency on the part of a variety of capitalists: investors,
stockbrokers, bill discounters, and, I would add, usurers. Poovey
explains that,

In part, the momentum behind [limited liability] legislation reflects the
achievement of a critical mass of support for Ricardo's position: according to this sentiment, the economy *is* a mechanism, which left alone,
will produce and distribute the nation's wealth. Partly, the momentum
behind the limited liability legislation suggests a growing conviction
among England's legislators that, even if the economy was amoral, investors were moral agents, capable of self-regulation and judicious discrimi-
nation.[15]

Dickens's fluctuating anxieties about the transformative powers of
capital seem rooted in the contradictory definitions of political
economy Poovey identifies. That the personal autonomy and
moral integrity of the capitalist-washerwoman is perpetually at
odds with the individual turned into commodity, the human body
worried into fat, finally provides the most compelling reason that
novels like *Bleak House* are so divided in their representations of
the avunculate.

Expanding on Poovey's line of argument that calls attention to
an essentially binarized definition of political economy, I would
suggest that the uncles of Dickens take their shape from contemporary cultural anxieties about the affective ravages of capitalism.
After all, by the time the will that finally calls an end to the Jarndyce suit is found in the oily depths of Krook's shop, the contro-

versy over the pawnbroker's social influence was in full swing. Exemplified by Dickens's characterization of "My Uncle," defenders of the pawnshop often justified the broker's role in the community by appealing to the social philosophy of "self-help" popular with the middle class at mid-century: that is, by transforming "passive capital" into "active capital" Uncle kept entire families, entire neighborhoods from seeking the demoralizing forms of assistance offered by charity guilds and poor-houses. With the help of "My Uncle," a common coat could miraculously take the shape of a bank deposit, and an old pair of boots could be readily translated into shillings. Furthermore, as Dickens explains, the pawnbroker's transformative powers were not limited to the pieces of furniture and wearing apparel deposited by his clients. By helping working-class families convert commodities into currency, "My Uncle" was even able to redefine the economic status of his clients themselves: recollect that although a "washerwoman has no money at all," she could become, "thanks to My Uncle, *a capitalist* while she possesses a flatiron."

The avuncular euphemism hits a distinctly unaffective register in the transformative nexus of the pawnshop, allowing us to read Victorian anxieties over pawnbroking, moneylending, and usury as schisms in the father-centered simplicity of family/society tropes. While in *Bleak House* Dickens demonizes brokering as a process that inevitably commercializes kinship and commodifies the human body—even converting the love letters from Esther's mother, Lady Dedlock, to Esther's father, Nemo, into a salable commodity at the hands of usurer Smallweed—in his *Household Words* essay, as in others of the Victorian period, the pawnshop emerges as a place where the stigmas of gender and class could be strategically discarded; a place where ready capital alone had the power to confer identity; a place where the self could be made—and remade. Indeed, although all varieties of usury were understood, as we will see, to be a collective challenge to social and economic paternalism as well as to the affective family, the pawnbroker's function was especially identified with commercial self-making because his business entailed the conversion of objects into money, and in the case of Dickens's washerwoman, the transformation of use value into exchange value. For Marx, moreover, money is a "radical leveler[16]; a form of currency that entirely elided the difference between commodities and their traders. In a passage of *Capital* that addresses the "the fetishism of commodities," Marx explains that while the commodity represents the social character of human labor, the conversion of the commodity into money erases the specific history of that labor:

When they thus assume the shape of values, commodities strip off every trace of their natural and original use-value, and of the particular kind of useful labour to which they own their creation, in order to pupate into the homogenous social materialization of unindifferentiated human labor. From the mere look of a piece of money, we cannot tell what breed of commodity has been transformed into it. In their money form, all commodities look alike.[17]

With the transformation of her property into money, the washerwoman is no longer a personification of her labor; the piece of money she now possesses simultaneously erases the history of her flat-iron and the history of her class status.

Although the homogeneity conferred by the money-form was distrusted by Marx, it was especially celebrated by defenders of the pawnshop. Because he elided the mutual history of pledger and commodity, "Uncle" was not only a rhetorical alternative to the law of the father, he was a radical alternative to paternalist philosophy: a "broker" of individual identity who offered a socially liberating denial of origins by undoing the organizing motif of Victorian society, the parent-child relationship. And just as the pawnshop was perceived to provide personal empowerment for the individual, it also seemed to promote economic independence for the nation: the laissez-faire commercial freedom to be found in English pawnshops epitomized "the spirit of the age" for writers such as A. Keeson, whose 1854 comparison of the religious and government-run Monts de Piété ("banks that take pity") of France and Ireland and the private pawnshops of England concluded that the "parental system" of government was completely at odds with "the gigantic commerce" currently enjoyed by "the greatest commercial nations of the age," England and America.

While the former profess to consider the State as a paternal Institution which ought to do all things for all men; the latter put their own shoulders to the wheel, and only desire that their respective Governments will leave off meddling with Trade, and permit it to enjoy the unrestricted development of its own resources.[18]

In Keeson's text, the private pawnshop becomes a symbol of national pride, the natural result of a highly evolved commercial system: where capital is "abundant" and "competition intense . . . the trade of lending money upon pawn may be . . . safely entrusted to private hands, although such a course may be dangerous, or even impossible, in other countries, from the paucity of respectable capitalists willing to embark on it."[19] Both the successful transition to national capitalism for England, and personal autonomy for the washerwoman, depended upon a permanent overthrow of the repressive benevolence of paternalistic government, and a widespread advocacy of shoulder-to-the-wheel self-reliance.

Similarly, Jeremy Bentham's famous "Defence of Usury" implies that government intervention deprived working-class men of their ability to function within society as adults: "No man of ripe years and sound mind, acting freely, with his eyes open, ought to be hindered, with a view to his advantage, from making such a bargain."[20] Without the ready help of the pawnbroker, the self-esteem and independent spirit of the working-classes would be dissolved under the infantilizing brands of aid offered by charity. An anonymous essay that appeared in the *Pawnbroker's Gazette* in 1871 denounced the poor-rates as a permanent blight on the self-esteem of members of the working class, insisting that it was impossible to "retain a mind erect" and ask for public assistance at the same time:

Dependence breeds servility, and he who stoops to charity, if at all avoidable, is rarely just to himself. The want of self-respect is a preparation for every evil. If degraded in their own and others' esteem, the poor are removed from the salutary restraint of opinion, and having no caste to lose—no honour to forfeit—often abandon themselves recklessly to vice and crime."[21]

Because economic individualism was—apparently—the only thing standing between an otherwise honorable individual and a life of crime, the pawnbroker, by transforming washerwomen into capitalists, became a virtual savior of souls. He arrested the "downward spiral" that so many middle-class moralists identified as the inevitable result of thriftlessness and poverty, making "redemption" his order of business in more ways than one.

Uncle, in other words, was more than just a pawnbroker, he was an alternative social philosophy that had been empowered by

modern capitalism; a visible symbol of the way that competition
and autonomy were replacing patronage and thralldom in the vocabulary of commercial interaction. This cultural evolution, however, was not universally received as an improvement upon the
paternalistic hierarchy of the past. By epitomizing the capitalist
mantra of "buy cheap, sell dear," the pawnbroker became a convenient scapegoat for all industrial age commercial inequities, and
"uncle" a familiar euphemism for any individual who made his
living from interest or profit margins. For example, T. Turner's
1864 exposé *The Three Gilt Balls: or My Uncle's Stock in Trade
and Customers* elided all differences between Uncle and more socially acceptable schools of brokerage.

In the present day our greatest capitalists are the greatest pawnbrokers;
and our greatest merchants, their best customers. If we could only get at
the facts, it would enable us to claim many as our Uncles, who forego
the honour, and never display their dignity by mounting the three gilt
balls. . . . The broad acres which give titles to many of our aristocracy,
and the mansions in which they live in splendour, and receive the hom-
age of their less dignified brethren, are as much in pawn as the flat iron
on which my Uncle lends his four-pence . . . Every mortgage deed is but
another name for a pawn ticket . . . The bill of exchange, or promissory
note, is but another form of pledging.[22]

As a concept of the avunculate begins to dilate in Turner's attack
on the pawnshop, the broader implications of my argument should
also become more apparent: under industrial capitalism, a socioeconomic philosophy founded upon the law of the father was
threatened by a competition-based commercial code that took its
shape from the law of the uncle. Especially valuable here is a concept I discussed in the introduction: the shift from "brotherhood"
to "otherhood" theorized by Max Weber in his sociocultural history of usury.[23] Because the modern "Science of Exchange" legiti-
mized a system of "accountability" in which one person's profit is
another person's loss, it was, in John Ruskin's assessment, "probably a bastard science—not by any means a *divina scientia*, but
one begotten of another father, that father who, advising his children to turn stones into bread, is himself employed in turning
bread into stones, and who, if you ask a fish of him . . . can give
you but a serpent."[24] Both Ruskin's alternative father and Dickens's Uncle of *Household Words* are functionaries in the mystical
process of exchange, but while the latter's transformations em-

power the working classes, the former's are described as perverse acts of economic sabotage practiced upon a pitiful legion of trusting children. According to Ruskin, even economic relationships carried familial responsibilities, duties that the commercial patriarch perpetually overlooked: "men of business . . . don't know . . . what other losses or gains far away in dark streets are dependent on theirs in lighted rooms."[25] As harbingers of a new capitalist doctrine of personal accountability and laissez-faire competition, Ruskin's "men of business"—the usurious fathers who were steadily replacing the benevolent feudal patriarchs—exemplified the alternative family/society motif I have been identifying as avuncular.

Moreover, the homogenizations of the avunculate were just as distrusted by Dickens as they were by Marx and even Ruskin. Dickens's anxiety about an economic process that could systematically dissolve Captain Hawdon into Nemo, disintegrate the human body, deny patriarchal heritage, surfaces not only in *Bleak House*, but in novels like the 1865 *Our Mutual Friend*. The commercial threat to bodily integrity is nowhere more apparent than in Mr. Venus's workshop of bone articulation, where Silas Wegg goes in search of his amputated leg, and finds Venus trying to fit it into a "miscellaneous" skeleton: "I have just sent home a beauty—a perfect beauty—to a school of art. One leg Belgian, one leg English, and the pickings of eight other people in it."[26] If Venus isn't literally a pawnbroker, his combination of various human bones into individual "articulations" mirrors the process of homogenization that is endemic to Uncle's workings. Just as the pawnshop dissolves paternal origins, social class, economic heritage, Venus's articulations place human identity under erasure, forcing individual bodies to lose integrity in order to reconstitute body fragments within anonymous, miscellaneous human shapes. Not only do these shapes reflect a social anonymity similar to Nemo's in *Bleak House*, but Venus's shop literalizes *The Merchant of Venice*'s moral conundrum about usury. "I bought you in open contract," Venus insists to Mr. Wegg, only to have Wegg naively respond: "You can't buy flesh and blood in this country, sir; not alive you can't . . . Then query, bone?" (351) Wegg's assumptions about the limits of commodification are summarily belied when Venus's workshop proves that capitalism has worried the human body into salable fragments, subjecting it to the same blockages, amputations, homogenizations, multiplications that are endemic to more commercial forms of circulation.

Yet even in the context of *Our Mutual Friend*, it is impossible to tell whether the perpetual mutations of human identity engendered by endless capitalist circulation of labor, commodities, and money erode economic individualism and material identity, or rather force it abruptly into existence. Certainly a mechanized view of the pawnshop is at work in the description of the way that female pawnbroker, Pleasant Riderhood, has a "ragged knot" of hair "constantly coming down behind" that prevents her from entering upon any form of business without first "winding herself up with both hands" (407–8). Again, the Jew Riah who serves as a beard for usurer Fledgeby offers what can only be considered a mantra of determinism in response to his clients' every plea for mercy: "I do as I am directed. I am not the principal here. I am but the agent of a superior, and I have no choice, no power" (635). Yet despite these signs of commercial automation, the transformations enabled by the Uncle of Dickens's *Household Words* essay appear thematically intact when John Harmon appears in Pleasant Riderhood's illicit pawnshop disguised by facial hair and the clothing of his attempted murderer, sailor George Radfoot. Harmon is attempting to unravel a series of events that have transpired to rob him of both his identity and a vast paternal inheritance, and a drug Radfoot procured at this pawnshop from Pleasant's father, Rogue Riderhood, seems to be the origin of a series of transformations that have forced Harmon to perpetually refigure himself as Julius Hanford, John Rokesmith, and now the inquisitive "Captain." Considering that Pleasant's "leaving shop" is a panorama of piecemeal identities, where "handkerchiefs, coats, shirts, hats, and other old articles 'On Leaving,' had a general dim resemblance to human listeners,"[27] it is appropriate that Harmon traces the fragments of his own lost identity to a place that greatly resembles the new home of Silas Wegg's amputated leg.

While it is certainly the case that the continuum of male multiplicity enabled by the leaving shop in *Our Mutual Friend* initially serves economic individualism by advancing *criminal* self-interest, it also launches Harmon on a process of self-making that may have been denied him if he had come into his paternal inheritance unencumbered. For example, the paralyzing effects of patrilineage are bemoaned by the morally and socially ambivalent Mortimer Lightwood when he contemplates himself and his equally passive friend, Eugene Wrayburn: "My own small income (I devoutly wish that my grandfather had left it to the Ocean rather than to me!) has been an effective Something, in the way of preventing me from turning to at Anything. And I think yours has been much the same" (885). Indeed, it is Harmon's mistrust of his father's wealth, of the wife that his father's will makes a condition of his inheritance, of his own ability to resist a paternal heritage of cruelty, avariciousness, and family disaffection, that makes him initially eager to temporarily transform himself into George Radfoot, "testing" the value of his allotted wife and old friends, the Boffins, before giving in at last to the law of the father.

The question whether bodily disintegration or patriarchal disinheritance can ever actually inaugurate selfhood is one that Helena Michie asks of *Bleak House*, although certainly with a different set of objectives. Taking on the disfiguring effects of Esther Summerson's illness, Michie argues that Esther "comes to selfhood at the expense of both face and mother . . . wrench[ing] herself free from her mother's fate through a rejection of physical and emotional "likeness":

Esther is, in effect, resisting the "familiar" in her scarred face and enacting the paradox of selfhood through erasure. The mirror of her mother's past remains broken despite Esther's discovery of the "mystery" that informs it; its very fragmentation allows Esther—painfully—to construct a "self."[27]

While it is true that Esther's defacement prevents her from mirroring her mother's body and hence her mother's life, her reconfigured identity draws her closer to her father's life as Captain Hawdon, his death as no one, and the way her own identity has been in pawn ever since her godmother "bred her in secrecy from her birth . . . blotted out all trace of her existence," and had sent John Jarndyce a letter requesting him to "finish what the writer had begun" (181). When Esther's godmother—who is really Lady Dedlock's sister, and therefore Esther's aunt—asks Jarndyce to finish by unfinishing, to make by unmaking, she is asking him to participate in a transformative process endemic not only to fairy godmothers in general, but to the avunculate, and endemic, as Elaine Scarry argues, to a capitalist economic system that keeps the human body perpetually in pain:

The large all-embracing artifact, the capitalist economic system, is itself generated out of smaller artifacts that continually disappear and reappear in new forms: out of the bodies of women and men, material objects emerge; out of material objects, commodities emerge; out of commodities, money emerges; out of money, capital emerges. In the first phase, the original work of creation entailed a double consequence, the projection of the body onto the material object and the reprojection of the object's power of disembodiment back onto the about-to-be-remade human body . . . In its final as in its first form, the artifact is a projection of the human body; but in its final form, unlike its first, it does not refer back to the human body because in each subsequent phase it has taken as the thing to which it refers only that form of artifact immediately preceding its own appearance.[28]

Scarry's teleology of capitalist exchange should throw some light on Krook's stock-in-trade and Venus's articulations: capitalism is, in general, a threat to any natural, even falsely naturalized human body, as well as to any individual features that work to constitute identity. In this context, the morally ambivalent logic of the pawnshop—its habitual homogenization of personal objects into money, washerwomen into capitalists, grown men into orphan children, human bodies into grease—provides a compelling spectacle of political economy as mechanism, or rather, as factory.

Yet this process of bodily alienation, reanimation, and eventual homogenization should also remind us of the myriad dangers of exchange, not only in Marx's idiom of capitalist abstraction, but in *Mansfield Park*'s idiom of foreign trade. Just as Sir Thomas's conversion to a home trade at the end of the novel successfully replaces the sexual excesses of the Bertram family with a kind of savings, Jarndyce's hyperactive domestication of Esther in *Bleak House* protects her from embarking upon a potentially dangerous path of alienation where she can be only governess, teacher, or what is infinitely worse: an overcirculated commodity like Lady Dedlock. Counteracting the godmother's radical unmaking, an erosion of selfhood that could have only resulted in Esther's conversion into the kind of fat so sadly represented by Jo, Jarndyce sets up a thriving home trade, "a whole little orderly system of which you [Esther] are the centre" (403). From her first morning of residence at Bleak House, Esther is thoroughly relegated to an economy of use, taking possession at once of the keys, domestic accounts, and such a litany of occupational nicknames—Old Woman, Little Old Woman, Cobweb, Mrs. Shipton, Mother Hubbard, Dame Durden—that her "own name soon became quite lost among them" (74). Distancing Esther from the false name that italicizes her illegitimacy and thus her marginalization from the supposedly protective culture of patriarchy, Jarndyce's "good" avuncular guardianship roots her firmly in domestic rather than political economy, utility rather than exchange. In this way, Esther's association with sexual excess is effectively neutralized by her enforced embodiment of the domestic principles of saving and waste prevention: "'There never was such a Dame Durden,' said my guardian, 'for making money last'" (633).

Remembering that all commodities, especially women, may come undone under the ravages of capitalism, and that, recalling Irigaray, the process of women's "development" from use to exchange can never take place easily, it is important that Jarndyce waits until the literal and figurative death of Esther's mother before he initiates his ward's safe transition to marriage. Moreover, Jarndyce minimizes the risks inherent in capitalist circulation by refusing to exchange Esther at all. Instead, Jarndyce exchanges Woodcourt for himself and the new and identical version of Bleak House for the old, allowing its mistress to pass from use to use, while never even entering an economy of exchange. Aware of the trail of abstraction commodities inevitably follow in the economy of the avunculate, Jarndyce even refuses to take on paternal status until Esther's final and most necessary transformation is all but complete, waiting till she is safe at the new Bleak House with Allen Woodcourt before he encourages her to "Lie lightly, confidently, here, my child . . . I am your guardian and your father now" (649).

Returning now to the question of whether the alienations of the capitalist economic system make or unmake individual identity, we may want to remember that it is the pawnshop's slow digestion and elimination of Esther's wasted father that enables her to break free of her paternal history and to be absorbed into an economy of savings provided by the "good" uncle. Like John Harmon's, Esther's paternal heritage requires avuncular modification: a series of transformations that disfigure in order to refigure, disembody in order to resurrect. At any rate, Dickens's multiple and contradictory anxieties about the radical unmakings and makings of the avunculate can continue to be measured against Victorian clamor over the family disaffection engendered by the pawnshop, as well as the commercial homogenizations of that "larger, all embracing" system of political economy of which my uncle the pawnbroker is only the most egregious representative

≺ II ≻

### Nicholas Nickleby and the Victorian Shylock

The image of an interest-hungry usurer as a virtual anti-father pro-liferated in the nineteenth century, redressing Shakespeare's tale of Shylock and Jessica in the appropriate metaphors and tropes of capitalism. For example, in the Reverend W. P. Scargill's 1832 no-vella *The Usurer's Daughter*, the rich usurer Erpingham attempts to compel his daughter Margaret to marry an aristocrat of his choosing, and disowns her when she does not comply. As Marga-ret and her new husband, Harry Worthington, slip further and fur-ther into debt and poverty, Erpingham repeatedly refuses to help because, like Ruskin's father, it is his business to traffic in dis-tress: "He had seen wretchedness in palaces, and wretchedness in prisons, but he had not looked on it as wretchedness, but as the means of his own wealth."[29] Halfway through Scargill's parable, however, the plot of the usurer and his daughter begins to dissolve in rather unexpected ways. Margaret and her husband Harry Wor-thington move to Naples for the sake of economy, and are lost within a Radcliffian panorama of banditti and evil monks. When the Worthingtons finally emerge from this gothic disruption, the familial tensions of the novel have drastically shifted: Erpingham dies, leaving his money to one Lord Singleton, a man who is re-vealed to be the insidious younger brother of Harry Worthington's unfortunate father. Harry, and not Margaret, is thus revealed to be the true victim of family conspiracy, and the actual villain of the piece is not the usurer, after all. The individual truly guilty of converting family bonds into economic bonds is Lord Singleton, and *The Usurer's Daughter* ends with neither usurer, nor daugh-ter, but with the deathbed reconciliation of Harry Worthington and his reprobate Uncle. By way of excusing his crime, Uncle Singleton pleads the familiar plight of the second brother, forced upon the cold, commercial world to make his own way, while his elder brother enjoyed the patrimonial effects of wealth and status. Thus when the bad Uncle plot absorbs the family narrative already set in motion by the plight of the usurer's daughter, usury becomes a heavy-handed metaphor for a host of anxieties about primogeniture and its effect on family sentiment, and an inevitable byproduct of a dystopian commercial system in which even family members can be sacrificed for profit. In Scargill's novel, uncles once again disrupt a paternalistic system of signification by subverting the laws of inheritance that normatively transfer property from father to son.

Even more canonical tales of usury tend to represent the plot of the moneylender as this inevitable disruption of the paternal family. Dickens's 1839 *Nicholas Nickleby*, for example, begins, appropriately, with an avuncular legacy that divides two brothers in temperament as well as in favored applications of capital. While Nicholas eventually takes over his father's farm and invests his inheritance in its modest improvements, Ralph "commenced usurer on a limited scale at school; putting out at interest a small capital of slate-pencil and marbles, and gradually extending his operations until they aspired to the copper coinage of this realm, in which he speculated to considerable advantage."[30] As Ralph increases his wealth, his suspicion that his financially unstable brother will eventually want to borrow money extinguishes his feelings of affection, and he forgets about Nicholas entirely until he hears of his death, and is implored by his sister-in-law for help. It is at this point that the plot of the usurer begins to converge with the synchronous plot of the bad father: Uncle Ralph's first action is to separate young Nicholas from his mother and sister by sending him off to serve as underteacher for the reprehensible Mr. Squeers at Dotheboys Hall, an aptly named Yorkshire repository for all variety of disowned, illegitimate, or inconvenient sons. As the subplots of *Nicholas Nickleby* begin to multiply in true Dickensian fashion, Nicholas runs away from Dotheboys Hall with the unfortunate Smike: a boy who had been abandoned by his parents years ago, and subsequently abused into a state of simple-mindedness by the Squeers. Uncle Ralph ends up helping Squeers violently regain Smike, who is rescued but soon dies of consumption, and through a series of plot twists we learn that the usurer's final and most serious crime is that he "has persecuted and hunted down *his own child* to death" (emphasis mine; 789). When the neglected and abused Smike is revealed to be Ralph's son from a marriage kept secret for the sake of money, bad fathering is again shown to be a vice endemic to the workings of usury.

On the other hand, *Nicholas Nickleby* does not subsequently suggest that bad fathering is a vice endemic to all brands of capitalism. True to Poovey's distinction between a mechanized and a morally autonomous definition of political economy, true also to Levin's identification of the good and bad uncles of Dickens, Ralph's abused nephew is provided with a more satisfactory set of uncles in the elderly Cheeryble brothers.[31] Rather than illustrating the anti-commercial ideology that circulation and investment of capital is antithetical to family affection, these large-scale importers of foreign goods actually use their capital to promote affect and domestic harmony in a series of campaigns that seems more reminiscent of Fanny Price's domestic management than the profit-driven prescriptions of free-trade political economy. When the Cheerybles hire Nicholas to work in their counting house, they enable him to support Mrs. Nickleby and Kate by renting him a cottage well under the market value. At first, brother Ned suggests that because they are rich they should charge no rent at all, but brother Charles improves the plan.

"Perhaps it should be better to say something, brother Ned," suggested the other, mildly; "it would help to preserve habits of frugality, you know, and remove any painful sense of overwhelming obligations. We might say fifteen pound, or twenty pound, and if it was punctually paid, make it up to them in some other way. And I might secretly advance a small loan towards a little furniture, and you might secretly advance another small loan, brother Ned; and if we find them doing well—as we shall; there's no fear, no fear—we can change the loan into gifts. Carefully, brother Ned, and by degrees, and without pressing upon them too much; what do you say now, brother?" (457)

Charles Cheeryble well understands the multiple uses of capital, not only the way its correct application can produce the proper habits of frugality, but the way a little money in circulation is a surer way to produce affection between employer and employee than the paternalistic and demoralizing strategy of circulating no

money at all. This same economic scheme is used by the Cheerybles to help Madeleine Bray, the daughter of the only woman
brother Ned ever loved, who is under the control of her spend-
thrift, invalid father:

they had at last come to the conclusion, that the best course would be to
make a feint of purchasing her little drawings and ornamental work, at a
high price, and keeping up a constant demand for the same. For the fur-
therance of which end and object it was necessary that somebody should
represent the dealer in such commodities, and after great deliberations
they had pitched upon Nicholas to support this character. (601)

By artificially inflating the value of Madeleine's "commodities,"
the Cheerybles take care to preserve her feelings of economic independence and self-worth: ". . . perhaps, if you did it very well
(that is *very* well indeed), perhaps she might be brought to believe
that we—that we made a profit of them. Eh? Eh?" (602). Moreover,
by creating a fiction of use, the good uncles keep Madeleine in the
sphere of private production rather than foreign exchange, the
same strategy that *Bleak House*'s John Jarndyce used to protect his
ward Esther from her maternal association with the exchange-
driven economy of prostitution.

Similarly, the farcical home trade constructed by the Cheerybles should be specifically contrasted with Ralph Nickleby's attempt to force his niece Kate into a series of roles that resemble
the commercial circulation of the prostitute. Like the Cheerybles,
Ralph creates a narrative of use for Kate and her mother when he
enlists his niece as an apprentice to a dressmaking establishment:
"Dressmakers in London . . . make large fortunes, keep equipages,
and become persons of great wealth and fortune" (120). Yet the
usurer's fiction of utility masks his attempt to fix Kate in the
realm of exchange, and the riches he attributes to seamstresses
sound increasingly like the profits of prostitution: "walk as fast as
you can" Ralph advises his niece, "and you'll get into the step that
you'll have to walk to business with every morning" (121). Although the occupations of seamstressing and streetwalking become as dangerously similar for Kate as they were believed to be
for Victorian women in general,[32] she is ironically more at risk in
her uncle's home where she is situated as a sexual "decoy" for the
young, aristocratic clients who come for the usurer's money. She
is made the subject of improper bets and threatened with violent

sexual circulation under the orchestration of her uncle, a man who is "proof against all appeals of blood and kindred" (244).

Kate Nickleby and Madeleine Bray begin to double for each other more vigorously when we learn that Madeleine's father is heavily in debt to Ralph Nickleby's fellow usurer, Arthur Gride, and the two have hatched a plot to cancel Mr. Bray's debts if he gives Madeleine in marriage to Gride. Believing she has a paternal duty to undertake all that her father asks of her, Madeleine is on her way to being "sold for money: for gold, whose every coin is rusted with tears, if not red with the blood of ruined men, who have fallen desperately by their own mad hands" (698), when the interference of true love, Nicholas, and her father's timely death rescue her at the eleventh hour. Still, the reader bears witness to the fact that while the Cheerybles brand of capitalism can indeed reverse the affective ravages of political economy, Uncle Ralph's bad fathering reproduces itself in other families, turning fathers into brokers and children into commodities.

Dickens's literary condemnation of usury is like Scargill's and most others of the nineteenth century in that it casts the usurer as a bad father in order to highlight the disaffective results of rampant economic individualism. This rhetorical ploy was so powerful that pro-pawnbroking literature was forced to insist that the opposite was actually true, and that pawnbrokers could, indeed, be good fathers. For example, Charles Lamb's 1830 contribution to the "Merchant of Venice" mythography was a short story called "The Pawnbroker's Daughter" written for *Blackwood's Magazine*, a tale that forestalls the plot of *The Usurer's Daughter*, only stopping short of the gothic disruption that brings on the evil avunculate. Instead, Flint (the pawnbroker) has a change of heart toward Marion (the daughter), demanding that "the prejudiced against our profession acknowledge that a money-lender may have the heart of a father . . . and that in the casket, whose loss grieved him so sorely, he valued nothing so dear as one poor domestic jewel."[33] Nevertheless, the cultural anxiety underscored by all versions of the Shylock and Jessica fable is identical: under a laissez-faire commercial code that is, by definition, usurious, all interpersonal ties are potentially fraught with economic demands, and sentimental notions of family and community are accordingly threatened.

In "fact," as well as in fiction, the work of the usurer was repeatedly shown to be antithetical to family, to community, and finally to nation, as suggested by an anonymous 1825 tract called *Reasons Against the Repeal of the Usury Laws.* The unspecified writer described the process by which a usurer comes into being as a thorough purgation of all emotional ties to family and home.

. . . the unhappy being, whose baneful calling it is to speculate on men's miseries, and like them because they are profitable; to traffic in distress, that he may distill it into gain; must begin by expelling and excluding from his bosom all emotions like these, must violently sunder the ties and feelings which connected and identified him with mankind, and stand amidst the human race, unpitying, callous andalone, feared, shunned and hated.[34]

Even in cases where usury is a family operation, the family itself is a sphere of economic accountability rather than sentimentality: in *Bleak House*, for example, members of the Smallweed family—who inherit not only Krook's pawnshop but generations of usury—would each "sell the other for a pound or two" (637). And what the usurer practiced himself, he also preached to his employees: the inexperienced young boys who were apprenticed to Uncle in the pawnshop were supposedly indoctrinated with their master's anti-family proclivities, and were even discouraged from marrying. "I know the fact, and assert without fear of contradiction," declared another anonymous essayist in 1825,

that no Pawnbroker will take a married man into his service, if he knows him to be married. It is possible, that if he marries while in his service, he may be kept afterwards; but experience has shewn that to be an occurrence extremely rare in the trade . . . What strangely perverted ideas those men must have, to regard, with such antipathy, in their servants that which most others consider as one of the strongest ties of social intercourse, and in itself a sort of guarantee for the steady conduct of the person employed.[35]

The resonances of the term "perverted" in this passage bring the antisocial, metaindividualistic figure of the pawnbroker into the realm of sexuality, suggesting that Uncle somehow represents a carnal alternative to the legitimate social intercourse of marriage. Of course, this suspicion that the usurer's crimes against humanity were sexual as well as social has a long philosophical and economic history. Following Aristotle, many nineteenth-century writers were opposed to usury on the grounds that it was contrary to "natural law." As explained by J. B. C. Murray in his 1866 *History of Usury*, "money being naturally barren, to make it breed money is preposterous and a monstrous perversion from the end of its institution, which serves the purpose of exchange and not increase."[36] When interest is metaphorically biologized, likened to an unnatural breeding method because it is a site of increase without animation, the usurer becomes guilty of appropriating and perverting yet another manifestation of family affection: sexual intercourse. Again in *Bleak House*, the usurer's capacity for natural reproduction is thrown into question by the "gratifying fact" that the house of Smallweed "has no child born into it, and that the complete little men and women whom it has produced, have been observed to bear a likeness to old monkeys with something depressing on their minds" (219). Certainly, this unusual recipe for reproducing a family of usurers suggests a new interpretation of Grandfather Smallweed's lower body paralysis. In the absence of affective marriage, but more often, in the absence of women, the pawnbroker, along with the young men and boys he prefers to employ, carries on a form of reproduction untrammeled by natural law, and as a result the pawnshop is often described as a place of inherent ribaldry. "Did they hang out their balls for the purpose of serving the world or serving themselves?" inquires one 1824 opponent of pawnbroking, enjoying his own pun so thoroughly that he cannot resist predicting the decline of the pawnbroker as the "bruising" of the balls.[37] James Greenwood's 1867 essay "An Evening with My Uncle" evinces a similar penchant for innuendo when describing the inner workings of the pawnshop, especially the "spout" at the center of the store that allowed deposited items to be warehoused on the story directly above the trading floor. Disingenuously collapsing the pawnbroker's sexual and economic largesse, Greenwood observes that "to accommodate Uncle Gawler's enormous business, his spout is of enormous size."[38]

≺ III ≻

*Self-Help, Social Determinism, and
the Rhetoric of Addiction*

These satirical representations of Uncle's corruptive influences existed side by side with more sincere attempts to demonize pawnbroking, and these latter forms of attack were all the more powerful because they adopted and redeployed the rhetoric of self-help
initially used by proponents of the pawnshop. As described by
Dickens's essay "My Uncle," the transformative power of pawnbroking reads as a natural component of the brand of self-making
that Samuel Smiles was advocating at mid-century. First published in 1859, Smiles's *Self-Help* quickly became a manifesto of
personal empowerment, promoting providence, free-will, and
thrift as the materials of commercial success. Above all, Smiles
emphasized the possibility that an otherwise disenfranchised man
could rise above his social origins, disregard his economic background, and triumph within modern society through industry,
diligence, and self-denial.[39] But despite his anti-paternalistic philosophy, his disparaging view of charity, and his signature image
of the "self-made" man, Smiles was decidedly against the brand of
debt-driven autonomy conferred by the pawnbroker:

The man who is always hovering on the verge of want is in a state not
far-removed from that of slavery. He . . . is in constant peril of falling
under the bondage of others and accepting the terms which they dictate
to him . . . It is easy enough for a man who will exercise a healthy resolution to avoid incurring the first obligation; but the facility with which
that has been incurred often becomes a temptation to a second; and very
soon the unfortunate borrower becomes so entangled that no late exer-
tion of energy can set him free.[40]

Although Smiles never mentions the pawnbroker by name, it is
clear that his trademark horror of debt spills over into a contingent
antipathy to borrowing. Like the Dickens of *Household Words*,
Smiles views moneylending as a potentially transformative process, but if Dickens envisions the pawnshop as a place where a superficially conferred identity can be discarded or exchanged,
Smiles understands borrowing as a process by which integral,
autonomous self-hood is enslaved to an addictive pattern of pledg-

ing, as well as to an usurious rate of interest. Instead of conferring identity, the Smilesian moneylender invariably eroded it.

Consequently, while proponents of the pawnshop used the discourse of self-help to characterize the economic autonomy provided by Uncle, anti-pawnshop propagandists resorted to the infamous "downward spiral" motif to drive home the rhetorical link that writers like Smiles made between pledgers and addicts. Indeed, the pawnshop was so embedded in the Victorian conception of alcoholism and addiction that pawnbroking was often looked upon as the virtual alpha of the downward spiral: for example, in Trollope's 1879 novel *John Caldigate*, Mrs. Shand is told that she should not send her emigrant son, a Queensland shepherd, any money because he is an alcoholic, so she instead decides to send him a dozen shirts because "he couldn't drink the shirts out there in the bush. Here, where there is a pawnbroker at all the corners, they drink everything."[41]

Likewise, anti-pawnbroking tracts of the nineteenth century repeatedly insisted that habitual recourse to the pawnshop directly promoted other, more dangerous addictions. In 1846, an anonymous pamphlet entitled *The Poor Man's Four Evils* dramatically proclaimed that "the pawn-shop and gin-shop are the twin brothers of darkness; they support each other and combine to ruin thousands."[42] Mrs. Henry Wood's 1862 temperance novel *Danesbury House* described a more topographical kinship between the pawnshop and a gin-palace known as the Golden Eagle:

If that house was the Golden Eagle, the one at the opposite corner of the narrow street might be called the Golden Balls. It was a pawnbroker's shop. Do you ever see the two far apart? And many a one visited that before they visited the Golden Eagle. Numbers were passing into it that Saturday night, carrying with them incongruous articles—flat-irons and children's clothes, pillows and timepieces, wedding rings and men's boots, Dutch ovens and chimney ornaments. Some pressed in there from sheer necessity, others, to obtain means of gratifying their fiery craving for drink.[43]

Earlier in the century, John Woodyer's *Treatise on Pawnbroking* casually equated pledging with alcoholism, and even self-murder: "Who can esteem it improbable that pawning leads to the 'water, the razor, or the rope,' to free the wretched from so miserable an existence?"[44] The loss of self-control initiated by the pawnbroker was only the first in a series of declensions to which the pledger was inevitably subjected; furthermore, because the pledger was enmeshed in a nexus of obligations that began with his family, his loss of self-control eventually became a social problem. *The Poor Man's Four Evils* includes criminal behavior among the roster of disorders the pawnshop could potentially produce, and is quick to connect individual corruption with family decay. Just as the combination of alcohol and pawning produced crime, alcoholic parents who frequented the pawnshop produced socially deviant offspring: "Families whose subsistence is consumed by the publican, the quack-doctor and the pawn-broker are nurseries for our prisons. A wasteful mother and a drinking father are sure to have bad, disorderly, vicious, and criminal children."[45]

In 1868, "Truths from a Pawnbroker" expressed a similar conviction that pawning led directly to drinking, and drinking, "where carried to an excess in men . . . tends to reduce the family to beggary and want, while in women the example is more frequently followed by members of the family, and the effect is felt more in the debasement of their morals."[46] What is more, for T. Turner, this erosion of family morality was exacerbated by the way children were often used to "gratify" their parents' perverse desires:

I have known a man to compel his wife to strip his children and pledge their clothing, to procure him the means of gratifying his base appetite. I have known a woman to do it while her husband has been hard at work. You may put it down as certain that every drunken man or woman among the lower classes knows the pawn shop as well as the gin shop.[47]

If the hand-to-mouth conversion of children's clothing into drink insinuates that the pawnbroker was literally stripping away the moral and bodily integrity of both the pledger and his entire family, the idea that he could make a mother deprive her own children suggested that Uncle had a role in what was popularly believed to be the inherent depravity of the working-class family.

The easy transformation of clothing into liquor, moreover, suggested that the pawnbroker had a hand in the sexual immorality of working-class women in particular. Because women tended to have the least valuable possessions to use as security, their pledges most often took the form of their own clothing: "I blush to state it," wrote Turner in 1864, but "women, when all their

money is gone, are known to slip off some article of dress, and
hand it to the landlord as a security for the maddening beverage he
calls porter."[48] Similarly, in Wood's *Danesbury House*, when a girl
"scarcely seventeen" with "the plague spot of intemperance" already on her face is refused credit at the gin-palace, she leaves for a
few minutes only to return,

and flinging down a shilling on the counter, demanded a half-quartern of
"mountain dew." The gin was served out to her and the eightpence
change. She had taken off her cotton gown in the street, and pledged it
for a shilling at the opposite pawnshop. "Who says I am to be done?"
cried she, when it was swallowed, turning round and holding out her
scant petticoat, as if she were preparing to dance a minuet.[49]

As female pledging and burlesque become suddenly identical, the
friendly, neighborhood pawnbroker takes on all the insidious characteristics of both publican and panderer. Rampant prostitution
emerges quite easily from this vision of women disrobing in pubs,
and Turner warns his readers that these unfortunate pledgers

are not limited to any class—their ranks are filled from every grade.
Some have been nursed in comfort—trained with care—lived in the enjoyment of every luxury the heart could desire, and owe their degradation
to a false step—to disappointed hopes—to cunning schemers—to the
formation of habits which not only admit, but compel a downward tendency, until the last stage is reached, when destitute of shame they seem
to possess only the power to resist every effort to elevate and bring back
to a position of comfort and respect.[50]

Using the idiomatic downward spiral of social determinism debates, Turner maps his teleology of female degradation against the
destructive workings of the pawnshop, epitomizing the way that
women, and not only working-class women, often took the brunt
of anti-pawnshop propaganda. Although statistical evidence did
point to the fact that women were Uncle's primary customers, the
causal relationship established by Turner and other writers between pawnbroking and prostitution, pawnbroking and maternal
disaffection, was a rhetorical deflection of social anxieties about
female empowerment onto the culturally sensitive ideology of the
Victorian family. For example, moral anxiety about women
"pledging" their own bodies for drink may be displaced economic
concern about women's legal and social right to own and dispose
of their own property. Apparently the pawnshop could not only

liberate the working-classes from an economic heritage of poverty and subservience, but it had the power to free women from the social imperatives imposed on them by gender: given that before the Married Women's Property Act was passed in 1882 all of a wife's possessions legally belonged to her husband, "a wife was alienating not her goods but his at the pawnbroker's."[51] While the difficulty of proving spousal consent rendered any official regulations virtually impossible, it is nevertheless apparent that female access to pawnshops, like working-class access to pawnshops, directly threatened a certain philosophy of ownership which was endemic to the mid-nineteenth century, when as Jeff Nunokowa argues, "the right to alienate ha[d] become the centerpiece of proprietorial prerogative."[52]

## ≺ IV ≻

### 'Oliver Twist' and the Illegitimate Commodity

In Dickens's 1837 *Oliver Twist*, the Victorian philosophy of ownership is directly threatened by female access to the pawnshop, and, in fact, illicit female alienations are twice responsible for prolonging the resolution of the novel's foundling plot: first, when the workhouse nurse robs the corpse of Oliver's mother, and pawns "a little gold locket: in which were two locks of hair, and a plain gold wedding-ring"[53] and later when workhouse matron, Mrs. Corney, finds a crumpled pawnticket in the dead fingers of the same nurse and redeems the items secretly, burying them away for future use. The fact that the stolen items represent the final tokens of Oliver's patriarchal heritage, the last signs by which he could ever be identified as his father's child and potential heir, points both to the homogenizing mechanisms at work in the pawnshop as well as to the threat that female alienation posed to the stability and integrity of patriarchy. In fact, the foundling plot of *Oliver Twist* is also initiated by the problem of female abstraction, reminding us that Oliver's anonymity is always coterminous with his illegitimacy. This thorough alienation of Oliver's heritage throws him solidly into the world of the avunculate, first in the context of the parish workhouse, where his food and his future are scantily doled out by "the kind and blessed gentlemen which is as

so many parents to you, Oliver, when you have none of your own"
(17). Following a familiar Dickensian thematic, the social institutions of *Oliver Twist* are perpetually revealed to be bad parents,
parents that subject the affective, biological family to ruptures,
elisions, and abstractions in the name of better economy and increased utility. The workhouse board that should serve as Oliver's
parents, in fact, is depicted by Dickens as the sole initiator of the
Poor Law of 1834, a series of acts that, among other things, separated families while they were in the workhouse, and did not hold
fathers responsible for the production of illegitimate children:

The members of this board were very sage, deep, philosophical men; and
when they came to turn their attention to the workhouse, they found out
at once, what ordinary folks would never have discovered—the poor people liked it! . . . 'Oho!' said the board, looking very knowing; 'we are the
fellows to set this to rights; we'll stop it all in no time.' So, they established the rule, that all poor people should have the alternative . . . of being starved by a gradual process in the house, or by a quick one out of it
. . . They made a great many other wise and humane regulations, having
reference to the ladies, which it is not necessary to repeat; kindly undertook to divorce poor married people, in consequence of the great expense
of a suit in Doctor's Commons; and instead of compelling a man to support his family, as they had theretofore done, took his family away from
him, and made him a bachelor! (9)

Just as *Bleak House* constructed a parallel between Krook's
avuncular pawnshop and the falsely paternalistic Court of Chancery, *Oliver Twist* finds an analogy for the bad parenting of the
parish workhouse in the second scene of Oliver's misadventures.
From the rural workhouse Oliver finds his way to London, and to
a den of child-thieves presided over by the Jew Fagin, a hoarder of
stolen merchandise as well as a fencer of stolen goods. It is here
that the problem of commercial alienation, especially female alienation, dovetails with the downward spiral of the social determinism debates, showing us how one of Fagin's former pupils
traces her fall into prostitution back to its origin in the pickpock-
eting and petty-thievery she performed as a child at the instigation
of the notorious fence.

bitter as were her feelings towards the Jew, who had led her step by step,
deeper and deeper down into an abyss of crime and misery, whence no
escape; still, there were times when, even towards him, she felt some re-
lenting, lest her disclosure should bring him within the iron grasp he had

so long eluded, and he should fall at last—richly as he merited such a fate—by her hand. (283)

While Nancy is clearly marked as fallen by her sexual transgressiveness, her prostitution is less important to the criminal teleology of the novel than her powers of transformation and alienation: her ability to assume the shape of Oliver's sister at crucial moments in the narrative, and eventually to use the idiom of affective siblingship to snatch him from the protective custody of the good uncle, Mr. Brownlow. Nancy owes her powers both to Fagin's training and to his "inexhaustible stock" (79) of stolen goods, articles and the accouterments of a thousand alienated identities: a clean white apron, curl-papers under a bonnet, a little covered basket, a miscellaneous key, are the stock and trade that enable Fagin to transform his band of thieves into false versions of the private family, as well as legitimate members of the social family.

If Fagin's dealings in stolen goods do not constitute him a legitimate pawnbroker, as a fence he occupies a cultural position that Victorian opponents of pawnbroking felt was coterminous with the shadier aspects of uncle's work. By providing the power of commercial alienation to anyone in possession of portable property, the illegitimate pawnbroker was believed to provide the thief with the ideal mechanism for homogenizing stolen property into the neutral money form.[54] Indeed, when we enter Fagin's infamous den of thieves, we see that fencing is also a process that makes by unmaking: not only in the way that it makes Nancy a thief and prostitute by initiating her social and sexual downfall, but in the way that Charley Bates, the Artful Dodger and the rest of Fagin's crew of children work to "make" things like handkerchiefs and leather wallets, first by stealing them and then by carefully alienating them from their original owners. By way of explaining the mysteries of the trade to the baffled Oliver Twist, Fagin inspects the fruits of Charley's labor:

'And what have you got, my dear?' said Fagin to Charley Bates.
'Wipes,' replies Master Bates; at the same time producing four pocket handkerchiefs.
'Well,' said the Jew inspecting them closely; 'they're good ones—very. You haven't marked them well, though, Charley; so the marks shall be picked out with a needle, and we'll teach Oliver how to do it. Shall us Oliver; eh? Ha! ha! ha!'
'If you please, sir,' said Oliver.

'You'd like to be able to make pocket-handkerchiefs as easy as Charley Bates, wouldn't you, my dear?' said the Jew.

'Very much indeed, if you'll teach me, sir,' replied Oliver. (56)

Although he invents a fiction of production to displace and disguise the perpetual mutation of the commodity, stolen goods pass through Fagin's workshop as if "through the melting-pot" (91): handkerchiefs, snuff-boxes, jewels, plate, alike metabolized into the gold sovereigns that the Jew distributes to Bill Sikes and his other skilled housebreakers. Moreover, Fagin's homogenization of stolen goods is described in a way that resonates with the pawnbroker's power to elide the social origins and personal histories of not only products but people. Just as the general neighborhood of Fagin's lair is filled "with a good many small shops; but the only stock in trade appeared to be heaps of children, who, even at that time of night, were crawling in and out of the doors, or screaming from the inside" (49), Fagin's band of children are commodities as well as procurers of commodities and easily degraded into homogenous units of thievery, units that can be consigned to Sikes or any other housebreaker on account of their size, appearance, or stealth. The process of alienation inherent in Fagin's transformation of children into thieves is most specifically underscored by the way that the fence is offered a sum of money by the evil Monks to initiate Oliver Twist into a life of crime. As Oliver's older half-brother, Monks is aware of a will that their father made on his deathbed and was later destroyed by his mother, a will that left the illegitimate Oliver the sum of their father's inheritance "only on the stipulation that in his minority he should never have stained his name with any public act of dishonour, meanness, cowardice, or wrong" (332). By transforming Oliver into a thief, Fagin would unmake the child's paternal heritage as easily as he disguises the origins of stolen handkerchiefs and wallets: homogenizing Oliver's identity in the melting-pot of avuncular abstraction.

When Brownlow is revealed to be Oliver's father's oldest friend, the perpetual shuttling of the orphaned commodity back and forth between different economies of the avunculate takes the shape of the now familiar battle over the two definitions of political economy, the moral and the mechanistic. Both Fagin and Brownlow are repeatedly referred to as the "old gentleman" in the novel, but while Fagin's goal is the obfuscation of Oliver's origins within his perennially heated melting pot, Brownlow's is precisely the opposite: "the discovery of Oliver's parentage, and regaining for him the inheritance of which . . . he has been fraudulently deprived" (265). Dickens is careful to curtail Oliver's eventual share of his paternal inheritance, however; not only has Monks's wastefulness and mismanagement made the fortune much smaller than it was, Brownlow magnanimously insists that the remaining monies be shared between the two brothers. Projecting the sexual excesses that are part and parcel of Oliver's parental heritage upon his brother's wasteful tendencies, Brownlow cleanses Oliver's inheritance of stigma, and erases the stain of his illegitimacy through the convenient legal fiction of adoption.

Yet the economic lessons of *Oliver Twist* remain similar to the lessons of *Bleak House*: as the most resonant symbols of enforced individualism and requisite social autonomy, the illegitimate children of Dickens are perpetually beset by the commercial forces that make and unmake identity, perennially exposed to the morally ambivalent forces of capitalism, and a culture of surrogacy dictated not by the affective law of the father, but by the political economy of uncles. Playing out the battle between commerce and sentiment within the arena of the family, Dickens's novels participate in a cultural struggle over more than dominant tropes, metaphors, or euphemisms, over even more than the ever-binarized forces of good and evil. At the counter of the all-encompassing nineteenth-century pawnshop, a sometimes empowering, sometimes disfiguring, but always terrifying series of negotiations could take place: negotiations that could sever an individual from his family, history, and identity, reducing the accouterments of selfhood to a commodified miscellany of bones, skin, and hair. In other words, in the economy of the avunculate, anonymity exists as both a threat and a promise.

# Turning Bones into Spoons

### JEWS, PAWNBROKERS, AND 'DANIEL DERONDA'

> To avoid therefore the evils of inconstancy and versatility,
> ten thousand times worse than those of obstinacy and
> blindest prejudice, we have consecrated the state, that no
> man should approach to look into its defects or corruptions
> but with due caution; that he should never dream of
> beginning its reformation by its subversion; that he should
> approach to the faults of the state as to the wounds of a
> father, with pious awe and trembling solicitude. By this wise
> prejudice we are taught to look with horror on those children
> of their country who are prompt rashly to hack that aged
> parent in pieces, and put him into the kettle of magicians, in
> hopes that by their poisonous weeds, and wild incantations,
> they may regenerate the paternal constitution, and renovate
> the father's life.
>
> Edmund Burke,<br>*Reflections on the Revolution in France*

THIS CHAPTER begins where Victorian narratives of usury are surprisingly at odds with our most enduring Western stereotypes about the usurer. While the Shylock and Jessica fables discussed in Chapter Three resemble Shakespeare's play in plot and in substance, *The Usurer's Daughter*, "The Pawnbroker's Daughter," and *Nicholas Nickleby* differ from "The Merchant of Venice" in one important respect: in none of these texts about usury is the usurer actually Jewish. Reverend Scargill repeatedly refers to Erpingham's Catholicism, in fact, and neither Lamb nor Dickens suggest that usury has a religious heritage. In fact, even in *Our Mutual Friend*, a novel partly conceived by Dickens as a kind of reparation for the perceived anti-semitism of *Oliver Twist*, the Jew Riah is forced by the heartless Christian moneylender Fledgeby to pretend he is the proprietor of Pubsey and Co. in order to promote a false ideology that the face of usury is always Jewish. "Shylock perenially holds the English imagination in thrall," Michael Ragussis explains in his book *Figures of Conversion*, "perenially mediates, regulates, and displaces Jewish identity for the English mind."¹ As we have seen, however, the Victorian tendency to Christianize the plot of "The Merchant of Venice" displaces that displacement, making usury, pawnbroking, and moneylending into cultural synecdoches for capitalism rather than for Jewishness, and all but banishing the Jew usurer from nineteenth-century textual representation.

The one Victorian reinscription of the Shylock and Jessica parable I have found that maintains the Jewishness of the usurer is an 1850 conversion narrative by a Mrs. Kemp entitled *Rachel Cohen: The Usurer's Daughter*. In Kemp's text, the Moretons, "an attached and happy family . . . that implied a Christian household,"² are seen cheerfully putting money in their "Jewish Missionary Box" and going on missions of charity to Jewish streets filled with people "sunk in ignorance and vice" (9), when they suddenly find themselves in debt to the notorious moneylender, Isaac Cohen. As usual, the usurer's power over the family violates the sanctity and integrity of kinship, and when Cohen calls in his financial bond, the family bond is necessarily disrupted: the father, Walter Moreton, stays in London to find work while his wife and children depart for a stay of indefinite length with friends in the country. Throughout his misfortunes, however, Mr. Moreton remains convinced that the Jews are capable of spiritual redemption, and even the Jewish workers who arrive to strip the Moretons' house of valuable items are engaged by the debtor in religious conversation. One especially sensitive laborer replies to Moreton's questions about Jewish history and heritage in an idiom that should now be familiar to us:

Ah! Sir, you can little understand the feeling with which a poor Jew regards that glorious country, the land of promise . . . the birthplace of his fathers, and sees it wrested from him and made desolate by the unjust usurpation of Gentile strangers, when the rightful heirs, the natural descendants of Abraham, are scattered far from their inheritance, strangers even in the land that gave them birth; for whatever country may be his dwelling place, a faithful Jew can never forget that Jerusalem is his rightful home. (50)

Kemp's working-class Jews are exceedingly articulate about their usurped paternal inheritance: scattered and desolate, the "natural descendants of Abraham" are strangers perpetually banished from the fatherland. Moreover, the anti-paternalist rhetoric of Kemp's novel proliferates when her Jews begin to discuss the biggest stumbling block in the Jewish path to conversion. As one of Cohen's lackies declares to Mr. Moreton, "We never can acknowledge the carpenter's son, the crucified, as our Messiah" (52). The Jewish race is thus doubly disaffected in Kemp's narrative: they are spiritually and geographically separated from their own paternal heritage, but persist in denying the redemptive paternal tie always available through conversion. In this way, all anti-paternalist economic philosophy as well as all anti-family sentiment is labeled usury by Kemp's narrative, and can be traced to these fundamental failures of affective faith.

As Ragussis observes, nineteenth-century proselytism was part and parcel of a larger process of regenerating British identity: "during the Evangelical revival, the conversion of the Jews functioned at the center of a project to reform the English nation, which had become wicked and profligate during the eighteenth century."[3] Accordingly, the process of reformation in *Rachel Cohen* is set successfully into motion by reversing the Deuteronomic code: "If you wish to gain a Jew," the narrative instructs, "treat him as a brother" (69). As the prodigal "elder brethren" of Christians, the Jew's "reconciliation to our common God and Father" (143), is the ardent desire behind all proselytism. By transforming strangers back into brothers, the economic machinations that destroy family affection and national integrity will be disrupted, and the Usurer's power will disappear. Just as we might expect, it is the responsibility of Rachel, the usurer's daughter, to "soar above Judaism" (5) in good Jessica fashion from the outset of the narrative, and to simultaneously convert to Christianity and cancel the Moretons' debts after the Usurer's unrepentant death at the end of the novel.

Of course, the Jewish component of "The Merchant of Venice" is also maintained in George Eliot's 1876 *Daniel Deronda*, where the Jewess Mirah Lapidoth escapes from a father who scorned his religious heritage, abandoned his wife and son, and attempted to pay off his gambling debts by selling his daughter to a French Nobleman.[4] Given the novel's Zionist objectives, Lapidoth's com-modifications of kinship situate his actions within an economy of usury even though he is not actually a usurer: that is, in *Daniel Deronda*, any Jew who denies his religious and cultural heritage *is* a usurer, and consequently an outcast from both the private family and the spiritual family. As Lapidoth's abandoned son, Mordecai, will teach Daniel Deronda,

What is the citizenship of him who walks among a people he has no hearty kindred and fellowship with, and has lost the sense of brotherhood with his own race? It is a charter of selfish ambition and rivalry in low greed. He is an alien in spirit, whatever he may be in form; he sucks the blood of mankind, he is not a man. Sharing in no love, sharing in no subjection of the soul, he mocks at all.[5]

In Mordecai's opinion, the only way for Jewish culture to redeem itself is by reforming the nation of Israel as an affective familial ideology rather than a geographical entity: "to consecrate it with kinship: the past becomes my parent, and the future stretches to-ward me the appealing arms of children . . . When is it rational to say 'I know not my father and mother, let my children be aliens to me'" (587–88). Like *Rachel Cohen*, *Daniel Deronda* reforms the culture of usury in order to resanctify the affective family, yet Eliot's novel stops short of the conversion narrative proffered by evangelical Mrs. Kemp. Instead, just as *Our Mutual Friend*'s Riah drives a wedge between usury and its stereotypical Jewish facade, *Daniel Deronda* suggests that spiritual Judaism is in pawn to Jew-ish economic identity, held hostage to ideologies that work in concert with the logic and rhetoric of nineteenth-century capital-ism rather than with the religious inheritance of the Jews.

This binarized concept of Jewish identity first coalesces in Eliot's careful inscriptions of Jewish bodies, bodies that inevitably connect the urban world of *Daniel Deronda* back to the rural envi-rons of *Adam Bede*. While the idiom of fatness in *Adam Bede* ex-posed a series of economic anxieties about the status of kinship and the circulation of capital amongst nineteenth-century land-lords and tenant farmers, fat in Eliot's last novel accumulates within the pawnshop of Ezra Cohen: a greasy site of commercial interaction more in keeping with the labyrinthine stomach of Krook's Rag and Bottle shop than with the Poyser's spotless dairy. Recall that Daniel's search for the remaining members of Mirah

Lapidoth's family ends at the counter of a Jewish pawnbroker,

> whose flourishing face glistening on the way to fatness was hanging over
> the counter in negotiation with some one on the other side of the parti-
> tion, concerning two plated stoppers and three teaspoons, which lay
> spread before him. Seeing Deronda enter, he called out "Mother!
> Mother!" and then with a familiar nod and smile said "Coming sir—
> coming directly." (438)

Turning from Cohen's "flourishing face," Daniel encounters the
pawnbroker's mother, and tries "to think away the fat which had
gradually disguised the outlines of her youth" (438), in order to
discern her possible likeness to Mirah. The appearance of another
customer occasions a call to Cohen's wife, who appears with their
"robust" son Jacob, a boy whose cheeks are often "very much
swollen with sweet-cake" (450). As three generations of Cohen fat
confront Daniel Deronda, the idiom of consumption gradually
links bodily images with capitalist economies, only to reach its
natural apex when Daniel finds who he is looking for—Mirah's
brother Mordecai—situated as an extended family member, living
on "thin tails of the fried fish . . . the sort of share assigned to a
poor relation" (449). Within the larger context of the novel, it becomes clear that Mordecai's thinness reflects his thematic status
as a quickly waning symbol of Jewish spirituality; an etherealized
force of historical consciousness and religious traditionalism that
is being overtaken by more secular icons of Judaism, most egregiously, the flabby pawnbroker. By situating an emaciated Jewish
heritage within the commercial corpulence of the Victorian pawnshop, Eliot uses fat in *Daniel Deronda* as she did in *Adam Bede*,
to analogize the process of commercial alienation, and to confirm
that the economic logic of nineteenth-century capitalism necessitates the digestion of all forms of inheritance: religious, historical,
and finally, familial.

Entering Cohen's pawnshop though the greasy portal of Chapter Three, discovering, with Daniel, the remnants of Mirah's alienated family amongst the flatirons and teaspoons of other disintegrated households, it also becomes clear that Eliot has come up
with a new way to exploit the avuncular metaphors of *Adam
Bede*. Like the myriad "uncles" of Dickens, Eliot's pawnbroker
possesses ambivalent powers of commercial transformation, and
threatens all paternal histories and paternalistic cultures with an-

nihilation. Although the novel's early depiction of Gwendolyn Harleth pawning a necklace with three turquoise stones that had "belonged to a chain once her father's" (48) introduces us to the way that the pawnbroker's economic alienations underwrite other, more affective disruptions, by the time Daniel enters the Cohen pawnshop we have been formally catechized about the danger that brokering poses to the family. Certain sacred materials, insists the epigraph to this latter chapter, should never pass the threshold of exchange:

'No man,' says a Rabbi, by way of indisputable instance, 'may turn the bones of his father and mother into spoons'—sure that his hearers felt the checks against that form of economy. The market for spoons has never expanded enough for any one to say, 'Why not?' and to argue that human progress lies in such an application of material. The only check to be alleged is a sentiment, which will coerce none who do not hold that sentiments are the better part of the world's wealth. (430)

This prohibition against capitalizing upon the remains of one's parents hits a variety of moral, social, and economic registers in Victorian culture: if the image of human bones being turned into spoons at once taps into a primitivist idiom of parricide and cannibalism, it also reflects certain contemporary anxieties about the commodification of the family, and the disappearing importance of heritage, genealogy, and "sentiment" in the progressive vocabulary of nineteenth-century economic identity. Karl Marx's critique of political economy is again useful in this context, articulating as it does a similar theory of economic transubstantiation:

Since money does not reveal what has been transformed into it, everything, commodity or not, is convertible into money. Everything is salable and purchasable. Circulation becomes the great social retort into which everything is thrown, to come out again as money crystal. Nothing is immune from this alchemy, the bones of the saints cannot withstand it, let alone the more delicate *res sacrosante, extra commercium hominum* [Consecrated objects beyond human commerce].[6]

In Marx's analogy, the capitalist system functions as a capacious mill stone grinding the consecrated artifacts of human history into the uniform and socially ambiguous currency of "money crystal." Less optimistic than the Rabbi, Marx does not mention the regenerative effects of sentiment; the new philosophy of political economy has already made sure that there is no object too sacred for the pawnshop, or too beloved for the ravages of commodity circulation.

After all, Daniel is initially drawn to Ezra Cohen's shop not because of the telltale name over the door, but because he catches sight "of some fine old clasps in chased silver displayed in the window," and thinks that his uncle's fat wife "Lady Mallinger, who had a strictly Protestant taste for such Catholic spoils, might like to have these missal clasps turned into a bracelet" (432). Here we learn that the pawnshop's transformative power does not discriminate among faiths: the remnants of Catholicism are just as susceptible as the legacies of Judaism to the avuncular ravages of commodification. Moreover, Daniel's mental conversion of the sacred artifacts of one religion into the trivial "spoils" of another suggests that the process of "brokering" does not distinguish between economic and affective value, and that even moral virtues such as family sentiment, religious faith, and paternal duty can be effectively alienated by the mercantilistic impulses of the nineteenth-century social world. Indeed, when Daniel redeems the wasted Mordecai from the Cohen family pawnshop, the broker's distinction between economic consideration and affective feeling is seemingly nonexistent: "you're taking some of our good works from us, which is a property bearing interest, I'm not saying but we can afford that, though my mother and my wife had the good will to wish and do for Mordecai to the last" (636).

Accordingly, this great commodifier of all human artifacts and existence provides the ideal meeting ground for the most incongruous and disparate of entities. Not only does the pawnshop draw Gwendolyn and Daniel into physical proximity within the multifarious plot of the novel, it links their stories thematically, disproving Leavis's infamous claim that the two narratives are mutually exclusive.[7] Indeed, when he redeems Gwendolyn's paternal chain from the homogenizations of the Leubronn pawnbroker, Daniel's heroic struggle though the novel that bears his name is revealed to be no smaller task than the resanctification of the law of the father: the redemption of the paternal family and the paternal nation from the modern state of economic disaffection epitomized by the pawnshop. The novel neatly accomplishes this seemingly enormous imperative by reducing its scope, initially at least, to Daniel's redemption of both Gwendolyn's and Mirah's family histories, as well as to the reclaiming of his own obscured heritage, a Jewish heritage all but nullified by a wide variety of avuncular transformations.

Moreover, when the anti-capitalist "redeemer" is revealed to be a Jew, the wedge between pawnbroking and Jewishness becomes more salient in the novel, effectively recasting the narrative of usury as endemic to England rather than Israel, Christians rather than Jews. By the end of the novel, Daniel chooses to invest himself in the construction of a new Jewish homeland that will respect the claims of cultural history and affective genealogy; of course, he must leave England to do so. "There are Ezras and Ezras in the world" (628), Eliot candidly reminds us, and when Daniel departs with one, dying Ezra and his sister Mirah for Jerusalem, he leaves the other one behind, palpably illustrating the schism in Jewish identity first imposed by inscriptions of bodily difference and unequal distributions of fat.

Yet it is not only the pawnbroker Ezra who is left to bear the stigma of usury in *Daniel Deronda*: what Daniel's Zionist pilgrimage makes fully and finally clear is that the narrative opposition of the two principal protagonists has worked from the beginning of the novel to project Daniel's problematic Jewish economic identity onto Gwendolyn Harleth. From the moment she pawns her paternal chain in the Leubronn pawnshop, to the way her actions and choices identify her as the "true" heir to Daniel's mother, the disaffected Jewish actress Alcharisi, Gwendolyn absorbs the ideological contaminations of usury so that Daniel can be cleansed. The ease with which this translation can occur acquires a certain degree of logic when we are reminded by Catherine Gallagher that the "whole sphere to which usury belongs, the sphere of exchange as opposed to that of production, is traditionally associated with women":

Women are items of exchange, a form of currency and also a type of commodity. Of course, in normal kinship arrangements, when the exchange is completed and the woman becomes a wife, she enters the realm of "natural" (in the Aristotelian sense) production. But the prostitute never makes this transition from exchange to production; she retains her commodity form at all times. Like money, the prostitute, according to ancient accounts, is incapable of natural procreation.[8]

Returning us neatly to Marx's notion of the homogenizing power of money, Gallagher complicates her argument by including the figure of the female author in this association of the usurer and the prostitute, pointing out that although money is a "sign of sterility, and even of outcast status . . . it is nevertheless an emblem of liberation from patriarchal authority."[9]

Although Gallagher is finally more interested in George Eliot's status as a female writer who escaped patriarchal authority by earning her own money than she is in the cultural and historical status of the Victorian pawnshop, it is important that her observations about money, usury, and the figure of the prostitute are made with reference to the economic morphology of *Daniel Deronda*. My own work introduces a concept of the avunculate to the debates surrounding usury and pawnbroking in order to indicate the extent to which non-nuclear, or at least non-normative, family structures were used to represent developing capitalist economies in the nineteenth century, and in doing so confirms Gallagher's point about the anti-patriarchal status of usury. As a catalyst of money's perpetual homogenization, the pawnbroker is a culturally resonant personification of the threat that commercialism and the rhetoric of self-help posed to social, biological, and economic paternalism. In this context, the story of Gwendolyn Harleth becomes a cautionary tale about the perils of female economic individualism. Attempting to trade her paternal heritage for the homogenized money form, Gwendolyn becomes a commodity rather than a capitalist, an emblem of exchange rather than of production. When read under the sign of the avunculate, moreover, the brokering process described by the rabbinical prohibition in *Daniel Deronda*—the transformation of parental bones into spoons—functions as a parable of nineteenth-century capitalism, outlining the way the affective law of the father is being replaced with the political economy of uncles, severing children from their parents by dissolving the links between past and future, origin and outcome, cause and effect.

The narrative structure of *Daniel Deronda* even replicates this thematic of mystified origins in that the novel opens with the Leubronn scenes of Gwendolyn losing all her money at the gambling table, and resorting to the pawnshop to repair her loss, only to abruptly refocus the narrative on a series of events that occurred *prior* to the incidents at Leubronn. Before the flashback, we are satisfied that Gwendolyn's recourse to the pawnbroker is an individualistic alternative to making "herself in any way indebted" (46) to the charitable compassion of her traveling companions, but Eliot destabilizes these initial assumptions by recontextualizing Gwendolyn's choice to pledge her father's chain within a process of paternal alienation that is well underway by the time Gwendolyn reaches Leubronn. "All my best ornaments were taken from me long ago" (319), Mrs. Davilow has admitted to her daughter, despite the fact that she "usually avoided any reference to such facts about Gwendolyn's step-father as that he had carried off his wife's jewelry and disposed of it" (319). When Mrs. Davilow's confession effectively resituates Gwendolyn's act of pledging along a continuum of paternal subtractions, it suggests that pawning the paternal chain simply perpetuates a project of divestment initiated not at the counter of the pawnbroker, but at the hands of another "bad" father, Gwendolyn's step-father.

In fact, Captain Davilow's gradual alienation of the Harleth family jewels is closely linked to the anxiety about pawnbroking that lies at the heart of both halves of *Daniel Deronda*. By literally functioning as a place where family affection can be commodified, the economic nexus of the pawnshop isolates and defines the inevitable teleology of modern capitalism "which left all mutuality," in the words of cosmopolitan musician Herr Klesmer, "to be determined simply by the need of a market" (283). In Gwendolyn's case, the market for family sentiment and paternal heritage was first determined by her step-father, and by the time *Daniel Deronda* opens, Gwendolyn's affective memory is as alienated as most of her biological father's remnants:

She would probably have known much more about her father but for a little incident which happened when she was twelve years old. Mrs. Davilow had brought out, as she did only at wide intervals, various memorials of her first husband, and while showing his miniature to Gwendolyn recalled with a fervour which seemed to count on a peculiar filial sympathy, the fact that dear papa had died when his daughter was in long clothes. Gwendolyn, immediately thinking of the unlovable step-father whom she had been acquainted with the greater part of her life while her frocks were short, said—

'Why did you marry again, mamma? It would have been nicer if you had not.'

Mrs. Davilow colored deeply, a slight convulsive movement passed over her face, and straightaway shutting up the memorials she said, with a violence quite unusual in her—

'You have no feeling, child.' (52)

While the mention of short frocks here, supplemented by Gwendolyn's apparent fear of sex later, has generated some critical speculation about the possibility that Captain Davilow's "spoilage" is sexual as well as economic, it isn't necessary to anchor such narrative traces of incest to psychological interpretations of *Daniel Deronda*. Like other nineteenth-century critics of capitalism and detractors of pawnbroking, Eliot combines the terminology of economic alienation with the rhetoric of sexual exploitation in order to highlight the paternal and patriarchal erosions taking place under the directives of capitalism. After all, within the economic conventions of nineteenth-century culture, a widow with a fortune is also a paternal relict, a bit of floating capital that cannot be repossessed without a great deal of anxiety about the degree of "proprietorial prerogative" still accruing to the deceased husband. Along with the more portable spoils of the Harleth jewelry box, Captain Davilow appropriated the dead man's wife and daughter, and there is little ambiguity about the moral status of this kind of paternal usurpation in the economically charged world of *Daniel Deronda*, a novel that will later characterize the courtship of a widow as "lurking about the battle-field to strip the dead" (778).

For my purposes, the shortness of Gwendolyn's frock in the above passage is less important than her truncated history lesson about her father. Captain Davilow's capacity for alienation is underscored by the way Gwendolyn's affective interest in her paternal heritage is instantly sidetracked by the invocation of her stepfather. It is also the case that Mrs. Davilow's angry response that her daughter has "no feeling" neatly encapsulates the problem with Gwendolyn—as well as the problem with the Alcharisi—that *Daniel Deronda* forces us to confront through the rest of the novel. Devoid of all sentimental attachment to the past, Gwendolyn epitomizes the disaffective results of modern economic philosophy, and the way that commercial factors work to mystify personal relations between individual people and among family members. If her willful ignorance begins with a fundamental lack of knowledge about her father, it extends into a more general failure to understand the connections between the private world of the family, and the economic world of capital. Although she is comfortable with the knowledge that her mother has a modest inheritance, she has "no notion how her maternal grandfather got the fortune inherited by his two daughters; but he had been a West Indian—which seemed to exclude further question" (52). Furthermore, it never "occurred to her to inquire into the conditions of colonial banking, on which, as she had many opportunities of knowing, the family fortune was dependent" (94). If Gwendolyn accepts the economic fact of her family fortune, she remains in devout ignorance about its origin in the sugar and coffee plantations of the West Indies, and about the enslaved race of people whose forced labor cultivated her family's commercial success.

For these reasons, Daniel Deronda's redemption of Gwendolyn Harleth's paternal history exceeds his initial, literal redemption of her father's turquoise chain from the shop of the Leubronn pawnbroker. Indeed, Gwendolyn's first encounter with Daniel is in the Leubronn casino, where he casts an "evil eye" on her play at the roulette wheel and makes her lose her stake as rapidly as she had won it. Although Gwendolyn experiences "a striking admission of human equality" (36) in the gambling hall, where, like the pawnshop, the rapid redistribution of money homogenizes social distinctions normatively maintained by nationality, class, and even gender, Eliot is unambivalent about the negative effects of such rampant republicanism:

The white bejewelled fingers of an English countess were very near touching a bony, yellow, crab-like hand stretching a bared wrist to clutch a heap of coin . . . And where else would her ladyship have graciously consented to sit by that dry-lipped feminine figure prematurely old, withered after short bloom like her artificial flowers, holding a shabby velvet reticule before her . . . There too near the countess, was a respectable London tradesman . . . Standing close to his chair was a handsome Italian, calm, statuesque, reaching across him to place the first pile of napoleons from a new bagful just brought him . . . the pile was in half a minute pushed over to an old bewigged woman with eyeglasses pinching her nose . . . But while every single player differed markedly from each other, there was a certain uniform negativeness of expression which had the effect of a mask—as if they had all eaten of some root that for the time compelled the brains of each to the same narrow monotony of action. (36–37)

As the now familiar idiom of addiction converts difference into sameness in this passage, Gwendolyn's abiding desire to access personal freedom and autonomy by "doing as she liked" is reabsorbed within a distasteful scenario of determinism: even the most exhilarating forms of pleasure become monotonous, boring, methodical when individuals become habituated to their rhythm. Moreover, when Eliot adds a little boy to this picture who "alone had his face turned toward the doorway," and his back to his mother, "a lady deeply engaged at the roulette-table" (36), the gambling hall is figured as yet another place where the sacred connection between parent and child is the price of admission. We hardly need Daniel's negative characterization of gambling as "raking a heap of money together, and internally chuckling over it, when others are feeling the loss of it" (383), to realize that the casino and the pawnshop function as analogous emblems of the capitalist system, each converting bones into spoons, and sentiment into specie.

Although Daniel is unable to stop Gwendolyn from marrying Grandcourt, and displacing the woman who has already borne Grandcourt four children, he will eventually teach Gwendolyn the human element of her economic crimes, and remind her of her paternal heritage in the process. "You wanted me not to do that—not to make my gain out of another's loss," Gwendolyn eventually realizes, transforming the redeemed necklace into a "memorial" that resembles a manacle, winding "it thrice around her wrist and ma[king] a bracelet of it" (495, 500). Moreover, at the height of Gwendolyn's marital unhappiness, when she and Grandcourt are yachting on the Mediterranean, she will remember Daniel's advice to stop being so self-absorbed, and attempt to "interest herself in sugar-canes as something outside her personal affairs" (735). In casting about for external interests, Gwendolyn ironically focuses on the economic foundations of her paternal heritage, the nexus of commercial exploitation that she has always profited by, but ignored. However unmotivated, Gwendolyn's new consciousness of the sugar-canes subtly marks a point of filial return, illustrating the way that Daniel's primary function in the plot of *Daniel Deronda* is to reconstitute the law of the father.

Indeed, we don't need to enter the hyper-commercial atmosphere of the pawnshop or the gambling parlor to visit the sphere of

brokerage in *Daniel Deronda*: just as Captain Davilow was the
first alternative father to alienate Gwendolyn from her place in the
paternal chain, a more literally avuncular sphere of influence continued the process of mystification when Mrs. Davilow moved
Gwendolyn and her four stepsisters to Offendene, a manor house
in the community where her brother-in-law is the current rector.
Immediately Uncle Gascoigne assumes responsibility for Gwendolyn's social and economic liberation from her past, arguing with
his wife that no expense should be spared in their niece's commodification:

This girl is really worth some expense: you don't often see her equal. She
ought to make a first-rate marriage, and I should not be doing my duty if
I spared my trouble in helping her forward. You know yourself she has
been under a disadvantage with such a father-in-law, and a second family
keeping her always in the shade. I feel for the girl. And I should like your
sister and her family now to have the benefit of your having married
rather a better specimen of our kind than she did. (66)

Superficially, Uncle Gascoigne's avuncular benevolence would
seem to counteract the bad parenting of Gwendolyn's reprobate
stepfather: indeed, he is quick to insist that there are no similarities between Captain Davilow and "better specimens" of fathering
such as himself. Yet the more we learn about Uncle Gascoigne,
the more we realize that he is as contradictory in his character as
he is in his physical profile: his "nose began with an intention to
be aquiline, but suddenly became straight," and "there were no
distinctly clerical lines in his face, no official reserve or ostenta-
tious benignity of expression, no tricks of starchiness or affected
ease" (59). The narrator suggests that these anomalies have a very
specific history, and that they may be traced to the fact that Uncle
Gascoigne was not born a clergyman, but became one through a
series of independent acts.

Perhaps he owed this freedom from the sort of professional make-up
which penetrates skin tones and gestures and defies all drapery, to the
fact that he had once been Captain Gaskin, having taken orders and a
diphthong but shortly before his engagement to Miss Armyn . . . Mr.
Gascoigne's tone of thinking after some long-quieted fluctuations had
become ecclesiastical rather than theological; not the modern Anglican,
but what he would have called sound English, free from nonsense: such
as became a man who looked at a national religion by daylight, and saw
it in its relation to other things. (60)

In other words, Uncle Gascoigne, or rather, Captain Gaskin, is more like that lesser specimen of fatherhood, Captain Davilow, than he admits. When we later learn "what nobody would have suspected, and what nobody was told," that Mr. Gascoigne's father had "risen to be a provincial corn-dealer" (176), it is clear that the social status of Gwendolyn's popular uncle is based upon a more figurative brokerage of the paternal chain than his niece's: a process of self authorization that enabled a disenfranchised boy to erase his paternal origins and alter his very subjectivity through a series of professions, an advantageous marriage, and a strategic transformation of surname. Like the pawnbroker, like Captain Davilow, Uncle Gascoigne is well versed in the transformation of bones into spoons, and he understands that the commodification of Gwendolyn is the process by which he will release his niece from the shadows of her paternal history.

Furthermore, it appears that the freedom from patrilineal identity enjoyed by Uncle Gascoigne is shared by many of his neighbors. Community gossip has it that "there's no blood on any side" of the Arrowpoint family, for example: although they are one of the wealthiest and most exclusive families in the area, "Old Admiral Arrowpoint was one of Nelson's men, you know—a doctor's son. And we all know how the mother's money came" (460)—from trade, of course. Although the same Arrowpoints also patronize a penniless German musician, Herr Klesmer, they disingenuously protest "the possibility of any longer patronising genius, its royalty being universally acknowledged" (135). Klesmer himself has "cosmopolitan ideas" (284), and responds to upper-class condescension by staunchly insisting that "[my] rank as an artist is of my own winning, and I would not exchange it with any other" (292). Of Sir Hugo Mallinger and his adopted nephew Daniel Deronda more will be said, but in the context of Diplow's rampant individualism it is worth mentioning that this particular uncle's advice to Daniel is to "remember Napoleon's *mot—Je suis un ancétre*" (201).

The social events favored by this neighborhood are, likewise, modeled upon seemingly republican principles: the tournament prizes of the archery club "were all of the nobler symbolic kind: not property to be carried off in a parcel, degrading honor into gain: but the gold arrow and the silver, the gold star and the silver, to be worn for a time in sign of achievement and then transferred to the next who did excellently" (134). When Gwendolyn Harleth joins the archery club under the sponsorship of her Uncle Gascoigne, who of course is already a member, she achieves "not the vulgar reward of a shilling poll-tax, but that of a special gold star to be worn on the breast . . . There was a general falling into ranks to give her space that she might advance conspicuously to receive the gold star from the hands of Lady Brackenshaw" (140). If the gold star destined for Gwendolyn's breast already resembles the medal of a military hero, the description of fellow archers and spectators "falling into ranks" to let Gwendolyn pass idiomatically reinforces the scene's connection to military service, where honor gained through skill can reshuffle class-based hierarchies, as it did for Nelson, Napoleon, and even Captain Gaskin.

Unfortunately, however, Gwendolyn soon learns that the carefully controlled competitions of the Brackenshaw Archers are mock scenarios of egalitarianism, primarily because women are usually shut out from the kind of self-making effected through public acts of heroism. "Women can't go in search of adventures— to find out the North-West Passage or the source of the Nile, or to hunt tigers in the East" (171), insists Gwendolyn to Grandcourt, attempting to stall his upcoming marriage proposal by diverting his pointed suggestions that she might not always live with her mother at Offendene.[10] "But a woman can be married," Grandcourt responds, simultaneously making his intentions clear and citing the only socially sanctioned kind of self-transformation open to a woman. If this proposal scene between Gwendolyn and Grandcourt sounds familiar, it is because the exchange replicates a prior proposal made to Gwendolyn by her cousin, Rex Gascoigne, in which Gwendolyn announces that marriage is antithetical to a woman's ability to do any of the things that she would like to do, such as "—go to the North Pole, or ride steeplechases, or go to be a queen in the East like Lady Hester Stanhope" (101). What is more important, however, is that Gwendolyn deflects both marriage proposals with a restless litany of possible or impossible identities for herself, roles that answer her abiding desire to "be something" (271) other than a requisite stopgap in the paternal chain: to create for herself an identity unrelated to the useful family functions of daughter, wife, or mother.

Central to the idiom of self-making is the familiar Victorian metaphor of theatricality, and it is no coincidence that Gwendolyn's youthful habit of staging herself in a variety of tableaux vivants—as St. Cecilia (55), as the famous actress Rachel (84), as Hermione (90)—becomes a full-fledged desire to become an actress in order to escape the multiple oppressions of marriage: "The inmost fold of her questioning now, was whether she need take a husband at all—whether she could not achieve substantiality for herself and know gratified ambition without bondage" (295). Gwendolyn's private audition for Herr Klesmer is an abject failure, however; like the regulated competitions of the archery club, the community theatricals in which Gwendolyn has taken part in the past have been scenarios of false republicanism, places where ladies can become actresses without the sacrifice of caste that is endemic to life on the public stage. Under Klesmer's criticism, Gwendolyn "wished she had not sent for him: this first experience of being taken on some other ground than that of her social rank and her beauty was becoming bitter to her" (300). Of course, the "other ground" on which Gwendolyn suddenly finds herself is the arena of nineteenth-century commerce: as we remember from *Mansfield Park*, "real" acting is a trade involving producers and consumers, and actresses, like prostitutes, are perpetually exchangeable commodities that never enter the sphere of use. Like the pawnshop, the public theater strips the self of patrilineal context and socioeconomic status, leaving female identity to fashion and refashion itself solely through the artistic renderings of *plastik*, a form of value that, according to Adam Smith, "perishes in the very instant of its production."[11]

If Gwendolyn's talent for *plastik* situates her and not Daniel as the proper heir to the exchange-driven imperatives of usury, it is also the case that the seemingly cosmopolitan Uncle Gascoigne and the rest of the Diplow community feel with Daniel's grandfather that women must be relegated to the arena of use for the sake of patriarchal coherence. They are necessary points of reference in the homosocial continuum between father and son, requisite links in a paternal chain that is constantly being forged with or without their approval. The Arrowpoints, for example, may pay lip service to the republican notion that artistic genius is the social equivalent of royalty, but when Catherine Arrowpoint informs her parents that she is engaged to the bohemian musician Klesmer, she is immediately told that her duty is to "think of the nation and the public good," and to prevent great properties from passing into the "hands of foreigners" (290). The self-made, liberal-minded Arrowpoints are actually hypocrites who view their daughter's marriage into an established English family as a way to permanently disguise the unseemly origins of her fortune: as Catherine so rightly interprets, it is the presumed duty of an heiress to "carry the property gained in trade into the hands of a certain class" (290). While the pawnshop converts paternal relics into capital, transforms the telltale objects of utility into the homogenous emblems of exchange, Catherine Arrowpoint's marriage to a nobleman will reverse the commodification process, transforming trade-gotten spoons back into the venerable bones of the British aristocracy.

Although Gwendolyn is not an heiress, and is not viewed as a financial "carryer" like Catherine Arrowpoint, the role that she seems similarly destined to occupy as a useful medium between father and son is foreshadowed by male reaction to her community debut, and it becomes clear that a beautiful woman's currency in the continuum of male homosociality is both sexual and economic.

'Who is that with Gascoigne?' said the archdeacon, neglecting a discussion of military maneuvers on which, as a clergyman, he was naturally appealed to. And his son, on the other side of the room—a hopeful young scholar, who had already suggested some 'not less elegant than ingenious emendations of Greek texts—said nearly at the same time, 'By George! who is that girl with the awfully well-set head and jolly figure?' (73)

Before Gwendolyn arrives, father and son appear to be separated by more than the length of the room. In fact, their only similarity seems to be the abiding anti-paternalism that loosely characterizes the entire male community: while the archdeacon, like Uncle Gascoigne, appears to have a military past, his more idealistic son is busy modernizing the plots and plausibilities of ancient Greek literature. Yet sexual desire for Gwendolyn spontaneously elides all differences between father and son, ironically subverting the way that Gwendolyn views her attractiveness to men as a form of personal empowerment that *removes* her from the paternal chain. Although Uncle Gascoigne wants to help his niece escape the negative ramifications of her paternal history, he wants to do so by

*reinscribing* her within a more socially acceptable set of patriarchal connections: like the Arrowpoints', Uncle Gascoigne's project is one of *repaternalization*, and he intends to disguise Gwendolyn's origins in the same way he elided his own, with a strategic
marriage and an alias, without encouraging her desire to become
something else.

Indeed, the alchemy of capitalism is not limited to the counter
of *Daniel Deronda*'s Jewish pawnbroker; the laws of political
economy here, as in *Adam Bede*, find their fullest representation
in the avunculate. When Daniel reclaims his familial inheritance
he learns that he was sacrificed to the now familiar opposition between sentiment and individualism that structures human interaction under capitalism: "I had not much love to give you," Daniel's mother, the famous actress Alcharisi, explains to her son
years after she abandoned him to pursue her career. "I did not
want affection. I had been stifled with it. I wanted to live out the
life that was in me, and not to be hampered with other lives"
(688). For the Alcharisi, the economic and social autonomy that
acting promises a woman is irreconcilable with affective ties to
family and the genealogical imperatives of the paternal chain.
Daniel's mother, in fact, preferred to enter this theatrical realm of
perpetually shifting identities, perpetually mutating incarnations
of the self, than to follow her father's mandate of utility and become the consummate Jewish woman "under pain of his curse":

To have this pattern cut out—"this is the Jewish woman; this is what
you must be; this is what you are wanted for; a woman's heart must be
pressed small, like Chinese feet; her happiness is to be made as cakes are,
by a fixed receipt." This is what my father wanted. He wished I had been
a son; he cared for me as a makeshift link. His heart was set on his Judaism . . . such men turn their wives and daughters into slaves. (694)

To prevent herself from becoming the "makeshift link" between
generations of patriarchy, from becoming the useful medium
through which a Jewish heritage of large-scale moneylending is
descended, Alcharisi resolved "to have no more ties, but such as I
could free myself from" (697). She pawns the remnants of her paternal chain more effectively than Gwendolyn, finding in Sir Hugo
Mallinger a willing Uncle who "would pay money to have such a
boy" (697) as her son Daniel.

It is finally one of the most fundamental ironies of *Daniel*

*Deronda* that the Alcharisi delivers her son from a patriarchal heritage of usury only to deposit him in the parallel world of the avunculate. Even more powerfully than Ezra Cohen, the novel's actual pawnbroker, Uncle Hugo epitomizes the force of modern individualism and the kinds of commercial brokerage that threaten the social, economic, and biological law of the father. Sir Hugo is unmarried and childless when he initially transplants Daniel to England, and though he does marry several years later, his wife produces no male offspring. The very existence of the Mallinger family is dangerously under erasure by the time Gwendolyn Harleth marries the next in line for Sir Hugo's fortune, his biological nephew, Grandcourt: "that fine families dwindled off into females, and estates ran together into the single heirship of a mealy complexioned male, was a tendency in things which seemed to be accounted for by a citation of other instances" (497). The family crisis here represented by Sir Hugo Mallinger's "dwindling" line of inheritance becomes a symbol of national crisis in *Daniel Deronda*, and of the way that the idiom of nephews is replacing the idiom of sons in the teleology of heirship.

Despite Uncle Hugo's apparent distress about Lady Mallinger's failure to produce a male heir, he is quite careless about conservative notions of lineage, heritage, and tradition. In fact, the English manor house in which Daniel was raised is the perfect setting for a variety of cosmopolitan transformations: described as a hybrid of "the undisguised modern with the antique," and a convergence of "various architectural fragments" (469), Uncle Hugo's country home was formerly a gothic abbey, but few of the old rooms still function as they were originally intended. In fact, "the finest bit of all is turned into stables. It is part of the old church. When I improved the place I made the most of every other bit; but it was out of my reach to change the stables, so the horses have the benefit of the fine old choir" (462). The Abbey, like the pawnshop, is a place where the remnants of ancient religions are converted into modern Protestant luxuries, and it is here that Uncle Hugo works the transformation of bones into spoons, converting a Jewish son into a Christian nephew by mystifying his origins and rescripting his genealogy.

This hybrid Abbey is also the scene of Daniel's first suspicions about his parentage. "Enclosed on three sides by a gothic cloister," a thirteen year-old Daniel is reading—appropriately—an History of the Italian Republics when he is prompted to ask his tutor, "Mr. Fraser, how was it that the popes and cardinals always had so many nephews?" Looking up—also appropriately—from his volume of political economy, Mr. Fraser gives the matter-of-fact answer: "Their own children were called nephews" (202–3).

Having read Shakespeare as well as a great deal of history, he could have talked with the wisdom of a bookish child about men who were born out of wedlock and were held unfortunate in consequence, being under disadvantages which requires them to be a sort of heroes if they were to work themselves up to an equal standing with their legally born brothers. But he had never brought such knowledge into any association with his own lot, which had been too easy for him ever to think about it—until this moment when there had darted into his mind with the magic of quick comparison, the possibility that here was the secret of his own birth, and that the man whom he called uncle was really his father. (205–6)

By schooling him from childhood in Napoleon's republican philosophy of self-making *"Je suis un ancêtre"* (201), Uncle Hugo has encouraged his nephew to forget the importance of biological parents by pointing out that the stigmas of heritage are rhetorically erased, and the paternal chain effectively broken, when an individual situates himself at the point of genealogical origin. But after learning that the idiom of uncles and nephews is a cultural euphemism for illegitimacy, "[t]he uncle that he loved very dearly took the aspect of a father who held secrets about him—who had done him a wrong—yes, a wrong" (206). Until he meets the Alcharisi, and learns the truth about his heritage, Daniel labors under the suspicion that Uncle Hugo's Napoleonic rhetoric of self-making is really a form of paternal disaffection, and that he, like the popes' nephews, is kept from his birthright by a father who does not want to acknowledge the stigmas of sexual excess.

This is the primary reason that Daniel is so offended when Sir Hugo summons him to sing for a group of his friends, and consequently inquires if his nephew would like to be "a great singer" when he grows up:

He knew a great deal of what it was to be a gentleman by inheritance . . . and now the lad had been stung to the quick by the idea that his uncle—perhaps his father—thought of a career for him which was totally unlike his own, and which he knew very well was not thought of among possible destinations for the sons of English gentlemen. (208–9)

Not only is the opera house a feminized sphere of exchange, it is also a site of patrilineal nullification, and Daniel takes his uncle's apparently casual comment as further proof that "there was something about his birth which threw him out from the class of gentleman to which the baronet belonged" (209). Although Daniel has the details of his parentage wrong, it is clear that he has the tenor of avuncular disinheritance right. Freed from the oppressions of the paternal chain and from the rigid, biology-is-destiny determinism of patriarchal inheritance, Daniel *is* his own ancestor, with "an apprenticeship to life which would not shape him too definitely, and rob him of that choice that might come from a free growth" (220).

What Eliot makes clear, however, is that Daniel's uninhibited sense of free-will and personal autonomy actually prevents him from creating an active identity for himself; instead, the radical homogenization of Daniel's patrilineal history leaves him wandering in a contemplative, philosophical "state of social neutrality. Other men, he inwardly said, had a more definite place and duties" (220).

A too reflective and diffuse sympathy was in danger of paralysing in him that indignation against wrong and that selectness of fellowship which are the conditions of moral force . . . as soon as he took up any antagonism, though only in thought, he seemed to himself like the Sabine warriors in the memorable story—with nothing to meet his spear but flesh of his flesh, and objects that he loved. (412)

While Gwendolyn's lack of paternal ties and affective memory leaves her devoid of all sentimental attachments, ready to capitalize indiscriminately on the fragments of her paternal history, Daniel's capacity for empathy is so expansive it threatens him with moral stagnation. Everyone is potentially a family member to Daniel, and any "antagonism" may risk turning the flesh of unknown family members into political, economic, or religious capital. This is finally the reason why Daniel, from the time he was a child, has been unable "to push his way properly," or to "swop for his own advantage" (218) in Uncle Hugo's competition-driven world of Whigs and Tories, supply and demand, gains and losses: without knowledge of his patrilineage he has no way of understanding the Deuteronomic commandments on usury, and cannot, after all, tell the difference between brothers and others.

Consequently, the excessive scope of Daniel's sympathy becomes a selfless desire to "redeem" other people, even at the expense of his own interests. It is not only Gwendolyn, but Hans
Meyrick, his college friend, who Daniel saves from "threatening
chances" (222) when he abandons his own course of study to help
Hans win a classical scholarship. Moreover, after Daniel rescues
Mirah from a suicide-by-drowning attempt, she compares him to
"the wonderful story of Bouddha giving himself to the famished
tigress to save her and her little ones from starving" (522). Mirah's
brother, the etherealized Jew Mordecai, will extend his sister's
analogy by seeing Daniel as a healthy body capable of absorbing
the enfeebled soul of Jewish historical consciousness: "You must
be not only a hand to me, but a soul—believing my belief—being
moved by my reasons—hoping my hope . . . You will be my life: it
will be planted afresh; it will grow" (557). Within the ongoing
panorama of cannibalism that *Daniel Deronda* stages, Daniel is
perpetually at risk of becoming food for other people's hunger, and
a feminized commodity for other people's use. In fact, the "apprenticeship to life which would not shape him too definitely"
risks leaving Daniel with no shape at all: "[M]y dear boy, it is good
to be unselfish and generous," Uncle Hugo warns his nephew,
"but don't carry that too far. It will not do to give yourself over to
be melted down for the benefit of the tallow-trade; you must know
where to find yourself" (224).

Throwing us abruptly back into Fagin's lair, this avuncular
analogy is initially interesting for its description of Daniel as a
commodity that is endlessly appropriable, pliable, and transform-
able. Yet it becomes even more significant when we consider that
tallow is a colorless, tasteless form of animal fat used in the making of candles. Unable to swop for his own advantage in the economy of the avunculate, Daniel is himself in danger of becoming an
object of exchange: it is no accident that when Eliot identifies Ezra
Cohen as a "Jeshurun of a pawnbroker" (575), she is invoking an
Old Testament figure who apparently "waxed fat" (n898). Moreover, Sir Hugo's anxiety about Daniel's tendency to put his own
identity under elision in the service of other people reflects an inherent fear that his nephew will eventually revert to Hebraic type,
or rather, stereotype. The pawnbroker's unlimited capacity for
"accommodation" cannot fail to remind us of Daniel's excessive

pliancy; after all, Ezra Cohen describes his family's specifically
Jewish talents as "a sort of cleverness as good as guttapercha: you
can twist it how you like. There's nothing some old gentlemen
won't do if you set 'em to it" (578). While Cohen is nominally associated with the sphere of commercial exchange—as a usurer, a
broker of commodities, a lender of money, a waxer of fat—he also
characterizes himself as a raw material rather than an actor in the
capitalist drama, a malleable personification of his own stock-in-
trade. Cohen explains to Daniel that he "began early . . . to turn
myself about and put myself into shapes to fit every sort of box"
(447), adding later that his business of accommodation has made
him "a sharp knife" (450). Within Cohen's idiom of perpetual mu-
tability, the pawnbroker's economic services finally become indistinguishable from his goods: "in point of business, I'm not a class
of goods to be in danger. If anyone takes to rolling me, I can pack
myself up like a caterpillar, and find my feet when I'm alone"
(636). Although Ann Cvetkovich has identified male Jewish identity as the only stable type of masculine subjectivity in *Daniel
Deronda*,[12] the pawnbroker's stability, like Daniel's, is founded
upon permanent instability. Like the Alcharisi, their reconstitu-
tions of self are perpetually enabled by social, economic, and national displacements.

When Grandcourt assesses Daniel as *"fat"* (475), he seemingly
intends the word to register in its French significance as "fop," but
his turn of phrase is finally more telling in its English sense.
Without paternal antecedents, Daniel *is* fat—tallow, *plastik*, guttapercha—and derives his identity from an un-English, un-
masculine capacity to assume the commodity form. In fact, because Uncle Hugo's metaphor of the constantly reconstituted matter of the tallow-trade connects Daniel's subjectivity with his
mother's (and Gwendolyn's) natural talent for *plastik*, it reminds
us that Daniel's makeshift position in the Mallinger family has
perpetually assigned him the feminine task of promoting patrilineal coherence. Not only does the bond between uncle and nephew
act "as the same sort of difference does between a man and a
woman in giving a piquancy to the attachment which subsists in
spite of it" (367), but Sir Hugo views Daniel in the aspect of a
prized commodity, "which, if found voice, might have said, 'You
see this fine fellow—not such as you see every day is he?—he be-

longs to me in a sort of way, I brought him up from a child; but you would not ticket him off easily'" (367). Furthermore, in the absence of the female figures that would normally mediate male relations, Uncle Hugo employs Daniel as the "medium" between himself and his biological nephew and heir-apparent, Grandcourt. Learning that Grandcourt is cash-poor, the baronet sends Daniel to propose that Grandcourt exchange all future interest in Diplow (a property that stands to be entailed away from Lady Mallinger and her four daughters) for "a good sum of ready money" (197). By sacrificing both past and future for his own present comfort, Grandcourt's patrilineal chain is brokered by Sir Hugo as effectively as Gwendolyn's, and the baronet ironically forces Daniel to become an instrument of the very kind of alienation he most deplores; an alienation that has already put his own past under erasure.

In this context, Sir Hugo's declaration that Gwendolyn Harleth is no more like Lady Cragstone, the infamous female-gambler, "because she gambled a little, any more than I am like a broker because I am a Whig" (368), only underscores more thoroughly the parallel between uncles and pawnbrokers that has guided the economic telos of the novel. Uncle Hugo's brand of alienation interrupts the paternal chain so thoroughly that even Daniel's longed-for reunion with his mother, the Alcharisi, is described in Marx's now-familiar idiom of commercial alchemy: "it made the filial yearnings of his life a disappointed pilgrimage to a shrine where there were no longer the symbols of sacredness" (723). Daniel's "filial yearnings" lose their hallowedness in the economy of the avunculate as easily as the Catholic missal clasps lost their religious significance in the economy of the pawnshop. The inevitable transformation of consecrated objects into capital proves too powerful a force for even Daniel to resist, and although he despises the modern mantra of buy cheap, sell dear, we learn that his years of social inaction and Hamlet-like self-scrutiny have been, ironically, "sustained by three or five percent on capital which someone else has battled for" (225). Realizing that his forgotten forefathers have "battled" for their money in the despised Jewish money-markets, the anti-commercial Daniel seems no better than an interest-driven usurer, after all. After accepting that the economy of the avunculate is the only sphere in which practical action and decision-making can occur, Daniel chooses to marry Mirah, only able to bring closure to the marriage plot by making Gwendolyn "the victim of his happiness," and by making Gwendolyn's loss into his own gain.

Finally freed from her destructive relations with patriarchy by the death of her husband, Grandcourt—a death that leaves his widow virtually penniless—Gwendolyn would prefer to disappear within the sororal embrace of her mother and sisters, but the commercial teleology of the novel has other plans. Clergyman Uncle Gascoigne, who mourns his past inadequacy as a father-figure to Gwendolyn, and baronet Uncle Hugo, who does not for-give his nephew Grandcourt for "the shabby way he has provided for your niece—our niece, I will say" (826), become fast friends, and Uncle Hugo emphatically provides the moral to the story of Gwendolyn Harleth, at least as far as he is concerned: "If you marry another niece, be it to the Archbishop of Canterbury, bind him down. Your niece can't be married twice over. And if he's a good fellow, he'll wish to be bound" (827). It is important that Un-cle Hugo's first lecture to the less worldly Uncle Gascoigne is a lesson about the economic rules that must precede affective ties, as well as about the proper distribution of commodities so that they need never re-enter an economy of exchange. As "our niece," Gwendolyn will again serve as the connective tissue between men, but instead of linking men vertically through patriarchally conferred roles of mother, wife, sister, or daughter, she connects men horizontally though avuncularism, dissolving class differ-ences in the new commercial world. Our last view of Diplow is shaped by the seemingly homogenizing social work of Uncle Hugo, who

was spreading some cheerfulness in the neighborhood, among all ranks and persons concerned, from the stately homes of Brackenshaw and Quetcham to the respectable shop-parlours of Wancester. For Sir Hugo was a man who liked to show himself and be affable, a Liberal of good lineage, who confided entirely in Reform as not likely to make any seri-ous difference in English habits of feeling, one of which undoubtedly is the liking to behold society well-fenced and adorned with hereditary rank. Hence he made Diplow a most agreeable house, extending his invi-tations to old Wancester solicitors and young village curates, but also taking some care in the combination of his guests, and not feeding all the common poultry together, so that they should think their meal no par-ticular compliment. (864)

Uncle Hugo's careful "combination" of guests is obviously guided by a desire to promote a kind of reform that takes place without revolution, and Eliot leaves us with somewhat more than a suspicion that the anti-paternalist promises of the avunculate, the radical self-making of economic individualism, are simply feudal ideals in progressive clothes. On the other hand, it is impossible to miss the simultaneous suggestion that modern political economy shapes the closing tableau of *Daniel Deronda*, giving the ideological force of the pawnshop center stage again. By forging family resemblances between people of disparate classes, religions, and nationalities, by engendering a cosmopolitan kinship based solely on the business of "accommodation," Uncle Hugo's combinations should remind us of the egalitarian work of Ezra Cohen, pawnbroker. Cohen boasts to novice pledger, Daniel Deronda,

Well, sir, I've accommodated gentlemen of distinction—I'm proud to say it. I wouldn't exchange my business with any in the world. There's none more honorable, nor more charitable, nor more necessary for all classes, from the good lady who wants a little more of the ready for the baker, to a gentleman like yourself, sir, who may want it for amusement. I like my business. I like my street, and I like my shop. I wouldn't have it a door further down. And I wouldn't be without a pawn-shop, sir, to be the Lord Mayor. It puts you in connection with the world at large. I say it's like the Government revenue—it embraces the brass as well as the gold of the country. (442)

As the undiscriminating "embraces" of the modern pawnshop replace the more traditionally affective connections of cultural history, national identity, and patrilineal "chains," we may be reminded of another of Marx's elucidations about capital: "the exchange of commodities breaks through all local and personal bounds inseparable from direct barter . . . it develops a whole network of social relations spontaneous in their growth and entirely beyond the control of the actors."[13] If the law of filiation is under erasure in the nineteenth-century social order, a new and more random "network" of affiliation has risen to take its place, a set of relations guided not by the patronage or sentiment of fathers, but by the political economy of uncles.

# "Send the Letters, Uncle John"

## TROLLOPE, PENNY-POSTAGE REFORM, AND THE DOMESTICATION OF EMPIRE

No, I don't have any big hypothesis about the conjoint development of capitalism, Protestantism, and postal rationalism, but all the same, things are necessarily linked. The post is a banking agency. Don't forget that in the great reformation of the "modern" period another great country of the Reformation played a spectacular role: in 1837 Rowland Hill publishes his book, *Post Office Reform: Its Importance and Practicability*. He is an educator; and a reformer of the fiscal system. What was he proposing? but the stamp, my love, what would we have done without it? The sticking stamp, that is, the uniformization of payment, the general equivalent of the tax, and above all, the bill before the letter, the payment in *advance*.

Jacques Derrida, *The Post Card*

IN THE SUMMER of 1839, a short pamphlet entitled *A Report of a Scene at Windsor Castle Respecting the Uniform Penny Postage* appeared for the first time in a monthly issue of Charles Dickens's *Nicholas Nickleby*. This fictional sketch, which would later prove to be the work of social reformer and art critic Henry Cole, is staged as a dramatic "scene" in which the young Queen Victoria sits at a large table in a council chamber at Windsor Castle "in deep study over 'Post Office Reform' by Rowland Hill," and surrounded by "Parliamentary and Commissioners Reports on Postage; Copies of the *Post Circular*; and Annual Reports of the American and French Post Office."[1] Lord Melbourne is depicted anxiously awaiting the Queen's opinion, which he receives in the opening lines of the sketch:

THE QUEEN (*exclaiming aloud*)—Mothers pawning their clothes to pay the postage of a child's letter! Every subject trying how to avoid postage without caring for the law! The Messrs. Baring sending letters illegally every week to avoid postage! Such things must not last.[2]

After summoning Lord Lichfield and Rowland Hill to give competing evidence about the prospective results of penny-postage reform, the Queen recommends to Lord Melbourne that Lord Lichfield be forced to retire from his duties as Postmaster General, and that Hill's plans be summarily adopted:

This interview, and what I have read, have convinced me that a Uniform Penny Post is most advisable. Sure am I that it would confer a great boon on the poorer classes of my subjects, and would be the greatest benefit to religion, to morals, to general knowledge . . . and that it would effectually put down the smuggling postman, and lead my people to obey and not to disobey the law. My Lord Melbourne, you will please to bear in mind that the Queen agrees with her faithful Commons in recommending a uniform penny post. If your Lordship has any difficulty in finding a minister among your party able to carry the measure into effect, I shall apply to my Lord Ashburton or my Lord Lowther, as circumstances may require. Mr. Hill, the nation will owe you a large debt of gratitude, which I am sure it will not be unwilling to repay.[3]

Within the context of the family/society tropes I have been exploring in previous chapters, the self-contained logic of Cole's imaginary "Scene" becomes particularly legible, first because it situates the unreformed Post Office and the pawnshop as points on the same continuum of family demoralization. The propaganda materials that so absorb the interest of Cole's Queen Victoria are full of references to the way that "mothers yearning to hear from absent children would pawn clothing or household necessaries rather than be deprived of the letters."[4] Moreover, the pawnshop and the post office appear to function identically in the 1840 testimony of a rural postmaster, who stated that "one poor woman offered my sister a silver spoon to keep until she could raise the money."[5] In this way, when the Queen in the above sketch summons Rowland Hill to her chamber, she heralds the penny post as a safeguard of the family integrity threatened by the pawnshop, positioning the two institutions as oppositional powers in the construction and redeployment of affect.

Yet the scene should also be recognizable within the larger context of *Avuncularism* as a text that appears to uphold affect over politics and biological motherhood over Victoria's role as Queen Mother. As portrayed by Henry Cole, the Queen's decision to champion Hill is finally a choice to regenerate one family, the affective, biological, lower-class family, at the expense of a socio-economically privileged, aristocratic "family" of which she is the head. Cole goes to great lengths to insist that any party consequences of the Queen's decision are secondary and irrelevant, and that penny-postage reform will greatly enhance the moral, sentimental, and intellectual progress of the English people by making all letters equivalent in the eyes of the law. In democratizing communication, however, the reformed Post Office finally has more in common with the anti-paternalistic, egalitarian pawnshop than our fictional Queen's initial opposition of the institutions would suggest.

By presenting the question of postal reform as an affective dilemma rather than a political challenge, Cole's penny-postage propaganda followed the ideological path that had been set in 1837 by the text that so influences his fictional Queen: Rowland Hill's *Post Office Reform: Its Importance and Practicability*. Beginning with a Malthusian observation that Post Office revenues had not been keeping up with increases in population, Hill concluded that lower postage would increase revenue and simultaneously "accelerate" the social and intellectual improvement of mankind, as well as the affectionate and morally uplifting intercourse between parent and child. Under Hill's plan, all inland, United Kingdom letters would be charged a mere penny for delivery, payable when the letter was posted rather than when it was received. "Fortunately this is not a party question," Hill asserts repeatedly throughout his text, downplaying the egalitarian philosophy that lurked at the center of postal reform:

When it is considered how much the religious, moral, and intellectual progress of the people, would be accelerated by the unobstructed circulation of letters and of the many cheap and excellent non-political publications of the present day, the Post Office assumes the new and important character of a powerful engine of civilization . . . Its object is not to increase the political power of this or that party, but to benefit all sects in politics and religion; and all classes, from the highest to the lowest.[6]

Not only was Hill's idea of penny postage immediately received as a relatively simple way to increase the revenue of the

Post Office, his "powerful engine of civilization" was also celebrated as a spontaneous remedy to many of the social and economic problems caused by overpopulation and rapid industrialization, especially the dispersion of the working-class family due to
migratory employment. By reducing the perimeters of overwhelming social and economic problems to the sentimental size of a
postage stamp, Hill's plans gained widespread support from reformers such as Cole who insisted that enabling poor families to
send and receive letters would reinstitute "natural" claims of duty
and affection within working-class communities.

So far, *Avuncularism* has argued that alternatives to the law of
the father and the oppression of patriarchy need to be theorized by
feminist critics and by historians, and has interrogated a variety of
nineteenth-century documents to suggest that familial tropes in
the Victorian period were more varied and comprehensive than
normative nuclear paradigms would suggest. The avunculate has
also been characterized as the site at which the economic claims
of the social world begin to intersect with the private family, introducing the family to the rites of exogamy, to the laws of exchange, and to the commodification of affection. The figure of the
Uncle, by extension, has been shown to be a vehicle of narrative
explication: a way to personify and make familiar the discourses of
anti-paternalism, anti-regency, and anti-monopoly. If on the one
hand, the penny post was conceived of as a government institution
that could defeat the commodifying powers of my Uncle the
pawnbroker, it was also, as Derrida notes in the epigraph, imagined as a "banking agency" that would circulate family sentiment
as economic, political, and cultural currency. Functioning as an
authoritarian alternative to the hegemonic paternalism and pro-
hibitive monopoly of previous postal regimes, the Penny-Post Office was designed to be an institution that would manage society
by managing the family: a site of discipline and power at odds
with the law of the father, but in step with the goals of avuncularism. Literally, the avuncular trope had widespread value for colonial agitators, who began to rally support for "Ocean Penny Postage" as soon as postal reforms had been passed in England. As we
will see, these penny post advocates turned to the avunculate for
an image of English benevolence and authority divested of the pa-

ternalistic proprietorship that would have been so objectionable to liberated American citizens.

But aside from these literal engagements with the avunculate in postal propaganda, this chapter traces the shift in national authority that occurred during the period of postal reform, and uncovers a parallel crisis in family coherence that was catalyzed by the unraveling of traditional models of patriarchal power. A written record of these related developments is provided by Anthony Trollope, literally and figuratively a man of letters, who worked for the central London Post Office in St. Martin's le Grand under the direction of Rowland Hill from the 1830s till the 1860s. Trollope credited himself with the introduction of pillar boxes to England in 1853, and many of his novels, as biographer Victoria Glendenning notes, described "with fascination, and some concern the effects of this change. The pillar box on the corner of the road . . . made private correspondences even easier for independent-minded wives and daughters."[7] Despite Trollope's complicity in Hill's reforms, his novels repeatedly suggest that the authority of the Post Office to maintain the integrity of the paternalistic family is an untrustworthy and ineffective fiction: an ideology of power that was finally belied by seditions and corruptions from within.

One of the few objections raised to postal reform at the time of Hill and Cole's agitation was that its ability to generate affect was in fact a mixed blessing: "Will clerks write only to their fathers, and girls to their mothers? Will not letters of romance or love, intrigue, or mischief, increase in at least equal proportions? Does any rational mind doubt that there will be, on this point of the question, a balance of good and evil?"[8] Indeed, by allowing unsanctioned "families" to form amongst blackmailers and victims, trade unions and striking workers, young girls and unsuitable men, the Post Office was a potentially dangerous catalyst of instant cousinship: an ambivalent uncle who could not be counted on for purely sentimental interventions. Turning to Trollope's *Autobiography* and to two of his novels, *The Claverings* (1867) and *John Caldigate* (1879), we will see how domestic integrity and nationalism reconcile themselves with the social discipline of the avuncular Post Office. By following the path of Rowland Hill's "civilizing engine" as it used affection to produce reform, and reform to produce dis-

cipline, this chapter will interrogate the way that the sentimentalized ideology of the Post Office disguised the political Post Office
long enough to foster a decentralized network of social control
that even today interprets the intersection of technology, nationalism, and family life.[9]

≺ I ≻

### Affect and Penny-Postage Reform

In 1838 Cole began publishing *The Post Circular*, a weekly news-
paper entirely devoted to the advocacy of penny postage. Along
with minutes from current Parliamentary hearings on postage
rates and occasional Hill-like assertions about the apolitical nature of postal reform, the Circular was packed with narratives of
family disaffection that repeatedly originated in high postage, and
these stories often took the shape of personal letters or testimoni-
als to the editor. In one issue addressed to the "Effects of Heavy
Rates of Postage on the Resident Clergy and Dissenting Ministers," a series of anonymous narratives appeared.

Mr. _____ is himself one of ten—the children of a pious and affectionate
couple, residing in the opposite extremity of the kingdom, who are deprived by the enormous tax from receiving that support and consolation
in their old age, which is the best and last hope and stay of pious Christians. Just examine all the ramifications by which the affectionate feelings of this family are damped, if not necessarily extinguished by the
unequal and unjust tax, and you will have a scene of moral mischief, for
which I do not believe any government is able to answer—as communication between any two members of this family costs *two shillings* and
*twopence!*[10]

By characterizing postal rates as a tax on family sentiment, Cole's
propaganda machine repeatedly suggested that the government-
controlled post office was actually responsible for commodifying
kinship, and for placing the moral "stay" of affection beyond the
economic reach of most working-class families. When children did
finally sit down to write to their parents, moreover, "they sit
down under the idea that they must write a letter that their father
may think worth the postage."[11] The minutes from a public meeting in Liverpool give a similar testimony:

When a child leaves the home of its parents, there was a natural anxiety on both sides for an interchange of sentiments; but a heavy rate of postage had a tendency to dry up the affections, which expired from a want of a cheap channel of communication.[12]

A letter to the editor from one John Rowland again asked readers to consider the anxiety of poor parents for their absent children's welfare, and to imagine

how gladly would they, from time to time, avail themselves of a cheap mode of communication to remind them of their duty and hear of their welfare, while at present they are debarred the indulgence of their paternal feelings by the knowledge that neither themselves nor their children have the means of paying for the letter by which the information could be conveyed.[13]

As one anonymous 1844 essayist pointed out, the proliferation of "touching anecdotes" in support of postal reform shows "with what dexterity the snare of cheap postage was spread; that it was represented as a case of feeling and won immediate access to the heart of a large class of people."[14] Indeed, the nearly hysterical repetition of such stories produced a disingenuous but powerful connection between the present postal regime and what the upper and middle-classes saw as the amoral and unsentimental behavior of poor families. Hill, Cole, and the other penny-postage propagandists bombarded the public with images of the family solidarity that would necessarily be the result of cheap postage, implicitly arguing that the newly regenerated post would become a vehicle for consolidating affect and generating long-distance versions of family life. Posters and petitions addressed to "MOTHERS and FATHERS that wish to hear from their absent children! FRIENDS who are parted, that wish to write to each other! EMIGRANTS that do not forget their native homes!" appeared everywhere, all with the familiar depoliticizing mantra "This is no question of party politics."[15] Moreover, the ideological force of these reform efforts continued to shape the penny post in the popular imagination of its admirers long after the reform was initiated. Throughout the century, the penny post was coterminous with more normative tropes of domestic happiness and middle-class sustenance, as one American rhapsodized:

To thousands and tens of thousands of family circles, in town, village and hamlet, the dispensation of the penny post comes almost as gratuitously and as silently as the morning dew upon the flowers that breathe and blush in the windows. Associating its benefits with enjoyments most necessary to nature, it serves up its messages of friendship and love as condiments of the morning meal. The administration of the tea-urn, under the presidency of the lady of the house, commences at the same time as that of the penny post at the other end of the table . . . The relish of this double repast is the refinement of that social enjoyment which England has procured for her millions by giving them the blessing of cheap postage.[16]

By insisting upon the morning-dew naturalness of cheap postage, and by suggesting that the tea-urn and the penny post were parallel emblems of domestic nourishment, the above passage continued the work of early reform propaganda: erasing the political and economic history of postal reform, even erasing the presence of the postman himself in this celebration of a nearly miraculous kind of postal "dispensation."

In the place of the Post Office's political and economic history, an affective history was generated. Although David Allam has noted that there is no evidence to suggest that the general public was in any way dissatisfied with the Post Office or the high cost of postage prior to 1837,[17] Hill and Cole's penny-postage propaganda was so powerful that it constructed a retrospective narrative of family disaffection that reformers and parliamentarians alike seem to have accepted as historical fact. "When you contemplate the enormous increase which has taken place in correspondence," asserted Lord John Russell in a 1848 House of Commons speech, "you may estimate the number of persons who were deprived of the benefit of communicating with their friends and of offering the interchange of domestic affections."[18] A similarly revisionist estimation of the regenerative powers of the penny post can be found in Benjamin Disraeli's 1880 novel *Endymion*, which begins by tracing the plight of a financially embarrassed family in the 1830s who are forced to retire to the country:

Parcels came down by the coach, enclosing not merely proof sheets, but frequently new books—the pamphlet of the hour before it had been published, or a volume of discoveries in unknown lands. It was a link to the world they had quitted without any painful associations. Otherwise their communications with the outer world were slight and rare. It is difficult for us, who live in an age of railroads, telegraphs, and penny posts and penny newspapers, to realize how uneventful, how limited in thought and feeling, as well as in incident, was the life of an English family of retired habits and limited means, only forty years ago. The whole world seemed to be morally, as well as materially, 'adscripti glebae'.[19]

In Elizabeth Gaskell's 1866 *Wives and Daughters*, moreover, the affective limitations imposed upon families before 1837 engender a whole system for the evaluation and quantification of sentiment. Speculating on the recent marriage of their neighbor Dr. Gibson and a former governess, the spinster sisters Browning are able to determine conjugal happiness from the number of letters the Doctor receives while his wife is away.

Now two letters during the week of her absence showed what was in those days considered a very proper amount of conjugal affection. Yet not too much—at elevenpence-halfpenny postage. A third letter would have been extravagant. Sister looked to sister with an approving nod as Molly named the second letter, which arrived in Hollingford the very day before Mrs. Gibson was to return. They had settled it between themselves that two letters would show the right amount of good feeling and proper understanding in the Gibson family: more would have been excessive, only one would have been a mere matter of duty.[20]

Through these kinds of fictional representations of the past, postal propaganda created a self-fulfilling prophecy, whereby benefits down the road were used as de-facto evidence of the morally and intellectually "limited" aspects of family life under high postage. This hindsight construction of pre-penny postage disaffection was partly enabled by the fact that Hill himself attributed the origin of his idea to a story he had heard about Coleridge on a walking tour of the Lake District, who paid the postage of a poor barmaid's letter, only to find that the envelope was empty, and was just supposed to serve as an outward sign that her brother was well.[21] The Coleridge story was told and retold in every account of penny-postage reform to be published, including one by Harriet Martineau, who mistakenly identified the Lake District samaritan to be Rowland Hill himself. Indeed, the desire to keep Hill the central figure of reform efforts and to locate him at the origins of reform led some psychobiographical historians to insist that the true alpha of penny postage was in Hill's childhood and in the bonds of family affection that made him so sensitive to issues of domestic harmony. As one happy philatelist observed as recently as 1955, "If Rowland Hill, as a very small boy, had not noticed his mother's worried look whenever a postman knocked at her door to demand a shilling or so for the letter he brought her, we might never have been able to collect postage stamps."[22]

Yet nineteenth-century historical narratives such as Harriet Martineau's *A History of the Thirty Years' Peace* did the primary work of historical revisionism by projecting images of family disaffection into the pre-reform years. While Disraeli and Gaskell went back only a few decades to depict families "limited in thought and feeling," Martineau conjured up an image that was even farther removed from her mid-Victorian perspective:

We look back now with a sort of amazed compassion to the old crusading times, when warrior husbands and their wives, grey-headed parents and their brave sons, parted with the knowledge that it must be months or years before they could hear even of another's existence. We wonder how they bore the depths of silence. And we feel the same way now about the families of polar voyagers. But, till a dozen years ago, it did not occur to many of us how like this was the fate of the largest classes in our own country . . . When once their families parted off from home, it was a separation almost like that of death.[23]

Just as penny postage had prevented such metaphoric deaths, it was also attributed with remedying widespread disease and literal death. "Who would now divine that high rates of postage could have any relation to the prevalence of smallpox?" marveled Hill in his autobiography. "And yet it was found that 'Practitioners and others in the country do not apply for lymph, in the degree they otherwise would do, to the institutions formed in London for the spread of vaccination, for fear of postage.'"[24] In retrospect, there was a never-ending litany of illnesses that the cheap circulation of letters had cured, ailments that infected the individual body and the social body alike. High postage, in the opinion of W. H. Ashurst, prevented scientists from gathering information from the working men who possessed it, and from in turn circulating knowledge amongst their intellectual peers:

the mine of facts which is now locked up in them cannot be brought forth; the results of the past and the seeds of the future, scientific, mechanical and moral fruit is wholly unproductive; the heavy rates of postage not only prevent an accurate record of facts from being transmitted, but actually prevent their being elicited . . . Indeed, intellectual seed is scattered among men with the same profusion that Providence supplies it for our physical wants: this has been shown wherever revolutions or any great exciting cause has thrown masses of men into new positions.[25]

If the Malthusian rhetoric of the above passage throws us back upon the pre-industrial world of *Adam Bede*, we should linger there long enough to note the anti-paternalistic message embedded in Ashurst's account of present scientific unproductivity. Intellectual seed may be found everywhere, amongst the lowest classes of men as well as the highest, and cheap postage will prove this egalitarian truth without the political violence that accompanies more standard scenarios of revolution.

≺ II ≻

*Politics and the Post Office*

Rowland Hill's divestment of politics from postal reform is partly explained by Mary Favret's study of the political function of the fictional letter in the Romantic period. Favret argues that the nineteenth century witnessed a transformation in the ideology of the letter, from an emblem of revolutionary politics to an anachronism that could not survive the modern Post Office. In Favret's understanding, the nineteenth century was a "post-epistolary age":

an age where one imagines the post where once there were letters, where one reads the movements of a mail coach, not the vagaries of the correspondence . . . it deliberately staged the death of the letter . . . and began to pay strict attention to the fiction of the Post Office.[26]

The Victorian "fiction of the Post Office" as designed by Rowland Hill and Henry Cole deliberately dislocated the letter from its eighteenth-century ideological history: instead of an emblem of revolutionary hostility and incendiary violence, the letter became a circulating token of affection that would renaturalize the demoralized space of the family and dispel social frictions between classes. In this way, Cole's fiction of the Queen authorized the fiction of the Post Office. By scripting the British monarchy's relinquishment of postal tyranny, Cole rewrote the revolutionary ideology of the letter that had previously circulated in the form of the French monarchy's *lettre de cachet*.

Cole's *Scene at Windsor Castle* was reprinted many times during the 1838–40 penny-postage campaign, and the imagined scene of Queen Victoria disregarding her Lords for the sake of commoners eventually gave way to the circumstance of the actual Queen not only giving up her own franking privilege but abolishing the franking system entirely. Apparently, when penny-postage was passed by parliament in 1840, the real Queen Victoria was "graciously pleased" as Rowland Hill remembered in his 1880 autobiography, "to abandon her privilege of franking, thus submitting her letters to the same rule as those of her humblest subject," and consequently "it was determined that all other privileges should cease at the same time."[27] Despite Hill and Cole's mutual denial of the political importance of reform, in both of their representations of the Queen's real or imagined reaction to penny postage the localized power of Victoria and her House of Lords is seen to be voluntarily replaced by a more amorphous type of authority signified by "the powerful engine of civilization" Hill had invented: a disembodied machinery of law enforcement that functioned without the police.

F. M. L. Thompson has argued that the postman did the opposite cultural work of the policeman in the Victorian period, characterizing him as "a friendly, unassuming, unobtrusive official; a member of the working class himself" who did not embody the main weight of the law.[28] Yet it was precisely by *not* embodying the law that the reformed Post Office could be so effective. As Cole's Queen implied, the law was being disobeyed during the unreformed postal regime, but under penny postage, the law would naturally compel citizens to behave properly, to give up the "smuggling postman" and to submit their letters to "friendly, unassuming, unobtrusive" channels of dispersion. In Hill's remembrance, likewise, the Queen subjects herself and her letters to an alternative "rule," and a decentralized, depersonified version of power can be seen taking shape in the mechanistic process of sorting, stamping, and delivering known as the Post Office.

These dual images of the Queen's ready acceptance of postal reform are important benchmarks of a radical shift in ideologies of authority that was catalyzed by nineteenth-century agitation for penny postage. The regenerated Victorian Post Office was invented and sustained along the same principles as Bentham's Panopticon, through which, as Michel Foucault has argued, a "collection of separate individualities" maintain "a power relation independent of the person who exercises it."[29] By appearing to relinquish power, the Queen and her minions would actually extend their authority; indeed, when postage reform came into effect, the penny stamp that authorized the egalitarian right of all British subjects to send and receive letters bore an image of the Queen's profile. Although some subjects expressed a certain amount of discomfort at the thought of "kissing or rather slobbering over Her Majesty's Back,"[30] most were "rather proud of sticking the Queen's head on their letters."[31] While these reactions to the Penny Black may seem radically different, they are identical in their suggestion that the apparent deflation of the Queen's power actually proliferated the visibility of her image and authority, making the effects of Victoria's rule tangible to all citizens in every part of the kingdom simultaneously.

In this context, Foucault's interpretation of the Panopticon, especially its ubiquity as a disciplinary architecture for a variety of nineteenth-century social institutions—the prison, the hospital, the madhouse—is instructive. "The body of the king," Foucault writes,

with its strange material and physical presence, with the force that he himself deploys or transmits to some few others, is at the opposite extreme of this new physics of power represented by panopticism; the domain of panopticism is, on the contrary, that whole lower region, that region of irregular bodies, with their details, their multiple movements, their heterogeneous forces, their spatial relations . . . At the theoretical level, Bentham defines another way of analysing the social body and the power relations that traverse it; in terms of practise, he defines a procedure of subordination of bodies and forces that must increase the utility of power while practicing the economy of the prince. Panopticism is the general principle of a new 'political anatomy' whose object and end are not the relations of sovereignty but the relations of discipline.[32]

By turning to Foucault's "political anatomy" here, to the "economy of the prince" that replaces and disperses "the body of the king" in this passage, it becomes apparent that the disembodied machinery of the Post Office similarly enforced discipline through diffusion and proliferated postal authority in the place of sovereignty.

In 1855, American citizen Pliny Miles celebrated Hill's engine of civilization precisely for its far-reaching ability to manage, to organize, and to control: "Like a giant possessing ubiquitous powers, like a Briareus with twice ten thousand hands, it is every-

where present, reaching nearly every house in the kingdom, receiving, distributing, and delivering whatever is entrusted in its
care, with a marvellous celerity that resembles the movements of
a pantomime."[33] By substituting a seemingly infinite number of
ubiquitous "hands" for the monolithic authority of the "head,"
the reformed Post Office became a carefully choreographed ritual
of social management, a disciplinary institution divested of individuality or personification. Significantly, Anthony Trollope's
fundamental point of discord with Rowland Hill was the way that
reform had projected an image of automation onto the civil servants of the Post Office. In his *Autobiography*, Trollope writes:

> With him I never had any sympathy, nor he with me. In figures and facts
> he was most accurate, but I never came across any one who so little un-
> derstood the ways of men,—unless it was his brother Frederick. To the
> two brothers the servants of the Post Office,—men numerous enough to
> have formed a large army in the old days,—were so many machines who
> could be counted on for their exact work without deviation, as wheels
> may be counted on, which are kept going always at the same pace and
> always by the same power.[34]

If the servants of the Post Office were once soldiers in a large
army, they now are automatons: the dehumanized, mechanized
"wheels" of Hill's great civilizing engine.

Trollope's view of the predetermined mechanization of the
postal service spurred him to put himself further out of favor with
Hill by delivering a lecture to the clerks in the General Post Office
on "the doctrine that a civil servant is only a servant as far as his
contract goes, and that he is beyond that entitled to be as free a
man in politics, as free in his general pursuits, and as free in opinion, as those who are in open professions and open trade."[35] This
indeterminate line between individual freedom and institutional
control was a subject that Trollope explored in his other career as
a fiction writer, expressing similar anxieties that Hill had replaced
the totalitarian monopoly of the pre-penny post with a disciplinary
regime that fostered artificiality, mechanism, and determinism
under the sign of family affection and social perfectibility.

In this way, reading the vicissitudes of Hill's postal reform
through Bentham's Panopticon, or even through Foucault's interpretation of panopticism, is appropriate. It may even be necessary,
considering that Hill's previous career as a schoolmaster and edu-

cational reformer met with high approval from Bentham, who frequently visited the school Hill and his brothers presided over in the mid- to late twenties.[36] Moreover, all of the Hill brothers perceived of reform in the spirit of "the great truth" that Bentham had advocated, "that the object of all government, and of all social institutions, should be the greatest happiness for the greatest number for the greatest length of time."[37] In this historical context, it is not surprising that Hill's Post Office prototype should yoke the greatest happiness principle and the disciplinary effects of the Panopticon to mobilize an image of the re-affected family in the service of social control. As Ann Cvetkovich has persuasively argued in her Foucauldian work on the political impact of Victorian sensation fiction, "If affect can be a source of resistance, it can also be . . . a mechanism for power."[38]

≺ III ≻

### Postal Discipline and Home Control

This is not to say that an affective model of the Post Office allowed the republican, revolutionary rhetoric of postal reform to go entirely unremarked or unchallenged. Hill's penny post did receive some conservative criticism, primarily from members of parliament who did not want to give up their franking privileges and from stationers who protested that cheap postage would drive down the price of paper.[39] But even Trollope's 1865 *Can You Forgive Her?* mocks the feminist and democratic potential of the penny post when Mr. Palliser describes to Alice Vavasor the weighty occupation that cheap circulation of mail has provided his spinster cousins, Iphy and Pheemy:

> Being women they live a depressed life, devoting themselves to literature, fine arts, social economy, and the abstract sciences. They write wonderful letters; but I believe their correspondence lists are quite full, so that you have no chance at present of getting on either of them . . . They don't at all seek people of note as correspondents. Free communication with all the world is their motto, and Rowland Hill is the god they worship. Only they have been forced to guard themselves against too great an accession of paper and ink.[40]

Along with Trollope's distrust of the belief that more letters simply equaled more knowledge, at least one 1839 article questioned the assumption that all forms of information were productive, or even benign:

are there no societies in this country which have other than religious, moral, and charitable objects—are there no societies which might wish to spread disaffection, irreligion, or faction? . . . Was the committee igno-rant—we think not—that the radicals in politics, and the sectarians in re-ligion, have been the warmest advocates—and indeed . . . the only very zealous advocates for this penny post? The reason is obvious; because at present such societies cannot circulate their venom without some kind of machinery and agency . . . it is Sedition made easy.[41]

To a certain extent, the author appears to have been right about the more "seditious" effects of reform. The radical leader of the Anti-Corn Law League, Richard Cobden, for example, wrote Hill a letter in 1843 praising the reformed Post Office as "a terrible en-gine for upsetting monopoly and corruption: witness our League operations, the spawn of your penny postage!"[42] Cobden's idiom replaces the sentimentalized family of reform propaganda with a depersonified, anti-paternalistic social family suggesting that pen-ny postage had not renaturalized the private family, but had in-stead spawned alternative combinations of people such as trade unions and political leagues. Indeed, thanks to Hill, Cobden was able to circulate approximately 40,000 League pamphlets; he "gave it as his opinion, that their objects were achieved two years earlier than otherwise would have been the case owing to cheap post-age."[43] When the Corn Laws were finally repealed in 1846, Cobden sent another evocative letter to Hill announcing the virtual disso-lution of his League:

I shall feel like an emancipated negro—having fulfilled my seven-year apprenticeship to an agitation which has known no respite. I feel that you have done not a little to strike the fetters from my limbs, for with-out the penny postage we might have had more years of agitation and anxiety.[44]

Although Cobden's rhetoric of slavery and emancipation di-rectly belies Hill and Cole's repeated insistence that penny-postage reform was inherently apolitical, for the most part, postal propaganda played down these incendiary images by suggesting that cheap postage would actually domesticate revolutionary poli-tics. The mob scenes usually associated with trade union agitation and labor strikes were appropriated and rewritten by reformers such as Cole, who described the scene at the General Post Office the night before the change in postage rates went into effect as an inverted riot:

The great hall was nearly filled with spectators, marshalled in a line by the police to watch the crowds pressing, scuffling, and fighting to get to the window first. The superintending President of the Inland Office with praiseworthy zeal was in all quarters directing the energy of his officers where the pressure was the greatest . . . When the window closed, the mob, delighted at the energy displayed by the officers, gave one cheer for the Post Office, another for Rowland Hill.[45]

Rowland Hill's Post Office could virtually rechannel the frenzy and potential violence of mob activity, making police officers less central to maintaining discipline and control than the postal officers who were cheered by the crowd for their efficiency and energy. Similarly, Hill's daughter described the scene of the Post Office on the first evening of the reform in an idiom that domesticates even the most pernicious emblem of the French Revolution:

When the last stroke of the hour had rung out, and the lower sash of every window had come down with a rush like a guillotine, a great cheer went up for penny postage and for Rowland Hill, and another for the Post Office staff who had worked so well.[46]

An 1838 report from the Select Committee on postal rates, moreover, had already determined that high postage actually kept working men "ignorant of the state of wages in different parts of the country, so they do not know where labour is in demand. This state of ignorance has a tendency to promote strikes and trade unions among them."[47] In this way, despite the inherently radical aspects of postal reform, most of its advocates insisted that its effects would be wholly anti-revolutionary: "Our greatest achievement of late has been the obtaining of the penny postage," wrote Harriet Martineau to an American friend. "I question whether there will be now time left for the working of beneficent measures to save us from violent revolution; but if there be, none will work better than this."[48] Thus, if the deployment of sentimental ideology advanced some liberal or radical causes like Cobden's Anti-Corn Law League, it also functioned conservatively, to enforce social control over an increasingly mobile and fragmented society. Martineau was especially interested in the pacifying effect that cheap postage had on men otherwise supposed to be violent and

unsentimental, repeatedly pointing out that soldiers are "more so-
ber and more manly, more virtuous and more domestic in their affections" when they are encouraged by their commanding officer
to correspond with their families.[49] Moreover, W. H. Ashurst testi-
fied that even the violent impulses of a hardened criminal would
be softened by the frequent correspondence with home and family,
asking, "How often from the criminal in the hour of condemnation do we here [sic] the first gush of misery break forth in, 'Oh
my poor mother!'"[50]

The domestic affections were more often than not personified
in this figure of the working- or middle-class mother, whose
higher claims both replaced and extended the Queen's authority.
Most noticeably, "mother" appears when the subject in need of
home control is a young girl: "give me a girl who left the parent's
roof pure," insisted one country clergyman in 1838, "and as long
as she writes freely to her mother, I shall scarcely fear for her virtue."[51] Martineau agreed that the disciplinary power made available by the penny post could be especially effective in the cases of
impoverished young women forced to leave their homes to seek
out work is distant places:

> If the governesses of this country (in whose hands rest much of the moral
> destiny of another generation) could speak of the influence of the reform
> upon their lot, what should we not hear of the blessing of access to
> home? We should hear of parents' advice and sympathy obtained when
> needed most; of a daily sense of support from the scarcely ideal presence
> of mother or brother; . . . while expense is no longer the irritating hin-
> drance of speech, the infliction that makes the listening parent deaf, and
> the full-hearted daughter dumb. . . who shall say to how many this privi-
> lege has been the equivalent to peace of mind—in how many cases to the
> preservation of innocence and a good name?[52]

In a parenthetical comment in his chapter on panopticism, Foucault tentatively suggests that "one day we should show how in-
tra-familial relations, especially in the parents-children cell, have
become 'disciplined,' absorbing since the classical age external
schemata . . . which have made the family the privileged locus of
emergence for the disciplinary question of the normal and the ab-
normal."[53] By generating a long distance version of family life and
doing away with any need for immediacy in the affective interaction between mother and child, postal reform provided a set of
principles by which first the family and then society were thor-

oughly disciplined. The penny post became the ultimate mechanism for the moral preservation and social control of all culturally
suspicious groups of people, from working men to criminals, governesses to revolutionaries.

≺ IV ≻

*Empire and the Avunculate*

After the passing of postal reform in 1840, moreover, activists realized that the reformed Post Office could be put to work in the
guise of a domesticated imperialism, carrying out colonial imperatives without the oppressive violence and tyranny that traditionally accompanied the promulgation of the British Empire. Hill
had, indeed, planted these seeds himself in a footnote to his original 1838 pamphlet, mentioning that cheaper postage between the
colonies and "the mother country" would remove some significant obstacles to emigration, and would "maintain the sympathy
. . . which is the only sure bond of connection."[54] As early as 1844,
the sitting House Committee on Postage began to formulate the
future objects of the postal system, making evident the extent to
which the moral and national integrity of British emigrants was a
central government concern:

To content the man, dwelling more remote from town with his homely
lot, by giving him regular and frequent means of intercommunication; to
assure the emigrant, who plans his new home on the skirts of the distant
wilderness or prairie, that he is not forever severed from the kindred and
society that still share his interest and love; to prevent those whom the
swelling tide of population is constantly pressing to the outer verge of
civilization from being surrendered to surrounding influences, and sink-
ing into the hunter or savage state; to render the citizen, how far soever
from [sic], worthy, by proper knowledge and intelligence, of his important privileges as a sovereign constituent of the government; to diffuse
throughout all parts of the land enlightenment, social improvement, and
national affinities, elevating our people in the scale of civilization, and
binding them together in patriotic affection.[55]

With the advent of penny postage came the idea that home and
civilization could be maintained in any wilderness that had a Post
Office, and that national identity could be preserved through a
constantly circulating medium of "patriotic affection." In the

same way that advocates of cheap postage appropriated revolutionary rhetoric in order to stress the nonviolent aspects of Hill's reforms, supporters of universal or ocean penny postage appealed to
a sentimentalized version of empire that could generate British nationalism through love and fellowship.

A faster, cheaper, and more technologically advanced postal
system was heralded throughout the nineteenth century as the
only means of maintaining the integrity of the British empire.
"What family in England to-day does not have a relative in the
colonies?" asked J. Henniker Heaton in an 1890 tract called *Ocean
Penny Postage*, moving quickly from the subject of affection to the
subject of empire:

It is often gloomily predicted that such a tremendous agglomeration as
the British Empire will inevitably fall to pieces and dissolve like its
predecessors . . . I venture to reply that, in the postal and telegraphic
services the empire of our Queen possesses a cohesive force which was
utterly lacking in former cases. Stronger than death-defying warships,
than devoted legions, than natural wealth, or wise administration, are
the scraps of paper that are borne in myriads over the waves, and the two
or three slender wires that lie hidden in the fathomless depths below.[56]

Similarly, in the 1907 book *Sentiment: The Bond of Empire*, W. R.
Malcolm insisted that the affective communalism fostered by
cheap postal rates would diminish economic and political "mis-
understandings" between nations, as well as "bring the scattered
members of the race together; to promote community of taste and
aspirations is to create identity of race feeling and sympathy, and
on this sentimental basis the empire will rest."[57] Of course, these
ideas about the way that the sentimental circulation of letters
would maintain national (or racial) communities and prevent the
hostilities of war had their roots in mid-Victorian reform efforts;
in fact, the prevention of international violence was one of the
primary objectives behind ocean penny postage.

By far the most sustained appeals to Britain for universal postage came from Americans, especially from "the learned blacksmith" Elihu Burritt, a self-made, Yale-educated working man
who visited London in 1847 and formed "The League of Universal
Brotherhood." His movement was "dedicated to promote friendship and good relations between countries and to work for the abolition of war."[58] Cheap postage was viewed as the potential key to

international peacekeeping, and in 1849, Burritt published *Ocean Penny Postage: Its Necessity Shown and Its Feasibility Demonstrated*, a tract that began with a prolonged ode to Hill and the people of Great Britain and ended with a series of appeals to the mother country.

> Every day this year nearly a thousand of her children will sail from her shores for these distant lands. These self-expatriated children are not prodigal sons, whose supercilious importunities have constrained her to divide with them a portion of her substance, that they might spend it in distant lands, in riotous living. No; they are her poorer children, whose hands are hardened, and whose shoulders are bowed with long years of labour, which they have bestowed on her green fields . . . They are going, portionless, to pioneer the English race, language, science, and commerce to these unclaimed continents and islands of the earth; to extend and elaborate the integrity of the British Empire . . . why should they not be treated as equal subjects of an integral empire in the matter of the penny post?[59]

In Burritt's text, the reformed Post Office clearly functions as an alternative method of maintaining empire and enforcing national "integrity," and the affective trope of mother and child is obviously central to his ideological objectives. Yet when the penny post's diffuse and expansive form of control began to be represented iconographically, the hegemony of power suggested by the rule of the Queen or the patronage of parents was unsuitable as a colonial emblem. A variety of pictorial envelopes was designed to propagandize for universal postage; most stressed an unpersonified image of home and community that could be established across oceans by the networks of the post. "The World Awaits Great Britain's Greatest Gift/An Ocean Penny Postage/To Make Home Everywhere and All Nations Neighbors," reads the message on one such envelope designed by London artist Henry Anelay around 1850.[60] In this way, the imperatives of empire were domesticated by the creation of an entirely postal version of home. It seemed to advocates that the very constraints of "time and space had begun to yield before increasing energy of the human mind, and it was reserved for [Hill's] administrative faculty to inflict upon them a new defeat by bringing the interchange of letters within the reach of all."[61]

Another envelope designed by Anelay, described in glowing detail by Burritt at the close of his pamphlet, testifies to the way that advocates needed to proselytize for universal postage with emblems and icons that avoided any association with paternalism or patronage:

John Bull, in the coziest mood of grandfatherly benevolence, is represented sitting in an arm chair, with his squat hat cocked urbanely, and his yellow-topped boots, looking to the life like the image of "the olden time." On one side a beautiful little fairy of a girl, with eyes as bright as diamonds, is looking askingly into his face, while she holds up a letter in one hand, subscribed "To cousin Jane in America," and with the other points to the American coast, which is dimly seen in the distance, lined with children, black and white, all with letters in their outstretched hands, and in the act of hailing an approaching steamer . . . bearing the English flag . . . At the bottom of the piece these words give language to its significance,—"Uncle John! Won't you please send my letter to cousin Jane in America, for a penny?"[62]

By personifying John Bull as an uncle, the artist was able to conjure up an image of English benevolence and authority divested of the paternalistic proprietorship that would have been so objectionable to American citizens. Uncle John Bull was a domesticated appeal to British Imperialism, just as the Post Office came to be perceived as a mechanism for peacefully fostering domestic and colonial discipline within an Empire that was increasingly unwieldy, in both size and temperament.

Indeed, appeals to this anti-paternalistic icon of sentimentality were quick to point out that affect was, in fact, a form of capital that could be put into circulation abroad as well as at home. A propaganda poem written in 1848 by the Englishman H. G. Adams, "Send the Letters, Uncle John," stressed Rowland Hill's philosophy that more frequent and cheaper access to sentimental interaction with family would actually increase and empower the commerce of the British empire:

> *Will it pay?* why, UNCLE! UNCLE!
> Can you doubt it? look at home;
> See how, from all parts, your mail-bags
> Daily weightier become:
> Hear how all your children bless you
> For the boon they here enjoy;
> Oh, extend it o'er the waters,
> And our eager pens employ!
> *Will it pay?* why, fifty letters

Will be sent instead of one:—
*Fifty* pence from *one* poor shilling,
Think of that, good UNCLE JOHN!
Think, too, how 'twill foster commerce,
And all friendly ties increase,
Binding nation unto nation
In the bonds of *Love* and *Peace*.[63]

Accordingly, Uncle John Bull was a useful icon in bridging the gap between an ideology of the affective, private family and the intrusive imperiousness of government control. "It has been said that the Government cannot weave the ties that bind us to our families," wrote a reporter for *The Lancaster Guardian* in 1838, "but how much may they not do towards strengthening and cherishing them?"[64] Through the agitation for penny postage, and eventually ocean penny postage, the government was reconceived as a network of support internal to kinship, rather than outside of it.

Another 1848 poem entitled "Sophie's Petition to Uncle John" was penned as a Christmas request from a child to her avuncular Santa Claus of postage, and includes a direct request to replace an international environment shaped by violence and commercial haggling with an affective economy mediated by the Post Office. After asking "Dear Uncle John" for a way to send cheap letters to her cousins in Australia, Canada, and America, "thy loving niece, Sophie" makes some economic observations about the high cost of waging wars overseas:

It costs some millions every year
To pay the men who fight;
'Twould be much better, uncle dear,
To set our pens to write.
Then kindly words of love and peace
Would reach from shore to shore,
Till men should learn they're brothers all,
And think of war no more.
Oh, uncle John! dear uncle John!
How very nice 'twould be
For ships with letters, not with guns,
To sail across the sea;
For cannon-balls, take letter-bags,
'Twould be a pleasant change
They'd reach a longer way, by far,
Than Captain Warner's "range."[65]

As the depoliticized, sentimentalized embodiment of the British empire, "Uncle John" accessed ideological notions of familialism without the taint of traditional, hierarchical models of power. Just as the avuncular term in debates surrounding pawnbroking signified the intersection of the affective world of the family with the commercial world of exchange, so Uncle John Bull is the figure chosen by propagandists to suggest that affect is not only a nicer and more civilized way to maintain empire than war, but that it is also a much more economically conservative strategy.

The avuncular trope resurfaces in novels such as Margaret Oliphant's 1861 *The House on the Moor*, a text that celebrates the reformed Post Office as a vehicle for introducing an isolated nuclear family into the rites and rituals of exogamous social life. Oliphant's novel focuses on a small, disaffected family living in an desolate corner of northern England: Susan and Horace Scarsdale are motherless siblings residing with their reclusive father who is "dark not so much in complexion as in sentiment."[66] When we learn that Susan has the affectionate, domestic disposition of her dead mother, but that she is unloved by her self-absorbed father and cruel brother, the blunt disavowal of Mr. Scarsdale's racial darkness resurfaces, implying that the initial anxiety of the narrative is that without love, Susan will inevitably succumb to the "dark" forces of the Moor that surround her. This threat is summarily neutralized by the sudden appearance of her mother's brother, Uncle Edward Sutherland, who has been a Colonel in the British army in India for twenty years. Fortunately for Susan, the sole point of Uncle Edward's return is to reestablish "reciprocity of honest affection and kindred between his own family and their nearest relatives" (vol. 1, 48). Beloved by her uncle, the colonial agent, Susan is at last able enjoy the sympathetic interaction of kinship, and when Uncle Sutherland is finally forced by his brother-in-law to depart, Susan can, for the first time in her life, take comfort in the daily dispensations of the post:

All had not disappeared with Uncle Edward. Here was a perennial expectation, a constant thread of hope henceforward to run through her life. Never before had Susan known the altogether modern and nineteenth-century excitement of looking for the postman. It gave quite a new interest to the day—any day that unknown functionary might come again to refresh her soul with this novel delight. She could see him coming across the moor, that celestial messenger! Not a cupid, honest fellow; but bearing with him all the love that brightened Susan's firmament . . . all was very different from that dead blank of her former life, in which she had no expectation. (vol. 1, 49)

By introducing his niece to civilization and to sentiment simultaneously, the avuncular visitor to *The House on the Moor* combines the colonial imperative of banishing foreign darkness in the name of empire with the postal imperative of redeeming the disaffected family.

Carrying mailbags instead of cannonballs, letters instead of guns, the "celestial messenger" of the nineteenth-century Post Office assumed a highly visible cultural role in the maintenance and expansion of the British empire: a circumstance that made the connection between postmen and policemen, postmen and soldiers, a point of metaphoric exploitation in a variety of Victorian texts. For example, Disraeli's 1844 novel *Coningsby* finds one ultra-conservative character, the Right Honorable Nicholas Rigby,

concocting, you could not term it composing, an article, a 'very slashing article,' which was to prove that the penny postage must be the downfall of the aristocracy. It was a grand subject, treated in the highest style. His parallel portraits of Rowland Hill the conqueror of Almarez, and Rowland Hill the deviser of cheap postage were enormously fine . . . There was never a fellow for giving a good hearty kick to the people as Rigby.[67]

Rigby's comparison of Rowland Hill, a general in the Peninsular War who died in 1842, and Rowland Hill the "deviser of cheap postage," would seem random and unmotivated without the context of the reformed Post Office's role in shaping and maintaining empire. By yoking the two disparate Hills in order to suggest that postal reform had more in common with violence than with sentiment, Rigby attempts to undo the domesticating rhetoric of Hill's advocates. In Rigby's establishmentarian assessment, penny-postage reform was no more than a war waged by Rowland Hill against the aristocracy.

But nowhere is the connection between the civil servants of the Post Office and the soldiers of the British Empire more telling than in Trollope's *Autobiography*. In 1851, Trollope returned from Ireland where he had been setting up colonial postal routes to begin working on similar networks in rural England: "During those two years," his *Autobiography* records, "it was the ambition of my life to cover the country with rural letter-carriers."[68] As a clerk whose primary function was the establishment of "postal networks which should catch all recipients of letters,"[69] Trollope was complicit in producing and extending the "powerful engine of civilization" Hill had created.

All this I did on horseback, riding on an average forty miles a day . . . I have often surprised some small country postmaster, who had never seen or heard of me before, by coming down upon him at nine in the morning, with a red coat and boots and breeches, and interrogating him as to the disposal of every letter which came into his office . . . In all these visits I was, in truth, a beneficent angel to the public, bringing everywhere with me an earlier, cheaper, and much more regular delivery of letters. But not unfrequently the angelic nature of my mission was imperfectly understood . . . Unless I came down suddenly as a summer's storm upon them, the very people who were robbed by our messengers would not confess the robbery, fearing the ill-will of the men. It was necessary to startle them into the revelations which I required them to make for their own good. And I did startle them.[70]

Trollope's representation of himself as a redcoated soldier, "interrogating" rural postmasters and startling country citizens into confessions about their mail delivery is, on the one hand, an ironic inflation of his socially demeaning occupation as a public servant. But on the other hand, if we think of the Post Office as an institution that had ideologically replaced the monarchy in order to extend its discipline, Trollope's mounted man of letters forces the political Post Office to resurface as a reconfigured army of civilization and empire. In Foucault's political anatomy, Trollope takes on the local authority of the prince, functioning not in the service of the Queen, but for an "earlier, cheaper and much more regular" circulation of information and affection.

≺ V ≻

*The Post Office and Trollope's Affective Family:*
*'The Claverings' and 'John Caldigate'*

Of course, Trollope's evident enjoyment of his power to "come down upon," to "interrogate," and to "startle" is seemingly at odds with his initial description of the reformed Post Office as a mechanized institution, staffed with clerks and postmen who were expected to do the work of automatons. Yet the two passages from his *Autobiography* are symptomatic of his conflictedness over postal progress mentioned by Glendenning. Trollope's enjoyment of the power that accrues to him as a navigator of postal routes, a soldier for intercommunication, is undercut by a nagging suspicion that he, both as a civil servant and as a British citizen, is subject to a specifically nineteenth-century brand of discipline enforced by heightened expectations for performance and participation. If the duties of a postal clerk under Rowland Hill were circumscribed by demands for ritualized and pre-determined actions and behaviors, the duties of a letter writer in the age of penny postage were governed by affective rules and regulations that were especially threatening to normative models of masculinity. "Women expect such a lot of letter-writing!"[71] mourns the vacillating hero of Trollope's 1867 novel *The Claverings*, who ultimately blames his engagement to two women at once on the fact that his first fiancé, Florence Burton, desired him to "live upon letters" (34) during a long engagement. "Dear Harry," Florence writes, "I am sure that we ought to wait . . . I fancy that I can be quite happy if I can see you two or three times a year, and hear from you constantly. It is so good of you to write such nice letters, and the longer they are, the better I like them" (90). When Harry begins to write shorter and shorter letters, and finally fails to write altogether for a few weeks, Mrs. Burton gets suspicious that her girl is being ill-treated and proposes a journey to London to find him. "It would look as if we were all afraid," Mr. Burton protests,

". . . and after all, what does it come to?—a young gentleman does not write to his sweetheart for two or three weeks. I used to think myself the best lover in the world, if I wrote once a month."
"There was no penny post then, Mr Burton."
"And I often wish there was none now," said Mr. Burton. (273)

The affective rituals of courtship have so accelerated under penny postage that male negligence and indiscretion are immediately perceptible not only to the lover, but also to the lover's entire family; moreover, the non-delivery of a letter can have just as many affective ramifications as a successful transmission. While postal relationships prolong the empowering period of a courtship for a woman, they increase the chances that men will go astray, or rather, in Trollope's idiom, that they will be caught in the act of going "to the wrong side of the post" (178).

As a policing agent that functioned nominally in the service of female sentiment, the penny post was often represented as the downfall of masculine autonomy. In Robert Surtees's 1858 novel, *Ask Mamma; or, The Richest Commoner in England,* the slowness of mail coaches is remembered as having been very conducive to the pulse of masculine lovemaking in pre-railway days, but the penny post and the railroad have given women all the power of romantic conquest. In light of this, the novel's titular "Mamma" has some important advice about courtship for her son, Billy Pringle:

> Be cautious too about letter-writing. There is no real privacy about love-letters anymore than there is about the flags and banners of a regiment, though they occasionally furl and cover them up. The love-letters are a woman's flags and banners, her trophies of success, and the more flowery they are, the more likely they are to be shown, and to aid in enlightening a Christmas party tea. Then the girl's Mammas read them, their sisters read them, their maids read them, and ultimately perhaps a boisterous, energetic young barrister reads them to an exasperated jury.[72]

While this passage reopens the ideological connection between the Post Office and the military, it also suggests that the female recipients of love letters are actually more like soldiers than the postmen who deliver them. The reformed, nineteenth-century Post Office, Surtees implies, has imposed an affective economy upon British citizens that circulates for the entertainment and legal benefit of women. Letters "enlighten" trivial Christmas parties, rather than intellectual circles, and, most egregiously, serve as evidence against young male writers in law suits. Once a letter is written it comes untethered from the context of its inception and may be absorbed in a variety of alternative economies: at any time, information or affection may "go to the wrong side of the post" with or without the knowledge of the writer.

If this is Derrida's point about postal economies ("a letter *can* always *not* arrive at its destination"[73]), it is also Trollope's point about nineteenth-century epistolary communication: "The word that is written is a thing capable of permanent life, and lives frequently to the confusion of its parent. A man should make his confessions always by word of mouth if it be possible."[74] Considering that only four years after the successful inauguration of penny postage, a secret, inner office was discovered at St. Martin's le

Grand where the letters of suspected political dissidents and foreign visitors to England were opened, Trollope's advice was motivated by more than the potential failures of interpretation. On the other hand, the possible interception of mail was just the most literal fracture engendered by postal communication. Although the popular ideology of the Post Office insisted that cheap postage could repair the disaffected family, a distinct counter-ideology suggested that it could also catalyze other, more linguistic breakdowns. As Alexander Welsh writes in his book on *George Eliot and Blackmail*,

The availability of the penny post probably lent impetus to greater literacy; at the same time, the increased use of the mails and of the telegraph placed a subtle strain on the trust between individuals. As in all uses of writing, the messages are loosed from their origin to be interpreted elsewhere.[75]

While holding the family and the nation together on the plane of ideology, the penny post engendered more "subtle" fractures at the level of the sentence and the paragraph. It was this loosening of origin from interpretation that opened up space for outside agents to wreak havoc on interpersonal relationships, especially relationships between and among family members.

For example, Trollope's 1879 novel *John Caldigate* introduces and upholds the hegemonic narrative of the Post Office's ability to reform the family, but ends with an ambivalent assessment of the interpretive loosenings that are inevitable within postal intercourse. The novel begins by telling the story of a family plagued by paternal disruptions: not only is John Caldigate's relationship with his father in ruins, but his father's relationship with his grandfather had been similarly fractured by general incompatibilities. While at college John has fallen in debt to Davis, an infamous Jew-usurer, and in light of his pre-existing problems with his wealthy father, has turned to his also-wealthy Uncle Babington for help. Uncle Babington does render some temporary financial aid, but John consequently finds that he is expected to recompense his uncle's family by marrying their eldest daughter, Julia. When John realizes he has merely proliferated his outstanding debts within the ledgers of a variety of uncles, he forfeits his future inheritance by selling his entail to his father for a sum of ready cash, and emigrating to Australia to dig for gold.

True to the ideology of postal reform, however, when John begins to send "rational, pleasant, and straightforward" accounts of his endeavors home to his father, "there was no touch or tone of the old quarrel."[76]

Letters came regularly, month by month, and were always regularly answered,—till a chance reader would have thought that no father and son stood on better terms with each other . . . each letter was regarded as the rising of a new sun . . . This went on not only from month to month, but from year to year, till at the end of three years from the date at which the son had left Folking, there had come to be a complete confidence between him and his father. (118–19)

The cheap and frequent circulation of letters between Britain and her colonies triumphs in the opening pages of *John Caldigate*, redeeming the alienated bond between father and son and simultaneously undoing the work of uncles.[77] The reformed Post Office makes the father "certain of the son's reform" (120), and the elder Mr. Caldigate happily reinstates John as his heir.

John returns home, marries Hester Bolton, and produces his own heir; but suddenly a letter signed "Euphemia Caldigate" arrives from Australia, threatening to expose a previous marriage if he does not return a large sum of money that he had received in payment for a now-defunct gold mine. John refuses and finds himself indicted for bigamy, the proof of which consists entirely of the testimony of the Lady and a single letter and an envelope, both in his handwriting; the envelope is addressed to "Mrs. Caldigate" (280). Despite the defense's plea that "a man does not marry a woman by simply writing his own name with the word mistress prefixed to it on an envelope" (294), the warnings of Billy Pringle's mother in *Ask Mamma* come true: John is convicted, and the power of the Post Office to prove family relationships appears hegemonic and infallible. In fact, the name on the envelope is all that is necessary to convince the Judge of John's guilt; if anything, the contents of the letter should throw doubt on the possibility of a marriage between John and Euphemia. They "referred almost altogether to money matters, though perhaps hardly to such as a man generally discusses with his wife. Certain phrases seemed to imply a distinct action. She had better sell these shares or those, if she could, for a certain price,—and suchlike" (281). The fact that John's letter to Euphemia has a strictly economic content has no bearing on the trial; as we know, the cultural work accomplished by postal ideology is the successful suggestion that every letter is a love letter.

In establishing the existence of an economic family, the Post Office denies the existence of an affective one, and Hester Caldigate's realization that she is no longer considered to be married registers as a confusion about how she will get her future mail: "what would they call her? When they wrote to her from Chesterton how would they address her letters?" (415). But it isn't long before Samuel Bagwax, Post Office clerk and authority on postage stamps, begins to suspect that something is wrong with the Australian stamp on the envelope addressed to "Mrs. Caldigate." To Bagwax, the envelope is indicative of the disaffection of one couple rather than the love of the other: "Every moment that I pass with that envelope before my eyes I see the innocent husband in jail, and the poor afflicted wife weeping in her solitude" (499). After months of careful study and research, Bagwax realizes and successfully proves that the "queen's-head" affixed to the envelope was not issued until long after the dated postmark (524). Despite the fact that the failures and corruption of the colonial Post Office have allowed blackmail and forgery to masquerade as bigamy, the police work of Bagwax realigns the sentimental family by proving bigamy to be forgery, after all. For his good service, Bagwax is sent to Australia to enforce greater postal inviolability between Britain and the colonies, and *John Caldigate* ends up supporting the same ideology it introduced: the sanctity of the affective family depends upon the reformation and maintenance of colonial Post Offices.

If, in *John Caldigate*, blackmail replaces bigamy in the novel's economy of crimes, in *The Claverings* we see that blackmail has replaced abduction and other forms of gothic brutality in the nineteenth-century economy of criminal behavior. In the middle-class parlor of the Burton family, the penny post is represented as a policing agent operating in the service of domestic affection, but in the hands of foreign personages, the penny post is as revolutionary in effects as the anachronistic *lettre de cachet*. Appearing in the pages of a late eighteenth-century gothic novel, the French-speaking Russian, Count Pateroff, would be the brutal and violent foreign villain, infiltrating the British parlor in order to kidnap a young, rich English maiden and force her hand in marriage. In

Trollope's *The Claverings*, however, Count Pateroff's tactics have altered to suit the temperament of mid-Victorian realism. Pateroff has attempted to propose to the rich British widow Lady Ongar on more than one occasion, but he has been consistently refused entrance to her London townhouse. Rather than abandon his pursuit, he turns his mind to alternative methods of manipulation, "feeling that he must operate on Lady Ongar through some other feeling than her personal regard for himself":

> He might, perhaps, have trusted much to his own eloquence if he could have seen her; but how is a man to be eloquent in his wooing if he cannot see the lady whom he covets? There is, indeed, the penny post, but in these days of legal restraints, there is no other method of approaching an unwilling beauty. Forcible abduction is put an end to as regards Great Britain and Ireland. So the count had recourse to the post. (280)

While the nineteenth-century legal system in Britain has terminated the practice of forcible family-making, the penny post has become an engine of alternative coercions: a tool for manipulating family bonds in the absence of affective feeling. In *The Claverings*, Trollope finally suggests that the penny post runs counter to the sentimental ideology that brought it into existence, and that the business of building kinship can be the chosen occupation of greedy gothic criminals as well as domesticated British families.

In other words, although the popular ideology of the Post Office was that it could bring the family together, it constantly threatened to bring the *wrong* family together: to solidify kinship bonds that were adverse to the claims of the "real" affective family. Moreover, the family relationships at risk in postal intercourse were linguistic as well as affective. Although the letter written by Count Pateroff is too long to be given to the reader (280), it is apparently a masterpiece of deliberate ambiguity, an example of the way that postal communication is subject to a plethora of loosenings between word and deed, intention and outcome, subject and object:

> His letter was very long . . . He began by telling Lady Ongar that she owed it to him for the good services he had done her, to read what he might say, and to answer him. He then gave her various reasons why she should see him, pleading among other things, in language which she could understand, though the words were purposefully as ambiguous as they could be made, that he had possessed and did possess the power of doing her a grievous injury, and that he had abstained, and—hoped that

he might be able to abstain for the future. She knew that the words contained no threat . . . but she understood also all that he had intended to
imply. (280)

Blackmail, consequently, was the economic and linguistic subversion of affective mail, the point at which the Post Office's republican accessibility became dangerous. "The temptation to blackmail
of the fictional employee of the Post Office is not what finally dis-
tinguishes them," Welsh insists. "Blackmail is an opportunity af-
forded to everyone by communication of knowledge at a distance."[78] This is certainly the conclusion reached by the dismissed
chaplain, Mr. Greenwood, in Trollope's last completed novel *Marion Fay*. Unsatisfied with the "beggarly stipend" granted him by
the Marquis of Kingsbury, Greenwood "remembered that though
it might be base to tell her ladyship's secrets, the penny post was
still open to him."[79] That "penny post" functions as a satisfactory
euphemism for blackmail in the above sentence is indicative of
how the cheapness and ubiquity of the first had, at least in Trollope's assessment, proliferated opportunities for the second. Like
Count Pateroff, moreover, Greenwood possesses secrets that could
significantly alter patriarchal alliances and family bonds: "her ladyship's secrets" are her plots and schemes to drive a wedge of
disaffection between her husband and his children from his first
marriage. Indeed, in its ability to engender a plethora of alternative
interpretations of the family, Trollope's representations of the
penny post are often reminiscent of Richard Cobden's letter to
Rowland Hill about the communities of angry citizens that the reformed post was capable of organizing: "witness our League operations, the spawn of your penny postage!"

Of course, Trollope's suspicions about the potentially dangerous proliferation of affective channels of communication are still
with us, most egregiously in the shape of online sexual predators
who suddenly have a new way to manipulate the interest of the
weak and unsuspecting. The easy and inexpensive circulation of
knowledge via cable television and the internet, moreover, has
again called into question the Victorian equation of diffusion of information and social advancement. But the avuncular project of
community building, of exogamous social exchange and the rapid
circulation of knowledge, is by now too embedded in our discourse
of contemporary family life to be dislodged. Indeed, the Victorian

ideology of kinship as frequent communication is not far removed from our late twentieth-century belief that kinship is *tele*communication. Even now, in the advertising campaign of MCI's Friends and Family Plan, kinship revolves around (and through) invisible networks controlled and maintained for our emotional benefit by a benevolent industrial agency. My favorite commercial for MCI features a very pregnant woman walking through various scenes of daily life (husband in fuzzy background), now with a cellular phone to one ear, now with a beeper going off on her belt, now at her computer reading email, in an ongoing conversation with parents, siblings, and multiracial friends about what to name her child. Fending off all suspicion that technology isolates, dehumanizes, disaffects, our telecommunications industry still extends the work of Hill's Penny Post, positioning itself at the very heart of the extended family, inaugurating the process of social exchange for the new millennium.

# Conclusion

## HOME TRADING REDUX: UNII6VERSAL
## BROTHERHOOD AND THE REDEMPTION OF UNCLE

The workers who begin to form themselves into co-operative
groups and think of trading must have an Uncle John to enable
them to borrow money at fair interest, and so prevent themselves
from getting under the thumbs of the Bastard Capitalist, who
would charge such a high rate of interest, or impose such unfair
conditions, that they would only be working for the "sweater" in
another form . . . Uncle John is not a sweater: he will be a FAIR
CAPITALIST and see fair play—he will be a fair Uncle, at least in
this conception.

Uncle John's Nephew, Universal Co-operation:<br>
A National "Uncle John" (1891)

I HAVE ARGUED throughout this book that the avunculate supplied the Victorian cultural imagination with a meaningful
commercial allegory. As figures at the threshold of family life,
Uncles could perpetually signify the flimsiness and permeability
of the private nuclear family, suggesting, through their very ubiquity, the sentimental fiction of the paternal family itself. In most
of the novels, essays, and articles cited, avuncular narratives function as ruminations about the vulnerability of local kinships and
communities under the transformative ethos of an increasingly
global capitalism. If in the first chapters, uncles signify the commercial limits of paternal and patriarchal discourse within pro-
grams of land privatization, female improvement, and colonialism,
later chapters examine how the pawnshop and the post office offered opposing evaluations of patriarchy under capitalism. In the
nexus of the pawnshop, commerce is a force of individualism and
self-interest that often sacrifices familial identity through an alchemical conversion of all relics into their neutral money form.

Conversely, in the post office, commerce works in the service of affective kinship: by lowering the tax on sentiment, penny postage reform supposedly circulated familialism instead of corporate profits and capitalist greed.

But what happened to avuncularism? What happened to the ideological struggle between bad and good uncles, between avuncularism that is dehumanizing and avuncularism that is kindness? For one thing, the pawnshop and the post office continued to stand in for alternative scenarios of capitalism for the rest of the century, often yielding a hybrid model of corporate familialism in the guise of avuncularism. Such an hybrid avunculate is evident as early as 1848 in Anna Maria Hall's allegorical novel *Uncle Sam's Money Box*, where the downfall of a nuclear family is predictably remedied by that convenient colonial visitor. After a great bank collapse, Mr. Hayward's money and credit disappear, and his eldest son Harold must work in a bank branch located at some distance from the family home. Unfortunately, for Harold, the economic ruin and separation of his family occurs before the institution of the national Penny Post. Looking back, Hall writes: "these are happy times when a letter from home—the sweetest of all luxuries!—cost only a penny! How earnestly Harold panted for his letter, though, in those days, it cost sevenpence! . . . more than once the youth . . . went without his dinner, that he might exchange his coin for the longed-for letter."[1] When Uncle Sam returns, of course, from India, rumors of his fabulous "money box" precede him, but it is some time before the reunited family realizes that his hoard of riches is primarily a metaphor for the knowledge, information, and multicultural interaction he gained working for the East India Company. "Once the mind of a young man becomes thoroughly saturated with the hope of acquiring knowledge, power, wealth, for the great purpose of USEFULNESS, I look upon him as safe. MY! How his happiness increases and his box fills!" (98). Decades spent traveling and living among indigenous peoples, learning their languages, and, most importantly, setting up systems of barter, made sure Uncle Sam's box was never empty when he was called upon to use it. In this way, *Uncle Sam's Money-Box* repackages the miser's wealth as a never-empty basket of loaves and fishes that circulates commodities in order to solidify the affective relations of classes and countries. For capitalism to function ethically, Hall implies, commerce must embrace the rhetoric and sentiment not of miserdom, but of reciprocity: "This is one of the firmest links between rich and poor—they are dependent on each other; one cannot prosper without the assistance of the other. The poor cannot get on without the aid of honest masters, and masters can never be rich without the co-operation of honest servants—all happiness to be real, must be reciprocal" (86).

This new language of "co-operation" combines the paternalist sentiment of Samuel Smiles with a capitalist agenda reminiscent of the "home trading" models of the early nineteenth-century, producing, by the end of the Victorian age, a coherent economic philosophy. In the 1890s, for example, the New Parcel Post publishing company of London printed a series of tracts on Co-Operation by "Uncle John's Nephew." *Universal Co-Operation*, as "Nephew" titled his first volume, would be a capitalist alternative to state socialism: an economic philosophy that preserved the fundamentals of trade while creating a "Brotherhood" of workers to defeat oppressive capitalists and middlemen.[2] Essentially, co-operative organizations would become alternative banking mechanisms for working-class members: if working men combined into co-operative groups, and if "fair-minded capitalists" were recruited to assist, co-operatives would charge only "fair" interest rates to help individual members begin businesses. Moreover, as "Nephew" makes clear, these banks would resemble not money-boxes, but pillar-boxes.

Referring again to my scheme, it must be borne in mind that before you can send goods by rail to a town the railway has to be made and a train must commence to run. Just the same with letters; the reason why you can post a letter in a pillar box in London and feel quite sure that it will reach Scotland in due course is because the National Postal System or organization extends to Scotland, and will do its allotted duty to your letter, through its servants both in London and Scotland. Therefore, let me earnestly point out, that before these great benefits which are here held out, and those which may, in the future, be added, the League and its Branches must be created, and its members must work in hearty response to this proposal.[3]

When the post office replaces the pawnshop as the favored model of capitalist circulation, the laws of Deuteronomy are also effectively reversed. "Uncle John's Nephew" insists that Universal Co-

Operation will eventually yield "Universal Brotherhood," resurrecting the bonds of affection between people, classes, and even Nations. "Nephew" also suggests that the fund of cash compiled through Co-operation be christened "Uncle John's Millions," and clearly explains the affective principles behind his new banking system:

> By creating your Uncle John, you have put just exactly the same law into operation for yourselves and your class as the well-to-do have for themselves and their families, viz., getting and keeping the money in the Family, and helping your own KITH and KIN, and you are getting and keeping the money, and also wisely helping the working-classes, of which you are a member, hold together for the common good.[4]

Under this benevolent capitalist Uncle, members of the working class become kin, and the economic allegiances they owe to each other will eventually challenge the patriarchal laws that keep money in the hands of the upper classes. Of course, such a personification of avuncular kindness would circulate not only in England, but in America, evolving into the most widely familiar and powerful Uncle in Western cultural imagination: Uncle Sam. In fact, in many American political allegories of the late nineteenth century, Uncle Sam appears as a good capitalist who engages and eventually defeats bad capitalist Uncle John Bull in economic debate. In Charles Elton Blanchard's *Report of Uncle Sam's Homilies on Finance*, for example, Uncle Sam argues that John Bull became a money-lender to the fledgling American States, and now controls much of the labor in her former colonies. Uncle Sam proposes an alternative system of financing American ingenuity and entrepreneurism: "we need an absolutely safe national bank where people could borrow easily on ample security, and at rates which would represent the actual cost of conducting business; people could leave their money, and the hoarding of money could cease."[5]

Such an autonomous, state-regulated banking system not only resonates with early theories of Home-Trading, it resembles socialism more than it embodies capitalism. Indeed, many American allegorical depictions of Uncle Sam are explicit about their pro-Socialist agenda, denouncing the rampant consumerism of England as the evil result of unregulated commerce. When José M. Aguirre's 1888 "open letter" on national and international politics,

*Uncle Sam in Pontifical Robes; John Bull Destitute of Attire*, declares that the governments of America and England have as little
in common as their eponymous icons, it describes "John Bull"
capitalism as sinister, supernatural, and compromised by the unproductive image of female prostitution Gallagher associated with
usury. Aguirre writes that England

> was born a shopkeeper, and that is her destiny and glory. It may be said
> that she has found the philosopher's stone of which the alchemists
> dreamt. She makes gold whenever it suits her, and gold always suits her;
> and she makes it of the virtues as of the vices, of talent as incapacity, of
> liberty as of slavery, of war as well as peace, and, in fine, knows how to
> convert into the precious metal even the misery, the hunger, the blood,
> of her own children.[6]

In language reminiscent of Ruskin, Aguirre describes the whole of
England as a veritable pawnshop; a place where the Father has
been dethroned by a witch who brokers affective relationships for
gold, and subjects the human body itself to the hideous alchemical
conversions of commodification. In America, Aguirre hopes, the
"sun and atmosphere" will purify the vitiated human body, de-
stroying the "moral microbes or germs of a deleterious nature that
are imported from old Europe," and reinventing "the mysterious
elements that constitute the moral individual."[7] The evils of the
feminized pawnshop will be repaired by "Uncle Sam in Pontifical
Robes," and the human body restored to health and wholeness in
the strong American sun.

This particularly American redemption of the avunculate is
also visible in an 1880 political pamphlet called *Uncle Sam and
Americus: A Dialogue of Land, Labor and Liberty*, where E. F.
Boyd returns us to the debate over land tenure we explored in the
first two chapters of *Avuncularism*. Here, Boyd outlines "a plan
for a New American National land and Labor Co-operative System, by which Land and comfortable Homes may be secured to
the poorest classes of every race."[8] Such co-operation will be
brought into existence by reviving a version of the closed system
of home trading, and eliminating the "oligarchy of landlords and
capitalists" who had undermined the sentimental obligations of
paternalism. In response to Uncle Sam's ignorant assertion that he
owns the public lands in America, the erudite philosopher, Americus, reminds him that he is but a trustee for the people:

You are the Nation's trustee; the guardian of the natural rights of the whole population; you are the trustee—not the owner really—of the public domain . . . I think there is something akin to blasphemy and mockery of the supreme ruler of the universe, when a man presumes the land—the common heritage of every child of the infinite Father; to assume proprietorship over it; to buy it or sell it as his own 'property,' forever, world without end.[9]

In Americus's analysis, private ownership is a violation of the most fundamental and divine father-child relationship; rather than usurping this law of the Father, Uncle Sam must act as a trustee, as a steward of the common good and heritage of all Americans. Significantly, Boyd's "Dialogue" uses the figure of a naïve Uncle Sam to depict the conversion of capitalism into co-operation; otherwise, to show how Uncle Sam, the caretaking icon of the American people, is really a communist in theory and in principle. Yet while Americus insists that Uncle Sam embrace communal principles of property stewardship, he also points out that the avunculate is still the transformative nexus of use into exchange and labor into wealth:

You are the greatest capitalist; the masses are your loyal laborers. Why should not these two mighty forces co-operate? It is the part of the capitalist to furnish the land, buildings, machinery, implements, domestic animals and so forth. Do that, and ere long you will possess hundreds and thousands of the biggest farms in the world.[10]

Although Uncle Sam is a great capitalist, he should be a capitalist in the service of the people, and Americus illustrates this version of avuncular kindness with a model that should be familiar, and even obvious to us by now. When Uncle Sam protests that he knows nothing of agriculture, Americus responds with an analogy we have learned to expect:

'It is just as practicable,' replied the sage, 'for you to cultivate the soil as to do numerous other things in which you have succeeded most amiably. You have been a common carrier of letters, newspapers and books almost a hundred years. You have hundreds of thousands of persons connected to that department. It works as regularly as clock-work. The people are accommodated very much by the wonderful amount and regularity of the postal service.'[11]

The primary objective of this project has been to loosen the nuclear family's hold upon Victorian culture, to suggest that under industrial capitalism ideologies of kinship were more complex and expansive than father-centered theories or histories will allow. Just as the uncle becomes the vehicle of exogamy and exchange for the closed, nuclear family, the avunculate marks the intersection of feudal, paternalistic culture with newly developing nineteenth-century discourses of economic individualism, free trade, and kinder, gentler versions of empire. That these discourses often spawned anxieties about female value, the rights of tenant farmers, the circulation of capital, and the revolutionary effects of trade unions suggests that avuncularism functioned as both ideology and counter-ideology: sometimes as a conservative, disciplinary supplement to the law of the father, and sometimes as a liberating promise of a life without father. In this context, the American emblem of "Uncle Sam" seems to be the ultimate ideological turncoat, reversing and redeploying the British discourse of home-control, becoming in the process a resonant personification of anti-English democracy and nationalism.

Of course, more work on the varieties of patriarchal authority in American literature and culture needs to be undertaken in order to determine whether avuncularism in nineteenth-century America proved to be an unambivalent force of religious freedom, social autonomy, and political justice. In contemporary American pop culture, where ideology tends to be most visible and hegemonic, avuncular metaphors certainly continue to shape the intersection of capitalism and familialism: witness the wildly popular mob miniseries *The Sopranos*, where fathers are scarce and the alternative "family" of mafia criminals is held together by the avuncular chain of Uncle Junior, nephew/Uncle Tony and nephew Christopher. But it also seems as though twentieth-century avuncularism is habitually situated at the crossroads of usury and prostitution, actively trading on the easy slippage between nieces and daughters, daughters and mistresses, first articulated by *Mansfield Park*. Looking back at John Huston's 1950 cops and robbers drama *The Asphalt Jungle*, for example, we find Angela (a very young Marilyn Monroe) living in a luxury apartment paid for by her much older and married sugar daddy, a man she calls Uncle Lon.[12] Uncle Lon, otherwise Alonzo Emmerich, is nominally a lawyer, but his real business is financing robberies and taking a significant cut of the profit. Huston's didactic film classifies Uncle Lon as a more heinous criminal than the working-class thugs he employs because

Emmerich has (as the police chief notes) used his expensive education and class status to avoid arrest, house a mistress, and maintain an elite social standing. In keeping with avuncular models, Uncle Lon is a capitalist who exposes the failure of social paternalism at the heart of usury. But he also typifies a brand of sexual capitalist that can be found in even more recent films about prostitution, exploitation, and sexual abuse.

"That goddamn trailer is more popular than uncle's day at a whorehouse," complains Carl, the manager of the Fat Trout Trailer Park, to FBI Agent Chet Desmond in David Lynch's 1992 prequel to the series Twin Peaks, *Fire Walk With Me*.[13] Given that the trailer belongs to the raped and murdered Theresa Banks, a young woman who worked as a prostitute, Carl's spectacular metaphor makes some sense: the avuncular euphemism gives older men access to young women, enabling a cycle of exploitation that flourishes under the guise of familialism. But add to that the fact that Theresa's murderer will be revealed to be Bob, the psychological/supernatural alterego of real estate lawyer Leland Palmer, Laura Palmer's father, and the colloquialism abounds with significance. By day, Leland helps client Ben Horne circumvent the law and sell off huge chunks of Twin Peaks to foreign developers; by night, Leland engages in a string of murders that are apparently incited by his twisted sexual desire for his daughter Laura; his first victim is Theresa, who looks like Laura, then Laura herself, then Maddy, Laura's look-alike cousin and his own niece. *Twin Peaks* was, among many things, a series that revealed small-town America, the idealized middle-class family, and especially the benevolent patriarch, to be convenient sentimental fictions that actually enabled a host of crimes including prostitution, blackmail, arson, drug trafficking, spousal abuse, incest, and murder.

Certainly there isn't much ambivalence about avuncularism in *The Asphalt Jungle* or *Fire Walk With Me*, but even less weighty Hollywood vehicles like Garry Marshall's 1990 comedy *Pretty Woman* are quick to locate the fictive avuncular metaphor at the intersection of economic and sexual commerce.[14] In order to successfully transform the prostitute into the lady, Barney, the manager of the Beverly Hills hotel must first transform the prostitute into a niece, using the avuncular metaphor to legitimize Vivian's relationship with Edward Lewis, and to persuade a saleslady to open the door of a fancy boutique to Vivian. During the first of the famous Pygmalion transformation scenes otherwise known as shopping, Vivian (Julia Roberts) confesses to the saleslady that the older, wealthy Lewis (Richard Gere) isn't really her uncle, and the saleslady sagely replies, "they never are, dear." By now, it seems redundant to mention that Lewis is a large-scale, Reagan-era capitalist, a man who buys failing companies in order to break them up and sell the pieces off at a profit. Like the affective alienations of the pawnbroker, Lewis's business profile transforms familial sentiment into capitalist profit; not only was his particular brand of commerce motivated by his hatred for his father, his father's company was the first he purchased and destroyed. Fortunately for Vivian, Marshall's tale is as crassly moralistic as Huston's: Lewis's father's recent death and his current callous pursuit of a kindly older man's family ship-building business (along with Vivian's "therapy") convinces him of the evil of his ways, and he repairs bad avuncular behavior by becoming a good paternalist after all (primarily by marrying Vivian and going into the ship-building business with his Cheeryble-style replacement father).

These modern capitalist fictions of familialism continue to articulate the goal of *Avuncularism* beyond the nineteenth century, revealing inherent instabilities in patriarchal ideology, and allowing us to catch glimpses of historical and cultural meanings that have been elided by psychoanalytically driven models of kinship. By calling into question the seamlessness of patriarchy as an ahistorical political institution, I am challenging feminist theory to develop an understanding of oppression that is more responsive to the material realities of gender, class, and culture, then and now. Like the knowing saleslady in *Pretty Woman*, we are already aware that familial metaphors obscure as much as they enable. Moreover, we have reached a historical moment when the heterosexually defined "nuclear" family is less definitive of kinship than ever before, and our abiding investment in patriarchal fictions of the past and the present demands to be fundamentally challenged and revised.

<>

# Notes

## INTRODUCTION: LIFE WITHOUT FATHER

1. See Stone's, *The Family, Sex and Marriage in England, 1500–1800* (New York: Harper & Row, 1977), 4. While Stone has very little to say about post-1800 family types, his progress narrative of family development suggests that the importance of extended kinship ties had all but evaporated by the late eighteenth century, and that those remaining were vestiges of older family models.

2. See, for example, Dianne Sadoff, *Monsters of Affection: Dickens, Eliot, and Bronte on Fatherhood* (Baltimore: Johns Hopkins, 1982); Marianne Hirsch, *The Mother-Daughter Plot: Narrative, Psychoanalysis, Feminism* (Bloomington: Indiana UP, 1989); Priscilla Walton, *Patriarchal Desire and Victorian Discourse: A Lacanian Reading of Anthony Trollope's Novels* (Toronto: University of Toronto Press, 1995); Carolyn Dever, *Death and the Mother from Dickens to Freud* (Cambridge: Cambridge University Press, 1998).

3. Catherine Gallagher, *The Industrial Reformation of English Fiction, 1832–1867* (Chicago: University of Chicago Press, 1985), 117.

4. Arthur Helps, *Friends in Council: A Series of Readings and Discourse Thereon* (Boston: James Munroe, 1849).

5. See Adrienne Rich, "Jane Eyre: The Temptations of a Motherless Woman," in *On Lies, Secrets, and Silence* (New York: W. W. Norton, 1979), and Sandra M. Gilbert, "A Dialogue of Self and Soul: Plain Jane's Progress," in *The Madwoman in the Attic* (New Haven: Yale University Press, 1979).

6. Charlotte Bronte, *Jane Eyre* (1848; reprint, New York: W. W. Norton, 1987).

7. Michel Foucault, *The History of Sexuality*, vol. 1, trans. Robert Hurley (New York: Vintage Books, 1990), 11.

8. Ibid.,113.

9. Ibid., 90.

10. Juliet Flower MacCannell, *The Regime of the Brother: After the Patriarchy* (New York: Routledge, 1991).

11. Lynn Hunt, *The Family Romance of the French Revolution* (Berkeley: University of California Press, 1992).

12. Anne McClintock, *Imperial Leather: Race, Class, Gender in the Colonial Contest* (New York: Routledge, 1995), 197.

13. Leonore Davidoff and Catherine Hall, *Family Fortunes: Men and Women of the English Middle Class, 1780–1850* (Chicago: University of Chicago Press, 1987), 321. For other critiques of Stone's model of family development, see David Cressy, "Foucault, Stone, Shakespeare and Social History," *English Literary Renaissance* 21.2 (1991): 121–33; James Casey, *The History of the Family* (New York: Basil Blackwell Inc., 1989); Jack Goody, *The Development of the Family and Marriage in Europe* (London: Cambridge University Press, 1983); and Jeffrey Weeks, *Sex, Politics and Society: The Regulation of Sexuality Since 1800* (New York; Longman Inc., 1981).

14. Ibid., 224–25.

15. Ibid., 223.

16. Juliet Mitchell, *Psychoanalysis and Feminism* (New York: Pantheon Books, 1974), 370.

17. Ibid., 375.

18. Claude Lévi-Strauss, *Structural Anthropology*, trans. Claire Jacobson and Brooke Grundfest Schoepf (New York: Basic Books, 1963), 48.

19. Mitchell, 377.

20. Mary Murray, *The Law of the Father?: Patriarchy in the Transition from Feudalism to Capitalism* (New York: Routledge, 1995), 27. For other examples, see Kaja Silverman's introduction to *Male Subjectivity at the Margins* (New York: Routledge, 1992), and Gayle Rubin's "The Traffic in Women: Notes on the 'Political Economy' of Sex," in *Toward an Anthropology of Women*, ed. Rayna Raiter (New York: Monthly Review Press, 1975).

21. Craig Owens, "Outlaws: Gay Men in Feminism," in *Men in Feminism*, ed. Alice Jardine and Paul Smith (New York: Methuen, 1987), 219–32.

22. Ibid., 227.

23. Eve Kosofsky Sedgwick, *Tendencies* (Durham: Duke University Press, 1993), 58.

24. Ibid., 71.

25. Ibid., 72.

26. Sheila Rowbotham, "The Trouble with 'Patriarchy,'" in *People's History and Socialist Theory*, ed. Raphael Samuel (London: Routledge & Kegan Paul, 1981).

27. Charlotte Bronte, *Shirley* (1849; reprint, New York: Penguin, 1987). All further references will appear parenthetically in the text.

28. Wilkie Collins, *The Woman in White* (1860; reprint, New York: Oxford University Press, 1973).

29. Not only does Marian feel her sister's forthcoming marriage will make her "*his* Laura instead of *mine*," she also takes Laura's inevitable defloration upon herself: "Drop by drop, I poured the profaning bitterness of this world's wisdom into that pure heart and that innocent mind, while

every higher and better feeling within me recoiled from my miserable task. It is over now. She has learnt her hard, her inevitable lesson. The simple illusions of her girlhood have gone, and my hand has stripped them off. Better mine than his—that is all my consolation—better mine than his" (166, 167).

30. Wilkie Collins, *The Moonstone* (1868; reprint, New York: Penguin, 1966). All further references will appear parenthetically in the text.

31. See Helena Michie's *The Flesh Made Word: Female Figures and Women's Bodies* (New York: Oxford University Press, 1987), for a discussion of ladylike anorexia and the link between excessive sexuality and female consumption of food.

32. Robin Fox, *Reproduction and Succession: Studies in Anthropology, Law, and Society* (New Brunswick: Transaction, 1993).

33. George Eliot, *The Mill on the Floss* (1860; reprint, New York: Oxford, 1980). Repeatedly, the rural community of St. Oggs is shown to be undergoing rapid industrial and commercial change.

34. See Margaret Homans, *Bearing the Word: Language and Female Experience in Nineteenth-Century Women's Writing* (Chicago: University of Chicago Press, 1986).

35. The question I am most commonly asked at this point in my argument is "What about aunts?" I have resisted including aunts for a variety of reasons, all stemming from my primary argument that uncles as fictions and as metaphors represent a commercial and political alternative to the law of the father in nineteenth-century social philosophy. Aunts may suggest lesbian subversions (such as Aunt Jemima Stanbury in *Trollope's He Knew He Was Right*), nasty maternal replacements (such as Aunt Reed in *Jane Eyre*), or wise maternal supplements (such as Aunt Gardiner in *Pride and Prejudice*), but the methodological possibilities are not nearly as uniform, nor as interdisciplinarily pervasive. After all, the "avunculate" is a fairly well-developed concept in both Victorian thinking about pawnbroking and anthropological theories of kinship. In the case of aunts, however, the terminology would have to be coined now (tantular? tarantular?) and the concept theorized in retrospect.

36. Karl Marx, *Capital*, vol. I (New York: Penguin, 1976), 182.

37. Ibid., 182.

38. Frederic Jameson, *The Political Unconscious: Narrative as a Socially Symbolic Act* (Ithaca: Cornell University Press, 1981), 152.

39. For Gallagher, see *The Industrial Reformation of English Fiction;* for Armstrong, see *Desire and Domestic Fiction: A Political History of the Novel* (New York: Oxford University Press, 1987); for Poovey, see *Uneven Developments: The Ideological Work of Gender in Mid-Victorian England* (Chicago: University of Chicago Press, 1988), and *Making a Social Body: British Cultural Formation, 1830–1864* (Chicago: University of Chicago Press, 1995).

40. Isobel Armstrong, in a 1999 presentation at the Harvard Center for Literary and Cultural Studies, made the point that the Victorian period is

an arbitrary segment of the past, useful for undergraduate survey courses but ultimately unhelpful for the exploration of those crucial slices of cultural history that are noteworthy for their stopgap status. "Let's Get Rid of the Victorians," March 23, 1999.

41. Jane Austen, *Pride and Prejudice* (1813; reprint, New York, W. W. Norton, 1993), 25. All further references will appear parenthetically in the text.

42. Mr. Bennet's inability to produce a male heir and protect the entail points to an innate problem with a system of inheritance that leaves women portionless, under the law. Moreover, the subsequent outcome of his failure to guide his children's intellectual and moral development is a direct critique of educational standards for the daughters of gentlemen at the turn of the century. This is also reflected in his own choice of a wife who was beautiful but essentially stupid, and incapable of contributing to his happiness or domestic economy.

43. "She had never seen a place for which nature had done more, or where natural beauty had been so little counteracted by an awkward taste. They were all of them warm in their admiration; and at that moment she felt, that to be mistress of Pemberley might be something!" (156).

44. Charles Dickens with H. G. Wills, "My Uncle," *Uncollected Writings from Household Words, 1850–1859,* ed. Harry Stone (Bloomington: Indiana University Press, 1968), 368–73.

45. Max Weber quoted in *The Idea of Usury: From Tribal Brotherhood to Universal Otherhood* by Benjamin Nelson (Chicago: University of Chicago Press, 1969), xvi.

46. Melanie Tebbutt, *Making Ends Meet: Pawnbroking and Working-Class Credit* (New York: St. Martin's Press, 1983).

47. George Eliot, *Middlemarch* (1872; reprint, New York: Penguin, 1988), 40.

48. Thomas Hardy, *Tess of the d'Urbervilles* (1891; reprint, New York: Oxford University Press, 1998), 42.

49. Eve Kosofsky Sedgwick, "Paranoid Reading and Reparative Reading; or, You're So Paranoid, You Probably Think This Introduction Is About You," *Novel Gazing: Queer Readings in Fiction*, ed. Eve Sedgwick (Durham: Duke University Press, 1997), 23. Using the terminology of psychologist Silvan Tompkins, Sedgwick labels the practice of close reading "weak theory" because it only attempts to account for local events and ideas. Sedgwick argues that this is preferable to the "strong theory" of Foucault, who presents a single totalizing narrative of discipline that is both tautological and paranoid because it retains the possibility of a reading pleasure rooted in surprise. For other affirmations of close-reading, see Joseph Litvak, *Strange Gourmets: Sophistication, Theory, and the Novel* (Durham: Duke University Press, 1997), and Mary Ann O'Farrell, *Telling Complexions: The Nineteenth-Century English Novel and the Blush* (Durham: Duke University Press, 1997). According to Litvak, close-reading, or "sophistication-affirming criticism," has been rendered offensive

by "its association with intellectuality and homosexuality, both of which are resented as by definition excessive, as self-indulgent and un-productive" (18).

50. Edward Said, *The World, the Text, and the Critic* (Cambridge: Harvard University Press, 1983), 19; McClintock, 45.

## Chapter 1: Home Trading

1. Jane Austen, *Mansfield Park* (1814; reprint, New York: Oxford University Press, 1970), 431. All further references to this edition will be made parenthetically in the text.

2. Avrom Fleishman, *A Reading of Mansfield Park: An Essay in Critical Synthesis* (Minneapolis: University of Minnesota Press, 1967), 62.

3. David Kaufman, "Closure in *Mansfield Park* and the Sanctity of the Family," *Philological Quarterly* 65 (1986): 215.

4. Ibid., 223–24.

5. Paula Marantz Cohen, *The Daughter's Dilemma* (Ann Arbor: University of Michigan Press, 1991), 25.

6. Ibid., 63.

7. Glenda A. Hudson, *Sibling Love and Incest in Jane Austen's Fiction* (London: Macmillan, 1992), 35.

8. Nina Auerbach, "Jane Austen's Dangerous Charms: Feeling as One Ought About Fanny Price," in *Jane Austen: New Perspectives*, ed. Janet Todd (New York: Holmes and Meier, 1983), 218.

9. Ruth Bernard Yeazell, "The Boundaries of Mansfield Park," *Representations* 7 (1984): 149.

10. Jane Gallop, *The Daughter's Seduction: Feminism and Psychoanalysis* (New York: Cornell University Press, 1981), 144. See also Helena Michie's *Sororophobia: Differences Among Women in Literature and Culture* (New York: Oxford University Press, 1992), 80.

11. Armstrong, *Desire and Domestic Fiction.*

12. Joseph Litvak, *Caught in the Act: Theatricality in the Nineteenth-Century British Novel* (Berkeley: University of California Press, 1992), 24.

13. Sarah Stickney Ellis, *The Daughters of England* (London: Fisher, 1843), 83.

14. Maaja Stewart, *Domestic Realities and Imperial Fictions: Jane Austen's Novels in Eighteenth-Century Contexts* (Athens: University of Georgia Press, 1993).

15. Adam Smith, *An Inquiry into the Nature and Causes of the Wealth of Nations* (1779; reprint, New York: Oxford University Press, 1993), 290, 289.

16. Ibid., 290–91.

17. T. R. Malthus, *An Essay on the Principle of Population* (1798; London: J. Johnson, 1803), 439.

18. William Spence, *Britain Independent of Commerce* (London: T. Cadell and W. Davies, 1807), 3.

19. Ibid., 80.

20. Ibid., 59.

21. William Cobbett, "Perish Commerce!" *Weekly Political Register* 12 (London: November 12, 1807), 802–24.

22. Arthur Young, Letters to the Editor, *Weekly Political Register* (London: February 24 and April 9, 1808), 376; 569.

23. Mr. Marshall, *On the Appropriation and Inclosure of Commonable and Intermixed Lands* (London: W. Bulmer, 1801), 87.

24. Samuel Beazley, *A General View of the System of Enclosing Waste Lands* (London: C. Chapple, 1812).

25. Agricola, *A Concise Essay on the British Constitution* (Taunton: Norris, 1812), 98.

26. Catherine Gallagher, "George Eliot and *Daniel Deronda*: The Prostitute and the Jewish Question," *Sex, Politics, and Science in the Nineteenth-Century Novel*, ed. Ruth Bernard Yeazell (Baltimore: Johns Hopkins, 1986), 46.

27. Armstrong, *Desire and Domestic Fiction*, 67.

28. Maria and R. L. Edgeworth, *Practical Education* (1801; reprint, New York: Garland Publishing, 1974), 523.

29. Ibid., 522.

30. Ibid., 545.

31. Hannah More, *Strictures on the Modern System of Female Education* (1799; reprint, New York: Woodstock Books, 1995), vol. I, 115.

32. Armstrong, *Desire and Domestic Fiction*, 72 (emphasis added).

33. More, vol. II, 5.

34. Ibid.

35. Armstrong, "The Rise of the Domestic Woman," in *The Ideology of Conduct: Essays on Literature and the History of Sexuality*, ed. Nancy Armstrong and Leonard Tennenhouse (New York: Methuen, 1987), 111.

36. More, vol. II, 3.

37. Ibid., Introduction, x.

38. Ibid., vol. II, 6.

39. Armstrong, *Desire and Domestic Fiction*, 79.

40. Luce Irigaray, *This Sex Which Is Not One*, trans. Catherine Porter (New York: Cornell University Press, 1985), 178.

41. For a twist on the rhetorical link between money and children, see Jeff Nunakowa's study of miserdom as a thematic inscription of masturbation and/or incest, "The Miser's Two Bodies: *Silas Marner* and the Sexual Possibilities of the Commodity," *Victorian Studies* 36.3 (1993): 273–92.

42. Jane Austen, *Pride and Prejudice* (1813; reprint, New York: Oxford University Press, 1970), 148.

43. Edgeworth, vol. II, 529.

44. More, vol. I, 70.

45. Ibid., vol. II, 166.

46. Of course, it is appropriate for a male heir who has already gambled away a portion of his brother Edmund's inheritance to have a tendency

toward excess; in fact, Tom's problems with waste will include a pro-
tracted illness brought on by a bout of drinking, an illness that forces even
his indolent mother, Lady Bertram, to ruminate upon "how little useful,
how little self-denying his life had (apparently) been" (390).

47. "Letter to the Right Honorable Sir Richard Brocas, Lord Mayor of
London, from an Unidentified Citizen" (London, 1730), quoted in Jonas
Barish, *The Anti-Theatrical Prejudice* (Berkeley: University of California
Press, 1981), 239.

48. Smith, 192.

49. Even the mode of self-education Fanny chooses reflects her broad
interest in economic relations, as Edmund at one time catches her reading
not the latest fashionable novel, but Lord Macartney's accounts of his
journey to China (140).

50. Humphrey Repton, *The Landscape Gardening and Landscape Design of Humphrey Repton, Esq.*, ed. J. C. Loudon (London: Longman, 1840),
113–14.

51. Alistair Duckworth, *The Improvement of the Estate* (Baltimore:
Johns Hopkins, 1971), 45.

52. Duckworth, 45.

53. Edmund Burke, *Reflections on the Revolution in France* (1790; reprint, New York: Penguin, 1984), 152.

54. Humphry Repton, *An Inquiry into the Changes of Taste in Landscape Gardening* (London: J. Taylor, 1806), 15.

55. Tom Williamson and Elizabeth Bellamy, *Property and Landscape: A
Social History of Land Ownership and the English Countryside* (London:
George Philip, 1987), 151.

56. Warren Roberts also notes that Mary and Henry Crawford are associated with the French Revolution "not so much as revolutionaries, as
aristocrats who are likely to provoke it." *Jane Austen and the French
Revolution* (1979; London: Athlone, 1995), 97–100.

57. Williamson and Bellamy, 153.

58. Anna Seward, "The Letters of Anna Seward," quoted in Williamson
and Bellamy, 153.

59. Marshall, 12.

60. Fraser Easton also makes this point in "The Political Economy of
*Mansfield Park*: Fanny Price and the Atlantic Middle Class," *Textual
Practice* 12 (3), 1998: 459–88.

61. Marshall, 35.

62. Repton, *The Landscape Gardening*, 63.

63. Irigaray, 185.

64. Fleishman, *A Reading of Mansfield Park*, 37; Moira Ferguson,
"*Mansfield Park*: Slavery, Colonialism, and Gender," *The Oxford Literary
Review* 13 (1991): 118.

65. Fleishman, 37–38.

66. Irigaray, 181.

67. See, for example, Anthony S. Wohl's "Sex and the Single Room: In-

cest Among the Victorian Working Class," *The Victorian Family: Structure and Stresses*, ed., Anthony S. Wohl (New York: St Martin's, 1978), 197–216.

68. Davidoff and Hall, *Family Fortunes*, 329.

## CHAPTER 2: REPRODUCTION AND MALTHUSIAN ECONOMICS

1. Sandra Gilbert and Susan Gubar, *The Madwoman in the Attic: The Woman Writer and the Nineteenth-Century Literary Imagination* (New Haven: Yale University Press, 1979), 496. See also Nina Auerbach's *Woman and the Demon: The Life of a Victorian Myth* (Cambridge: Harvard University Press, 1982), 175; and Helena Michie's *Sororophobia: Differences Among Women in Literature and Culture* (New York: Oxford University Press, 1992).

2. George Eliot, *Adam Bede* (1859; reprint, New York: Penguin, 1985), 143. All further references to this edition will appear parenthetically in the text.

3. By "Malthusian" I refer to economic theories put forth by Thomas Malthus's "principles of population," rather than to any debates surrounding contraception or abortion that Malthus's work has spawned. I have chosen to use Malthus's first *Essay on the Principle of Population* (1798) as a theoretical touchstone rather than any of the revised editions primarily because *Adam Bede*, although first published in 1859, attempts to account for economic and social changes occurring at the turn of the century—more specifically, between 1799 and 1807. Rather than asserting that Malthus is the definitive subtext of Eliot's novel, I am suggesting that the partial operations of Malthusian economic discourse can be traced within *Adam Bede* in a manner that assumes, in the words of Catherine Gallagher, "no fixed hierarchy of cause and effect." "Marxism and the New Historicism," *The New Historicism*, ed. H. Aram Veeser (New York: Routledge, 1989), 37.

4. Catherine Gallagher, *The Industrial Reformation of English Fiction: Social Discourse and Narrative Form, 1832–1867* (Chicago: University of Chicago Press, 1985).

5. Arthur Helps, *The Claims of Labour: An Essay on the Duties of the Employees to the Employed* (London: William Pickering, 1845), 157; J. S. Mill, "The Claims of Labour," *Edinburgh Review* LXXXI (April 1845): 498–525. The review was unsigned, but it has been identified as Mill's by subsequent bibliographers.

6. Mill, 374.

7. Ibid., 379.

8. Margaret Homans, "Dinah's Blush, Maggie's Arm: Class, Gender, and Sexuality in George Eliot's Early Novels," *Victorian Studies* 36 (Winter 1993): 161.

9. Irigaray, *This Sex Which Is Not One*, 178.

10. Ibid., 173.

11. Ibid., 185.

12. F. M. L. Thompson, "Landownership and Economic Growth in England in the Eighteenth Century," *Agrarian Change and Economic Development: The Historical Problems*, ed. E. L. Jones and S. J. Woolf (London: Methuen, 1969), 41–60.

13. Ibid., 59.

14. Christabel S. Orwin and Edith W. Whetham, *History of British Agriculture* (Devon: David and Charles, 1971), 153.

15. J. V. Beckett, "Landownership and Estate Management," *The Agrarian History of England and Wales*, vol. VI, ed. G. E. Mingay (Cambridge: Cambridge University Press, 1989), 597–98.

16. G. S. Lefevre, quoted in I. S. Leadam, "To the Tenant Farmers of Great Britain: Farmer's Grievances and How to Remedy Them at the Next Election" (London: National Press Agency, 1880), 5.

17. James Caird, *The Landed Interest and the Supply of Food* (New York: M. Kelley, 1967), 60.

18. James Caird, *English Agriculture in 1850–1851* (London: Longman, Brown, Green, and Longmans, 1852), 503.

19. Charles Higby Lattimore, "A Plea for Tenant Right" (London: Ridgway, 1848), 12–13.

20. As Caird notes, "the great proportion of English farms are held on yearly tenure which may be terminated at any time by a six months notice." *English Agriculture*, 503.

21. Leadam, 5.

22. Caird, *English Agriculture*, 505.

23. Lattimore, 17.

24. Caird, *The Landed Interest*, 149.

25. Wally Seccombe, *A Millenium of Family Change: Feudalism to Capitalism in Northwestern Europe* (New York: Verso, 1992), 21. Although Seccombe is specifically interested in working-class families, it is important to recognize that the Poyser household is working class to the extent that every adult member of the household labors on the farm or in the dairy. I am arguing here that the very "latency" of tenant farmers' capital kept farmers who rented their land (like Mr. Poyser) on the socioeconomic cusp of middle-class existence until much later in the nineteenth century, when tenant's right was finally codified.

26. Ibid., 21.

27. Irigaray, *This Sex Which Is Not One*, 177.

28. Eve Kosofsky Sedgwick, *Between Men: English Literature and Male Homosocial Desire* (New York: Columbia University Press, 1985), 170.

29. Helena Michie, *The Flesh Made Word: Female Figures and Women's Bodies* (New York: Oxford University Press, 1987), 27.

30. John Kucich, *Repression in Victorian Fiction: Charlotte Bronte, George Eliot and Charles Dickens* (Berkeley: University of California Press, 1987), 193.

31. Leonore Davidoff, "Class and Gender in Victorian England," in *Sex and Class in Women's History*, ed. Judith L. Newton, Mary P. Ryan, and Judith R. Walkowitz (London: Routledge & Kegan Paul, 1983), 18.

32. Davidoff, 19.

33. Adam Smith, *An Inquiry into the Nature and Causes of the Wealth of Nations* (1776; reprint, New York: Oxford University Press, 1993), 353.

34. Susan Walsh, "Bodies of Capital: *Great Expectations* and the Climacteric Economy," *Victorian Studies* 37 (Fall 1993): 73–98.

35. Ibid., 76.

36. Ibid.

37. Interestingly, the first sign of Squire Donnithorne's contemplated exploitation of Hall Farm occurs at the birthday feast for Arthur, when he appears to be uncharacteristically concerned about Mrs Poyser's health, and proceeds to give her medical advice: "he gave his most elaborate civility to Mrs. Poyser to-night, inquiring particularly about her health, recommending her to strengthen herself with cold water as he did, and avoid all drugs. Mrs Poyser curtsied and thanked him with great self-command, but when he had passed on, she whispered to her husband, 'I'll lay my life he's brewin' some nasty turn against us. Old Harry doesna wag his tail for nothin' " (328).

38. For example, see Nancy L. Paxton's chapter on *Adam Bede* in *George Eliot and Herbert Spencer: Feminism, Evolutionism and the Reconstruction of Gender* (New Jersey: Princeton University Press, 1991), 43–68.

39. Malthus's late eighteenth-century economic views are obviously more apocalyptic than Arthur Helps's mid-Victorian paternalist theory; on the other hand, Mill identifies Malthus's "Essay on Population" as the origin of the social paternalist movement because it represents the first time "the economic condition of the working classes had been regarded as susceptible of permanent improvement" (Mill, "The Claims of Labour," 366).

40. Thomas Robert Malthus, *First Essay on Population: 1798*, reprinted for the Royal Economic Society (London: Macmillan & Co., 1926), 14–15.

41. Ibid., 14.

42. Catherine Gallagher, "The Body Versus the Social Body in the Works of Thomas Malthus and Henry Mayhew," *Representations* 14 (Spring 1986): 85.

43. Ibid.

44. Malthus, *First Essay on Population*, 128.

45. Although Mrs Poyser is unable to recognize the fact that Hetty is pregnant, it is important that she *does* recognize a change in her niece that she unknowingly characterizes in the economic idiom previously associated with Arthur Donnithorne: "Mrs Poyser though she noticed a surprising *improvement* in Hetty. . . she thought much less about her dress, and went after the work quite eagerly, without any telling. And it was wonderful how she never wanted to go out now—indeed, could hardly be per-

suaded to go . . . it must be, after all, that she had set her heart on Adam at last" (398, emphasis added).

46. Malthus, *First Essay on Population*, 318.

47. Gallagher, "The Body Versus the Social Body," 97.

48. Malthus, *First Essay on Population*, 86.

49. If we know where to look for the fat at Hall Farm, it is also the case that we know where to find the lean—on the body of yet another niece, Dinah Morris. The "naked hills" (121) and scant natural resources of Snowfield are repeatedly contrasted with Hayslope's rich valleys and fertile farms: as Dinah warns Seth Bede when he offers to return home with her, "It's a bleak and barren country there, not like this land of Goshen you've been used to" (80). Just as Totty's fatness is a sign of the idealized economy of plentitude at Hall Farm, a plentitude that Hetty's unrecognized "fatness" ultimately belies, Dinah's thin "starved" body is a constant marker of Snowfield's struggling industrial work-force: a brand of labor against which the Poysers (via perpetual contrast) measure their own economic identity. Added to the Poysers' abiding fear that "she'll never marry anybody if he isn't a Methodist and a cripple" (555), Dinah's starved body takes on the signs of reproductive barrenness: an infertility that initially locates Dinah instead of Hetty as the weak link in the Poysers' economics of fat.

50. It is also the case that Malthus deplores the "Parish laws of England" because they undermine British individualism (67).

51. Squire Donnithorne's offer is little more than extortion, of course: Eliot informs us that summer flooding in the Midlands has rapidly driven up the price of bread and the Hayslope farmers currently have a unique opportunity to make the most of their cornlands (337). Furthermore, according to Adam Smith's 1776 *Wealth of Nations*, dairyland was generally believed to be less valuable than corn land in the eighteenth-century: "the dairy is not reckoned a more profitable employment of land than the raising of corn, or the fattening of cattle," 227.

52. Malthus refers to infanticide as an economic rather than criminal resource—a "check to population" directly resulting from insufficient food.

53. Homans, "Dinah's Blush, Maggie's Arm," 165.

54. Buttermaking was literally as well as figuratively uneconomical at the turn of the century. According to B. A. Holderness, in most circumstances profits from butter and cheese "were never ample and barely recompensed the dairyman for his trouble." *The Agrarian History of England and Wales*, vol. VI, 183.

## CHAPTER 3: IN LOCO PARENTIS

1. Charles Dickens, *Bleak House* (1853; reprint, Boston: Riverside, 1956), 204. All further references will appear parenthetically in the text.

2. See Tebbutt's *Making Ends Meet*, 123.

3. George Cochrane, *On the Economy of the Law; Especially in Relation to the Court of Chancery* (London: E. Wilson, 1855), 5.

4. Charles Dickens, *Martin Chuzzlewit* (1844; reprint, New York: Oxford University Press, 1982), 4–5.

5. Christine van Boheemen, *The Novel as Family Romance: Language, Gender, and Authority from Fielding to Joyce* (Ithaca: Cornell University Press, 1987), 107; Richard T. Gaughan, "'Their Places Are a Blank': The Two Narrators in *Bleak House*," *Dickens Studies Annual* 21 (New York 1992): 79–96; D. A. Miller, *The Novel and the Police* (Berkeley: University of California, 1988), 59.

6. Tebbutt, 46.

7. Kenneth Hudson, *Pawnbroking: An Aspect of British Social History* (London: The Bodley Head, 1982), 13.

8. Ibid., 17.

9. John P. Caskey, *Fringe Banking: Check-Cashing Outlets, Pawnshops, and the Poor* (New York: Russell Sage Foundation, 1994), 18.

10. Harry Levin, "The Uncles of Dickens," *The Worlds of Victorian Fiction*, ed. Jerome H. Buckley (Cambridge: Harvard University Press, 1975), 31.

11. Ibid., 7.

12. Ibid., 6.

13. Ibid., 32.

14. Poovey, *Making a Social Body*, 156.

15. Ibid., 156.

16. Marx, *Capital*, vol. I, 229.

17. Ibid., 204.

18. A. Keeson, *Monts De Piété and Pawnbroking* (London: Jackson & Keeson, 1854), 369.

19. Ibid., 387–88.

20. Jeremy Bentham, "Defence of Usury," *Works of Jeremy Bentham*, vol. IX, ed. John Bowring (Edinburgh: William Tait, 1839), 3.

21. *Pawnbroker's Gazette* (20 February, 1871).

22. T. Turner, *The Three Gilt Balls: or, My Uncle's Stock-in-Trade and Customers* (London: E. Marlborough, 1864), 4.

23. Benjamin Nelson, *The Idea of Usury*, xvi.

24. John Ruskin, *Unto This Last* (1862; reprint, London: George Allen & Unwin, 1960), 132–33.

25. Ibid., 39.

26. Charles Dickens, *Our Mutual Friend* (1865; reprint, New York: Penguin, 1985), 124. All further reference to this edition will appear parenthetically in the text.

27. Helena Michie, "'Who Is This in Pain?': Scarring, Disfigurement, and Female Identity in *Bleak House* and *Our Mutual Friend*," *Novel* 22.2 (1989): 199–212.

28. Elaine Scarry, *The Body in Pain: The Making and Unmaking of the World* (New York: Oxford University Press, 1985), 259.

29. W. P. Scargill, *The Usurer's Daughter* (London: Clarke Beeton, 1832), 10.

30. Charles Dickens, *Nicholas Nickleby* (1839; reprint New York: Oxford University Press, 1990), 3. All further references will be cited parenthetically in the text.

31. The avuncular euphemism becomes even more appropriate for the childless Cheeryble brothers when we meet their nephew and heir, Frank Cheeryble. Frank's actions often mirror Nicholas's throughout the novel, and more importantly, Frank eventually marries Nicholas's sister Kate, making the Cheerybles everyone's uncles after all.

32. On this point, see Mary Poovey, "Speaking of the Body: Mid-Victorian Constructions of Female Desire," in *Body/Politics: Women and the Discourses of Science*, ed. Mary Jacobus, Evelyn Fox Keller, and Sally Shuttleworth (New York: Routledge, 1990), 29–46.

33. Charles Lamb, "The Pawnbroker's Daughter," *Blackwood's Magazine* 27 (January 1830), 109.

34. *Reasons Against the Repeal of the Usury Laws* (London: John Murray, 1825), 34. The Usury Laws, which regulated the amount of interest a pawnbroker or moneylender could legally charge, were partially abolished in 1839 and completely repealed in 1854. This long-term legislative interest no doubt motivated much of the popular and literary focus on Uncle and his works.

35. *An Examination of the Present Modes of Granting Temporary Loans on Pledges by Pawnbrokers* by "A Retired Pawnbroker" (London: Effingham Wilson, 1825), 56.

36. J. B. C. Murray, *The History of Usury: From the Earliest Period to the Present Time* (Philadelphia: J. B. Lippincott, 1866), 22.

37. W. P. Chubb, *Usury v. Equity* (London: W. Chubb, 1824), 12.

38. James Greenwood, "An Evening with My Uncle," *London Society* 9 (1867): 140.

39. Samuel Smiles, *Self-Help: With Illustrations of Conduct and Perseverance* (London: John Murray, 1958).

40. Ibid., 285, 288.

41. Anthony Trollope, *John Caldigate* (1879; reprint, New York: Oxford University Press, 1993), 138.

42. *The Poor Man's Four Evils* (London: C. Fox, 1846), 7. The "four evils" are the pub, the quack-doctor, the pawn-broker, and waste of time.

43. Mrs. Henry Wood, *Danesbury House* (London: Ward, Lock & Co., 1862), 192.

44. John Woodyer, *A Treatise on Pawnbroking* (Manchester: Robert Smith, 1823), 26.

45. *The Poor Man's Four Evils*, 11.

46. Viscount Ingestre, "Truths from a Pawnbroker," *Meliora: or, Better Times to Come* (1868): 228–85.

47. Turner, 23.

48. Ibid., 7.

49. Wood, 197.

50. Turner, 9–10.

51. Tebbutt, 42. The suspicion that washerwomen were capitalizing on their *husband's* property was so disturbing to middle-class legislators that the 1870 Select Committee on Pawnbroking made female pledging their primary order of business.

52. Jeff Nunakowa, "*Daniel Deronda* and the Afterlife of Ownership," in *The Afterlife of Property: Domestic Security and the Victorian Novel* (New Jersey: Princeton University Press, 1994), 79.

53. Charles Dickens, *Oliver Twist* (1837; New York: Oxford University Press, 1966), 241. All further references will be provided parenthetically in the text.

54. Tebbutt, 123.

## Chapter 4: Turning Bones into Spoons

1. Michael Ragussis, *Figures of Conversion: "The Jewish Question" and English National Identity* (Durham: Duke University Press, 1995), 60.

2. Mrs. Kemp, *Rachel Cohen: The Usurer's Daughter* (Bath: Binns and Goodwin, 1850), 34. All further references will appear parenthetically in the text.

3. Ragussis, 16.

4. Accordingly, Daniel's "redemption" of Mirah does not begin and end with the prevention of her suicide: he successfully transfers her from an economy of commodification and alienation to the entirely female home of Hans Meyrick's sisters and mother, who, importantly, have nothing "that a broker would care to cheapen" (237).

5. George Eliot, *Daniel Deronda* (1876; reprint, New York: Penguin Classics, 1988), 587. All further references to this edition will appear parenthetically in the text.

6. Karl Marx, *Capital: A Critique of Political Economy*, vol. I, trans. Samuel Moore and Edward Aveling, ed. Frederick Engels (1867; reprint Chicago: Charles H. Kerr, 1906), 229, 123.

7. F. R. Leavis, *The Great Tradition: George Eliot, Henry James, Joseph Conrad* (New York: New York University Press, 1963).

8. Catherine Gallagher, "George Eliot and *Daniel Deronda*: The Prostitute and the Jewish Question," in *Sex, Politics, and Science in the Nineteenth-Century Novel*, ed. Ruth Bernard Yeazell (Baltimore: Johns Hopkins, 1986), 39–62.

9. Ibid., 46.

10. Considering Gwendolyn's ignorance about the history of her family, it is worth noting that both of these responses bespeak a certain amount of knowledge about the goals of Victorian exploration, and about the unwritten social codes that keep all but the most eccentric of women from participating in such projects.

11. Smith, *The Wealth of Nations*, 18.

12. Ann Cvetkovich, *Mixed Feelings: Feminism, Mass Culture, and Victorian Sensationalism* (New Jersey: Rutgers University Press, 1992), 153.

13. Marx, 126.

## CHAPTER 5: "SEND THE LETTERS, UNCLE JOHN"

1. Henry Cole, *Report of a Scene at Windsor Castle Respecting the Uniform Penny Postage* (London: Henry Hooper, 1839), 3.

2. Ibid., 3.

3. Ibid., 7–8.

4. Eleanor C. Smyth, *Sir Rowland Hill: The Story of a Great Reform Told by His Daughter* (London: T. Fisher Unwin, 1907), 61.

5. "Post Office Reform," *Edinburgh Review* (January, 1840), 543–73.

6. Rowland Hill, *Post Office Reform: Its Importance and Practicability* (London: Charles Knight, 1837), iv, 7, 66.

7. Victoria Glendenning, *Trollope* (London: Hutchinson, 1992), 372.

8. John Wilson Croker, "Post-Office Reform," *Quarterly Review* (Oct., 1839), 531.

9. Witness the contemporary advertising campaigns waged by telecommunications giant MCI, where the "Friends and Family Plan" is promoted to assuage any public anxieties that an increasingly complicated and mechanized postal network may be alienating people from each other instead of bringing them together.

10. *The Post Circular, or Weekly Advocate for a Cheap, Swift and Sure Postage*, ed. Henry Cole (Wednesday, March 28, 1838), 10.

11. Ibid., 11.

12. *The Post Circular* (Friday, May 4, 1838), 29.

13. *The Post Circular* (Tuesday, April 24, 1838), 27.

14. *The Administration of the Post Office* (London: J. Hatchard, 1844), 19.

15. Poster, "Uniform Penny Postage" (Hanbury: W. Potts, 1839).

16. Elihu Burritt, *Ocean Penny Postage: Its Necessity Shown and Its Feasibility Demonstrated* (London: C. Gilpin, 1849), 2.

17. David Allam, *The Social and Economic Importance of Postal Reform in 1840* (London: Harry Hays, 1976), 3.

18. Lord John Russell, Parliamentary Address (June 21, 1848). Reprinted in *Life of Rowland Hill and the History of Penny-Postage*, vol. 2, by Rowland Hill and Gregory Birkbeck Hill (London: Thomas De La Rue, 1880), 98.

19. Benjamin Disraeli, *Endymion* (London: Longmans, 1881), 48.

20. Elizabeth Gaskell, *Wives and Daughters* (1866; reprint, Penguin, 1986), 489.

21. *Life of Rowland Hill*, vol. 2, 239.

22. Norman Wymer, *Social Reformers* (New York: Oxford UP, 1955), 3.

23. Harriet Martineau, *A History of Thirty Year's Peace*, vol. 4 (London: George Bell, 1878), 11–12.

24. *Life of Rowland Hill*, vol. 1, 305.

25. W. H. Ashurst, *Facts and Reasons in Support of Mr. Rowland Hill's Plan for a Universal Penny Postage* (London: Harry Hooper, 1838), 3, 67.

26. Mary A. Favret, *Romantic Correspondence: Women, Politics, and the Fiction of Letters* (Cambridge: Cambridge UP, 1993), 197, 202.

27. *Life of Rowland Hill*, vol. 1, 388.

28. F. M. L. Thompson, *The Rise of Respectable Society: A Social History of Victorian Britain* (London: Fontana Press, 1988), 359.

29. Michel Foucault, *Discipline and Punish: The Birth of the Prison*, trans. Alan Sheridan (New York: Vintage Books, 1979), 201.

30. Quoted in L. N. and M. Williams, *The Postage Stamp: Its History and Recognition* (London: Penguin Books, 1956), 19.

31. *Life of Rowland Hill*, vol. 2, 91.

32. Foucault, *Discipline and Punish*, 208.

33. Pliny Miles, *Postal Reform: Its Urgent Necessity and Practicability* (New York: Stringer and Townsend, 1855), 25.

34. Anthony Trollope, *An Autobiography* (1883; reprint, New York: Penguin Books, 1993), 122.

35. Ibid., 123.

36. *Life of Rowland Hill*, vol. 1, 171–72.

37. Ibid., 193.

38. Cvetkovich, *Mixed Feelings*, 40.

39. Frank Staff, *The Penny Post: 1690–1918* (London: Lutterworth, 1964), 83.

40. Anthony Trollope, *Can You Forgive Her?* (1865; reprint, New York: Oxford University Press, 1990), 237–38.

41. Croker, 531.

42. *Life of Rowland Hill*, vol. 1, 478.

43. William Lewins, *Her Majesty's Mails: An Historical and Descriptive Account of the British Post Office* (London: Sampson and Low, 1864), 135.

44. *Life of Rowland Hill*, vol. 2, 31.

45. Henry Cole, *Westminster Review* (May 1840), reprinted in Staff's *The Penny Post*.

46. Smyth, 165.

47. *Third Report from the Select Committee on Postage* (August, 1838), 25.

48. *Harriet Martineau's Autobiography*, ed. Maria Weston Chapman (Boston: James R. Osgood, 1877), vol. 3, 249.

49. Martineau, *History*, 12.

50. Ashurst, 94.

51. *The Post Circular* (Friday, May 4, 1838), 34.

52. Harriet Martineau, letter to Sir Thomas Wilde, M. P. Reprinted in Pearson Hill's *The Post Office of Fifty Years Ago* (London: Cassell, 1887), 44–45.

53. Foucault, *Discipline and Punish*, 215–16.

54. Hill, *Post Office Reform*, 48.

55. *Report of the House Committee on Postage* (1844), quoted in Joshua Leavitt, *Cheap Postage* (Boston: Cheap Postage Association, 1848), 24.

56. J. Henniker Heaton, *Ocean Penny Postage* (London: Harrison and Sons, 1890), 23.

57. W. R. Malcolm, *Sentiment: The Bond of Empire* (London: Cassell, 1907), 22.

58. Staff, 108.

59. Burritt, 5–6.

60. Major E. B. Evans, R. A., *The Mulready Envelope and Its Caricatures* (London: Stanley Gibbons, 1891), 195.

61. M. Guzot, *Popular History of England: From the Accession of Queen Victoria, 1837–74*, trans. M. M. Ripley (Boston: Estes and Lauriat, 1881), 24.

62. Burritt, 27–28.

63. Ibid., 31.

64. *The Lancaster Guardian* (February 10, 1838).

65. Burritt, 32.

66. Margaret Oliphant, *The House on the Moor*, 3 vols. (London: Hurst and Blackett, 1861), vol. 1, 35. All further references to this edition will appear parenthetically within the text.

67. Benjamin Disraeli, *Coningsby* (1844; reprint, New York: Penguin, 1983), 438–39.

68. Trollope, *An Autobiography*, 82.

69. Ibid., 81.

70. Ibid., 83–84.

71. Anthony Trollope, *The Claverings* (1867; reprint, New York: Oxford University Press, 1986), 233. All further references to this edition will appear parenthetically in the text.

72. Robert Surtees, *"Ask Mamma," or, The Richest Commoner in England* (London: Bradbury and Evans, 1858), 173.

73. Jacques Derrida, *The Post Card: From Socrates to Freud and Beyond*, trans. Alan Bass (Chicago: University of Chicago Press, 1987), 123.

74. Trollope, *The Claverings*, 440.

75. Alexander Welsh, *George Eliot and Blackmail* (Cambridge: Harvard University Press, 1985), 55.

76. Anthony Trollope, *John Caldigate* (1879; reprint, New York: Oxford University Press, 1993), 118. All further references to this edition will appear parenthetically in the text.

77. It is also important that when Dick Shand's mother suggests sending shirts to her son in Australia because "he can't drink the shirts out there in the bush," John Caldigate tries instead to get her to send letters imparting motherly encouragement and kindness.

78. Welsh, 58.

79. Anthony Trollope, *Marion Fay* (Leipzig: Bernhard Tauchnitz, 1882), 317.

## Conclusion: Home Trading Redux

1. Anna Maria Hall, *Uncle Sam's Money-Box* (Edinburgh: William and Robert Chambers, 1848), 49. All further references will appear parenthetically in the text.

2. Uncle John's Nephew, *Universal Co-Operation (Instead of State Socialism): A National "Uncle John"* (London: New Parcel Post Publishing, 1891), 10.

3. Ibid., 104.

4. Ibid., 63.

5. Charles Elton Blanchard, *Report of Uncle Sam's Homilies on Finance: An Exposition of the True Functions of Money and Its Relations to the Industries and Society* (Cleveland: The Current Events Co., 1895), 160.

6. José M. Aguirre, *Uncle Sam in Pontifical Robes; John Bull Destitute of Attire* (New York: G. W. Dillingham, 1888), 86.

7. Ibid., 187.

8. E. F. Boyd, *Uncle Sam and Americus: A Dialogue on Land, Labor, and Liberty* (Cincinnati: Joseph Boyd, 1880), 9.

9. Ibid., 10.

10. Ibid., 9.

11. Ibid., 9.

12. *The Asphalt Jungle*, dir. John Huston, 112 min., Turner Entertainment Co., 1992, 1950, videocassette.

13. *Twin Peaks: Fire Walk with Me*, dir. David Lynch, 134 min., Columbia Tristar, 1992, videocassette.

14. *Pretty Woman*, dir. Garry Marshall, 125 min., Touchstone Home Video, 1990, videocassette.

< >

# Index